For Moham...
Your ...
big heart are such
big supports. Inspiring
Gratitude,
Nanci

The Gatherings

The Gatherings

REIMAGINING INDIGENOUS-SETTLER RELATIONS

Shirley N. Hager

and

Gwen Bear, Shirley Bowen, Alma H. Brooks,
gkisedtanamoogk, JoAnn Hughes, Debbie Leighton,
Barb Martin, Miigam'agan, T. Dana Mitchell,
Wayne A. Newell, Betty Peterson,
Marilyn Keyes Roper, and Wesley Rothermel
Afterword by Frances Hancock

ÆVO UTP

Aevo UTP
An imprint of University of Toronto Press
Toronto Buffalo London
utorontopress.com

© Shirley N. Hager 2021

Proceeds from the sale of this book will be used to foster understanding of Indigenous-
settler relations and to support Indigenous-led initiatives striving for justice.

Library and Archives Canada Cataloguing in Publication

Title: The gatherings : reimagining Indigenous-settler relations / Shirley N. Hager ;
    with Gwen Bear [and 12 others] ; and afterword by Frances Hancock.
Names: Hager, Shirley N., 1952–, author.
Description: Includes index.
Identifiers: Canadiana (print) 2020037737X | Canadiana (ebook) 20200377582
    | ISBN 9781487508951 (hardcover) | ISBN 9781487539399 (EPUB)
    | ISBN 9781487539382 (PDF)
Subjects: LCSH: Indigenous peoples – Maritime Provinces – Social conditions.
    | LCSH: Indigenous peoples – Maine – Social conditions. | LCSH: Maritime
    Provinces – Race relations. | LCSH: Maritime Provinces – Ethnic relations.
    | LCSH: Maine – Race relations. | LCSH: Maine – Ethnic relations. | LCSH:
    Intercultural communication – Maritime Provinces. | LCSH: Intercultural
    communication – Maine.
Classification: LCC E78.M28 H34 2021 | DDC 305.897/0715 – dc23

ISBN 978-1-4875-0895-1 (cloth)   ISBN 978-1-4875-3939-9 (EPUB)
                                    ISBN 978-1-4875-3938-2 (PDF)

Printed in Canada

We acknowledge the financial support of the Government of Canada, the Canada
Council for the Arts, and the Ontario Arts Council, an agency of the Government of
Ontario, for our publishing activities.

Canada Council   Conseil des Arts
for the Arts   du Canada

ONTARIO ARTS COUNCIL
CONSEIL DES ARTS DE L'ONTARIO
an Ontario government agency
un organisme du gouvernement de l'Ontario

Funded by the   Financé par le
Government   gouvernement
of Canada   du Canada

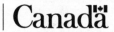

MIX
Paper from
responsible sources
FSC® C016245

For Elly Haney, who made her visions her policy

In memory of

Gwen Bear
JoAnn Hughes
Betty Peterson
Wesley Rothermel

and

for all who dare to cross the deep, vast chasm
of our fears of one another

There's a word in Mi'kmaq: *upisktwo*. We might say in English "forgiveness," but it means "we return to that original place, and let's try again."

Miigam'agan

Contents

THE GIVEAWAY BLANKET

Preface

Mawopiyane, in Passamaquoddy, literally means "let us sit together," but the deeper meaning is of a group coming together, as in the longhouse, to struggle with a sensitive or divisive issue. The word indicates an urgency to meet because the outcome is something very desirable, such as resolving a conflict or bringing about peace. It's a healing word.

We, the Wabanaki members of the group that guided this project, chose this word to describe those of us who came together to create this book. *Mawopiyane* is a word that is recognizable in all Wabanaki languages, and it reflects the collaborative nature of our effort.

In those long-ago Gatherings, and again in co-creating this book, our commitment has been to aid one another in navigating through the hundreds of years of malfeasance, genocide of Indigenous peoples, and theft of homelands that has occurred in both the United States and Canada under the pretense of law. In the Gatherings, we re-enacted the form of treaty-making that existed among our peoples before the arrival of the European invasion. Our treaties between and among our Nations enabled the *making of relatives* and included all Living Beings. Indigenous Nations extended this form of treaty-making to the incoming Europeans and the establishment of their settlements, but ultimately those treaties were broken. Our

Gatherings, described in this book, fulfilled the promise of our treaties, and they enacted the relations and the commitments that we are all collectively responsible to and for. Our commitment to one another in the Gatherings, and in creating this book, is a model for every Good Heart to follow and implement.

So much has happened since the start of this book project. Our small community has endured many challenges and losses, yet we persevered for each other. We are grateful for Shirley's dedication and patience, and for Frances's expertise and guidance.

We hope that people will see our story as an example of what alliances look like. From the beginning, we gave voice to our differences and began building something. It was like constructing a house together. We are excited to share the lessons that we learned over time.

This book is our gift to our children, our families and friends, and the future.

Miigam'agan
gkisedtanamoogk
Wayne A. Newell

With Gratitude

This book has had many guardians. First and foremost, it was made possible through the collaborative leadership of a planning group of Native and non-Native individuals who have known one another for over thirty years. The group consisted of Miigam'agan (who is Mi'kmaq), gkisedtanamoogk (Wampanoag), Wayne Newell (Passamaquoddy), Frances Hancock (a New Zealander of Irish descent), and myself (a White North American). I am deeply grateful to Miigam'agan, gkisedtanamoogk, and Wayne for giving themselves wholeheartedly to this project. In addition to their sustaining friendship, they invested their concerns, commitment, hopes, and aspirations in this book. I consulted them regularly and they generously shared their perceptions and opinions, as well as their descriptions and explanations of Wabanaki cultures. They embraced my questions with patience and honesty. Their insights, critical analysis, and belief in building alliances between our peoples are woven into the text. Without their wisdom and moral support this project could not have happened.

At every stage, this book was nurtured by the care, devotion, expertise, and wisdom of our New Zealand friend Frances Hancock. Originally intended to be our researcher and writer, Frances was derailed by a series of eye surgeries that rendered her unable to travel and, as a result, she encouraged me to step into these roles. By phone and e-mail from New Zealand, she persevered in her commitment by offering ongoing support as advisor. She drafted grant proposals, suggested questions and topics to pose at our planning meetings and in the personal interviews, and was an unfailing cheerleader on our monthly calls. Once able to travel, she returned to Maine in 2015 and accompanied me on visits with the book's contributors, taking meticulous notes on their suggested revisions to the manuscript. She was also the book's initial editor, giving feedback on both first and second drafts. It is fitting that she writes our afterword, drawing on her experiences working with and for the Māori, the Indigenous people of New Zealand, and reflecting on the universal elements of building alliances.

Four contributors to this book, Gwen Bear, JoAnn Hughes, Betty Peterson, and Wesley Rothermel, have since passed on, but thankfully not before they shared their experience with us. They are greatly missed and very much alive in the pages that follow.

Our deep gratitude goes to the board of the Eleanor Humes Haney Fund for their belief in our vision from the very beginning. They provided our seed money as well as additional funds at later dates that allowed face-to-face conversations among the widely dispersed contributors to this book and supported travel expenses for contributors to speak about and promote the book once it was published.

Many thanks to the eighteen individuals who were enthusiastic enough to fund our second planning meeting, and to Rachel Carey-Harper who, when approached for a donation, responded by saying "… and here's something extra for next steps."

Within and surrounding this book is a quiet, strong Quaker presence. The following Quaker entities provided support, both moral and financial, and their belief in us has been gratifying and humbling.

Winthrop Center (Maine) Friends Church and Farmington (Maine) Friends Meeting have both, at separate times, acted as our fiscal agent. They also made financial contributions, as did the Friends Committee on Maine Public Policy. A number of individual financial donors are Quakers as well. Winthrop Center Friends and its pastor, Maggie Edmondson, continue to provide spiritual oversight and support for me personally and for this project. A special thank you to Portland (Maine) Friends Meeting's Leadings Committee for their belief in me, and for the grant that funded the writing phase of this project. Quaker support for this book grows out of the historical and ongoing ally work of Quakers throughout North America, including the American Friends Service Committee and Canadian Friends Service Committee, who have long joined with Indigenous peoples to confront stereotypes, correct Westernized versions of history, and address injustices.

Thank you to The Rev. Dr. H. Roy Partridge, Jr., special assistant to the president for multicultural affairs at Bowdoin College, for his generosity, wisdom, and patience in exploring with me the multifaceted subject of race. Our conversations illuminated both the universality and the uniqueness of the themes in this book. Thank you also to the numerous "critical readers" who gave their time and expertise to review, critique, and sometimes correct the text.

A special appreciation goes to Harry Roper, who was interviewed for this book at the same time as his wife Marilyn, whose story is included here. Harry acknowledged that Marilyn's story spoke for him as well, and graciously deferred to Marilyn's inclusion. Harry's presence in our Gatherings is a tender memory for us, as he often accompanied our awakening for First Light with the sweet tones of his French horn.

Once the manuscript was completed, our book needed just the right home and just the right caretaker. We found both in the University of Toronto Press and acquisitions editor Jodi Lewchuk. Jodi's belief in, and enthusiasm for, our story has made it possible for us to share it with you, and we will be forever grateful. She is also a delight to work with. Terry Teskey's gentle but insightful copy-editing made the revision process actually pleasurable. The photos, which came from many sources and in many forms, were artfully made presentable by Paul Luise, extraordinary photographer that he is, who gave his talents to this project gratis.

Finally, deepest gratitude for my husband Dave. His support, patience, good humor, and unfailing faith in me made it possible to focus on this project, and to give it all the time it needed.

Notes on Terminology

Throughout our stories and commentary, you will see a variety of names for Indigenous peoples. Where specific to Indigenous peoples of Maine and the Maritimes, the name "Wabanaki" may be used, referring to one of the four recognized tribes: Penobscot, Passamaquoddy, Micmac (in Maine) or Mi'kmaq (in Canada), and Maliseet. In various places you will also see the more traditional spelling of Indigenous names paired with the anglicized version. Other general terminology is also used, and reflects differences between the United States and Canada (for example, "First Nations" and "Aboriginal" are terms commonly used in Canada but not generally in the United States) as well as regional, generational, and personal differences. Sometimes variation in terminology is used to avoid repetition.

"Native" is a term commonly used both in Maine and in Eastern Canada, and is preferred by many Indigenous people to the term "Indian." Conversely, to distinguish the other participants in the Gatherings, we often use the term "non-Native," as well as "White." The stories in this book speak to the relationship between Native North America and White North America – between the original inhabitants of this land and the descendants of European settlers as well as those of European descent who came after the original settlement. We do not attempt to address relationships between Native

North America and other ethnic or racial groups who came later from Africa or Asia.

All names for Indigenous peoples as well as for Whites and other ethnic/racial groups have been intentionally capitalized, except where appearing in direct quotations from other sources. Other nouns in specific contexts also have been capitalized to denote respect or reverence, such as "Elder," "Earth," "Fire," "Circle," and "Life."

Other differences between United States and Canadian terminology exist. In the United States, the term "reservation" is used for areas of land set aside by the government as tribal homeland; in Canada, the corresponding term is "reserve." In the United States, the governing body of a tribe that was established by act of Congress is referred to as the "tribal council"; in Canada, the corresponding body is referred to as the "band council."

The creation of the United States and Canada, and the resulting border, gave rise over time to these differences in terminology and political structures as they relate to Indigenous peoples, but throughout the years Wabanaki participants in the Gatherings reminded us that the border is simply an imaginary line created by two colonial governments. While this line had meaning for the United States and Canada, it divided and separated Wabanaki families, communities, tribes, sovereign governments, and territories that had, for millennia, existed as one.

In the text to follow, every effort has been made to distinguish clearly between the opinions of Native and non-Native participants of the Gatherings. As a non-Native author, I took care to speak only for myself or for "we non-Natives," and to attribute the thoughts and reflections of Native participants appropriately to them. I use the word "we" in certain places to refer to the group as a whole where

I am confident, based on the conversations that created this book, that the experience was shared by all.

Finally, in describing the original intention of the Gatherings, I purposely use the word "alliance" rather than, possibly, "coalition." Coalitions are generally formed around a common goal, and when that goal is met they can, and often do, dissolve. Elly Haney, the founder of the Center for Vision and Policy, defines "alliance" in her book *The Great Commandment*:

> Alliances are sustained commitments among groups and individuals to share experiences and insights, pain and rage, dreams and fears, and to engage in collective action for justice.[1]

It was upon this understanding of the concept of alliance that the Gatherings were founded.

Introduction

In the summer of 1986, I heard about a new organization in Maine called the Center for Vision and Policy (CVP). It was an ambitious name for a group with an ambitious agenda. Its mission was to develop a vision for the Gulf of Maine bioregion, one that would represent a more sustainable and more socially just way of life, and to explore ways to implement that vision. "Bioregion" refers to an area defined by characteristics of the natural environment rather than by political divisions. CVP, although based in Maine, had chosen to define its territory as the watershed, or bioregion, of the Gulf of Maine so that its recommendations would have environmental integrity. This territory includes Maine, New Hampshire, and Massachusetts as well as two Canadian provinces, New Brunswick and Nova Scotia. CVP's vision was to be created through conversations in community forums largely composed of the most disenfranchised – individuals and groups whose lives were most negatively impacted by existing economic, environmental, and social realities in the region.

At the time, I was active with a Quaker peace program based in southern Maine, and I thought that the two organizations should be introduced. I contacted the founder of CVP, Elly Haney, and we met one morning over pancakes at a local Portland diner. She filled me in on her background as a theologian and activist, as well as the assumptions underlying CVP, activities to date, and plans for the future. CVP's plans included a particularly notable decision for a primarily "White" organization: a commitment that any vision of sustainability should include the perspective of the Indigenous people who had lived for thousands of years, and continued to live, in the bioregion.

Currently the CVP board was mulling over the question of how to reach out and find Native individuals who would be interested in participating in this endeavor, and Elly admitted they were pretty much clueless about how to start. She planned to contact existing Native organizations as well as a few people whose names she had been given, but was feeling less than confident of a positive response. By this time, I was hooked. "Well, I'm going to a New England Quaker gathering in Amherst next week," I said, producing the brochure from my purse. "There's a Wampanoag man named gkisedtanamoogk" – whose name I couldn't yet pronounce – "speaking there. Maybe I could talk to him."

gkisedtanamoogk (who doesn't capitalize his name) was a young man then. He had been invited by the Quakers to present several sessions on Native spirituality at this, their annual New England gathering. As the conference was being held in Massachusetts, it was fitting that they had invited a Wampanoag to speak, and one of gkisedtanamoogk's Elders had encouraged him to accept. I signed up for all three of his presentations and, after the first one, I tentatively approached him. I described CVP's mission and their intentions to reach out to Indigenous people for their perspectives. He was, to my relief, intrigued by this idea, and possibly also by this earnest and persistent, if uninformed, White woman who attended all three of his presentations and was so full of questions. At the end of the conference, he suggested several names of Wabanaki individuals whom he thought would be willing to talk to me and to others from CVP; and he offered to stay in touch.

So began a year of correspondence between gkisedtanamoogk and me, in which he tried to educate me in the realities of our peoples' shared history and ongoing conflicts. At the same time, I and other members of CVP were reaching out to Wabanaki individuals in Maine and New Brunswick whose names we had been given (a number of whom are featured in this book: Gwen Bear, Alma Brooks, Barb Martin, Dana Mitchell, Wayne Newell). In our conversations, we found a common interest in critiquing the dominant culture's current priorities. At some point during the year, the idea emerged of a "Gathering" between Native and non-Native people in our region. We imagined this "Gathering" as a forum to educate non-Natives about Indigenous perspectives and concerns. We decided that a first step had to be education, as the non-Natives in attendance would have virtually no reliable information about the Wabanaki people who currently lived in and shared the territory.

Our first Gathering was held at a retreat center on the coast of Maine and funded by CVP. It consisted of a panel of Wabanaki speakers who offered an Indigenous perspective on our shared history and described current issues facing their communities. Panel presentations were followed by small-group discussions, sometimes dividing into "non-Natives only" and "Wabanaki only" to give participants freedom to speak openly, after which we would come back together. Meals were prepared by the retreat center where we all had overnight accommodations. Conversations tended to be tentative and formal as we approached one another cautiously outside of the activities. By the end, however, there was enough positive response that we decided to repeat the process the following year.

Our second forum looked much like the first – the Wabanaki up front, non-Natives in the audience. At the end of that second event, however, as people were packing to go home, I was approached by several of the Wabanaki participants with an observation and an invitation. Our efforts held promise, they said, but our way of meeting was not natural or comfortable for them. "Could we meet in a more traditional Wabanaki way?" they asked. They suggested that we hold our future Gatherings in a Council format – in a Circle, using a Talking Stick – and include ceremony during the weekend. The ceremonies, they said, would allow us to greet each day, offer thanks, and ask for guidance in our deliberations. They would be in charge of the ceremonial aspect as well as the form and structure of our meetings, while CVP should continue in its organizational role of finding the location and getting people there. Their invitation was accepted; and at that point, everything changed.*

The Gatherings grew initially out of CVP's intention to convene community forums among many different groups throughout the bioregion, but eventually they took on a life of their own. What began as an academic exercise – an educational forum – became, increasingly, a meeting of friends. We did not have an agenda. We did not come together to support a common cause, though shared actions did result over time. Instead, our primary objective became simply to know and understand one another.

---

* It is important to emphasize that the opportunity to participate in these Council Circles was by invitation of the Wabanaki, with the Wabanaki as the initiators and leaders of the ceremonial aspects of our Gatherings. Native people may or may not want to include non-Natives in ceremonies associated with gatherings or alliances, and non-Natives should not expect or seek this experience. While participants felt that our meetings were greatly aided by the way in which we met, many traditions contain the general principles we utilized. There are many ways to meet and dialogue that do not involve Indigenous ceremonial practices.

The Gatherings, with generally twenty to thirty Native and non-Native participants in attendance, ultimately spanned six years. During that period, we met twice a year for a total of eleven long (three-to-four-day) weekends. We alternated meetings between Maine and New Brunswick, and we depended upon participants who had sufficient land for camping, and who could accommodate a crowd, to be our hosts. People traveled hundreds of miles to be together, coming from towns and Indigenous communities spanning a region from Cape Cod, Massachusetts, to Halifax, Nova Scotia.

Ours is a story of unlikely friendships, unlikely because around five hundred years ago my ancestors, the houseguests from hell, arrived on the eastern threshold of this continent, walked through the door, and raided the metaphorical refrigerator – indeed, helped themselves to all the contents of the house without invitation or permission. The occupants of this home – those who survived the initial invasion – were confined to tiny rooms somewhere in the back of the house. In these back rooms, also known as reservations, many more died of starvation, disease, and broken hearts. We descendants of these settlers, as well as the beneficiaries of this occupation who arrived later on this continent, have gone to great lengths, continuing to this present day, to pretend that this land is our rightful home. As a society, we have paid virtually no attention to the sounds coming from those back rooms. It is a trespass and a violation that North America has never come to terms with, neither in relationship to the original inhabitants of this land nor within our own souls.

Here in Wabanaki territory, Indigenous people have experienced the longest occupation, but in the 1970s a miraculous thing began to occur. Young Wabanaki, ignited and inspired by an emerging nationwide Red Power movement, began to seek out their Elders who still remembered and, according to Native sources, even practiced in secret some of the Old Ways. Some began to travel out west, where traditions were stronger as the settler occupation there had been more recent, and they brought back traditions that became integrated into ceremonies and teachings here. Regained traditional knowledge was carefully guarded – guarded both from a non-Native culture that was becoming enamored with anything "Native American" as part of the New Age spirituality movement, and from many of their own friends and families as well as the Catholic Church. The church was and still is a major presence and influence in Native communities, and many Wabanaki who chose to pursue and practice their Native traditions at that time were condemned by the church as well as ostracized, even disowned, by their own relatives. While the Catholic Church is more accepting now toward Indigenous ceremony, even incorporating some aspects into the Catholic service, tensions remain in many communities.

In Maine, throughout the seventies, this re-emerging sense of tribal identity and power led to a historic land claim by two Wabanaki tribes, the Passamaquoddies and the Penobscots. The claim was finally negotiated and officially settled in 1980, amid much tension, conflict, and outright hostility aimed at Wabanaki peoples by politicians, the media, and the general populace. During the period of negotiation, old and ugly stereotypes of Native people were resurrected, and once the settlement was signed resentments remained, along with many misconceptions about what the settlement did and did not do for Native communities in Maine.

Against this cultural and political backdrop in the mid-1980s, our Gatherings began. We were told at the time by a visiting Seneca scholar, John Mohawk, who traveled all over the world, that he was not aware of any attempt such as ours occurring anywhere else.

In these Gatherings, over time, we discovered the power and strength in coming together. We shared our life stories, and also our talents, perspectives, and philosophies. Now, thirty years later, we find ourselves in a world that more than ever needs all of our knowledge and wisdom to address the developing crises around us. There is an ever-increasing drive to exploit natural resources while, at the same time, many are at last awakening to society's devastating impact on the lands, water, and air we mutually depend on. Our very climate is changing at an unsustainable rate. The voices that non-Natives tried to shut away in those back rooms are the voices of those who have lived on, and understood, this land for longer than our settler minds can conceive, and those voices have critical and significant insights to share.

Currently, throughout the United States and Canada, a number of environmental groups are forming alliances with Indigenous communities over concerns they have in common. In several recent instances here in eastern North America, the leadership in expressing these concerns has come from Indigenous communities asserting their legitimate claims to sovereignty within their homelands. Significantly, there has evolved among many Native Elders a willingness to share their knowledge and spiritual traditions in order to assist and support these new movements, so unlike the protectiveness that existed thirty to forty years ago.

Other Native/non-Native alliances are forming as well. Here in Maine, for example, Wabanaki child welfare workers, together with staff members of the State of Maine's child welfare system, began meeting in 1999 out of a shared concern for the impact of state policies that continued to remove Native children from their families and place them, typically, in White homes. These practices not only tore children from extended family members and others in their own communities where they could have been placed, but separated them from their culture and often also exposed them to physical, sexual, and emotional abuse. The joint efforts, over years, of this small group of Native and non-Native individuals resulted in 2012 in the formation of the first ever Truth and Reconciliation Commission (TRC) between Indigenous nations and a state government within US territory, and the only commission ever originating from a grass-roots movement rather than from a governmental action. The TRC officially fulfilled its mandate in June 2015, but its work continues through a cross-cultural collaborative (Maine-Wabanaki REACH) that exists to ensure its recommendations are considered and implemented.

We offer this book for efforts such as these – efforts where Indigenous and non-Indigenous peoples seek to come together to create mutually beneficial and honorable relationships.

We realize that not everyone has the opportunity, or the time, to gather in the way we did. In the United States and Canada, many Indigenous and non-Indigenous peoples do not live in proximity to one another (a result, of course, of the decimation of Indigenous populations described above, and their forced relocation onto reservations and reserves). Our experiences in the Gatherings gave us a window into one another's lives that is rare, and for that reason we are compelled to share the lessons we learned. It is our hope that, through this book, both Indigenous and non-Indigenous peoples may come to view one another with new eyes. We hope as well that, for those of us of European descent, this book can be the beginning of a journey to examine the legacy of colonialism that we inherited, and to understand how that inheritance serves to perpetuate the ongoing oppression of Indigenous peoples as well as to diminish our own lives. The stories contained here also provide insight into the astounding resilience of Native peoples living in North America today.

We believe that beginning to heal the wounds of our past – our separation, the violence done – is necessary for the spiritual well-being of us all. This deep divide between our peoples was created initially in the mindset of the settlers, my and possibly your ancestors, who arrived on these shores – the mindset that this land, being the home of "savages" and non-Christians, could be legitimately and morally appropriated by any Christian conqueror. It was a divide carved deeper over the years by the subsequent cruelty of the invaders, and the dislocation and near annihilation of the people indigenous to this land. And it is a divide maintained today through misunderstanding, suspicion, and fear of Native people … if we think about them at all. Wayne Newell, a long-time Gathering participant, says that if he had only one wish it would be that Native people would be more visible. My European culture, I believe, keeps Indigenous peoples invisible in our minds so that we don't have to confront, or admit, that the place we call "home" and the resources we benefit from today were taken without remorse from the original inhabitants of this land; and that the impact of this taking lives on in the intergenerational trauma experienced by Indigenous peoples today.

What we experienced in those Gatherings years ago is that, in spite of our history, understanding is still possible, trust is still possible, laughter is still possible. These rewards, however, do not come easily or quickly. Interactions are filled with anxiety and awkwardness. Misunderstandings and misinterpretations are inevitable. Truths dawn slowly as we visit in each other's homes and communities.

Patience, flexibility, and persistence are required. In spite of the challenges, we, both Native and non-Native, learned that the gifts we exchange when we come together in friendship are profound and varied – intellectual, emotional, and spiritual. And, in coming to know one another, we began to lay down the burden of our unresolved past, feeling the weight of that burden ease … just a bit.

What inspired this desire to be together? What kept us coming back to these Gatherings, in spite of a shared history that includes genocide, near annihilation, and the enduring oppression of Native peoples? What sustained our friendships and alliances all these years since the Gatherings ended?

We believe that what we learned through our anxieties, guilt, anger, embarrassments, and mutual affection are key to our shared future here in "North America." We need each other, and it is now more critical than ever that we reimagine Indigenous-settler relations.

GATHERING

Preparing

I am driving north. For the past several days I have been amassing camping equipment, throwing not-to-be-forgotten items into a duffle bag, shopping, baking, and talking for hours on the phone. The phone calls have been mostly with non-Natives who have expressed an interest in attending a Gathering for the first time. Since our decision to meet in a traditional Council format, around the Fire, we have been strict about preparing first-timers. We want to make sure they understand that this Gathering is about forming relationships and creating alliances, and not primarily about experiencing Native ceremonies.

People find out about the Gatherings through word of mouth. I send out invitations to those who have previously attended, announcing the date and location, and say that if they want to bring someone new they need to prepare them. Often, they suggest that the newcomer call me. When they do, I carefully explain the taboo of cultural appropriation, and that under no circumstances should they take what they experience at the Gathering and share it with others for financial gain or self-promotion. "If you were to attend a Catholic service for the first time," I ask, "would you feel qualified to go out and conduct a mass?"

The invitation reads, "This is our [sixth, seventh, etc.] Gathering in the Gulf of Maine Bioregion, the region corresponding to the Wabanaki Confederacy. We meet to continue to strengthen our friendships and to support one another's lives and work." The invitation also has an important, sometimes surprising, statement: "It is strongly requested that you abstain from all alcohol and non-medicinal drugs for at least four days prior to, during, and four days after the weekend, both in order to be fully present at the ceremonies and Council meetings, and out of respect for traditional ways." This is a critical request made by our Wabanaki participants. Alcohol and drugs have had a devastating effect in Indigenous communities, a consequence of poverty, oppression, and trauma. Some of the Indigenous Elders involved in the Gatherings have had their own brushes with alcoholism and drug abuse, and made conscious decisions to alter their course and become role models for others. Often, their reconnection with their own Indigenous traditions has been their path to recovery. It is in solidarity with their struggle, and with the struggle of many Indigenous people, that everyone abstains, but there is something deeper as well. We are told – and the non-Natives among us take this mostly on faith – that any drug or alcohol use, even several days prior to or after our Gathering, would interfere with the experiences, and integration, of the ceremonies that we will participate in together.

In my phone calls I also deliver another message to the women: women who are experiencing their Moon Time, or menstrual cycle, are asked not to participate in the ceremonies or in the Talking Circles, which are held around the Sacred Fire. They are still welcome to attend the Gathering, to socialize, and to listen to discussions from outside the Circle. This is a conflicting task for me, and I deliver this message out of respect for the relationship I have with our Wabanaki attendees, rather than from any real understanding or even agreement. I repeat what I have been told by several of the Native participants: that this tradition is based on a profound respect and reverence for the power of women at this time (of menstruation) and that, traditionally, women experiencing their Moon Time would have had their own time together in a separate women's lodge. Still, for the non-Native women who, like myself, have spent most of our lives fighting to be included in important matters, this is tough to swallow.*

Wabanaki participants, as well as non-Natives, have come and gone from our Gatherings, but there is now a core group of us who are attending regularly. Even with our increasing familiarity with one another, and growing trust, there are countless moments of uncertainty and anxiety in our encounters. I constantly seem, to myself, to be too loud, or talking too much. In phone conversations with gkisedtanamoogk, I keep reminding myself to "wait … wait …" for him to respond before I go barreling into my next sentence. I have come to understand that his pauses are due to the fact that he is actually listening to, and pondering, my words before he responds – a manner of communication I'm not used to in my everyday hurried interactions.

We charge no fee for attending a Gathering, and use funds raised by the Center for Vision and Policy to cover costs. It is important, especially to ensure the attendance of some Wabanaki participants, that we offer to help with travel expenses. We come from disparate and unequal financial circumstances that, we all recognize, are rooted in the historical injustices of our original relationship, and so it is more often the Wabanaki members of our group who need travel

---

* I have since learned from Native participants that many Indigenous women, and a few men also, felt uncomfortable with this practice. It was true that in former days, prior to European contact, women were revered during their Moon Time and went into lodges to experience the unique power of this time while the other women in the community cooked for them and took care of their children (sounds wonderful). However, Indigenous culture was not immune to patriarchal Western views of women, and slowly women's menstrual cycles came to be seen as unclean, even dangerous. Many now feel that excluding women from the ceremonies reinforces this misconception, and here in Wabanaki territory a number of Indigenous women have been confronting this practice. It has been many years since I have observed women sitting apart from the Fire.

funds in order to join us. At times, people come when they have just enough money to get to the Gathering but not enough to get home.

Of course, not all Wabanaki need or want travel expenses, but our sharing of resources, when it is helpful, is also out of respect for, and in support of, the work that our Native participants, many of them already considered Elders, do in the world. Many Indigenous Elders are often asked to travel in support of other tribal members in need, and the expenses they incur may be beyond their means but they respond anyway. Also, well-known Elders are often asked by non-Natives to be part of events, symposiums, and the like, but because they don't have the requisite titles or degrees, sometimes they are not paid as much as other "experts," or are given only travel reimbursement but no honorarium, while they share the stage with "professionals" who draw more-than-adequate salaries.

How we acknowledge and respond to our different needs without incurring resentment or embarrassment, and without perpetuating "haves" and "have-nots" in our own group, is a delicate dance to which I never quite know the steps until I'm doing it. In non-Native culture, someone's giving you money because you need it is usually a cause for shame. In Native cultures, the concept that "what is good for one is good for the whole community" still seems ingrained. You share what you have because that is what you do.

A contribution to a Wabanaki participant is generally received gratefully but without much comment or fanfare, possibly because of the trust and understanding that now exists among our group, but possibly a reflection of Native culture as well. A particular moment comes to mind: I was once at an outdoor musical event where we were all sitting on blankets in the grass. To get a little more comfortable, I shifted to lie face down and stretch out. A Native woman next to me, whom I didn't know, reached over and, almost automatically, pulled my blanket up and over my back. "Thank you," I said. She hesitated. "In my culture," she said, "we don't say thank you. We just do for each other."

When I arrive at a Gathering, because I am now the designated "coordinator" of these events, and an incurable organizer, I am filled with questions for our host: "Where would you like people to set up?" "What time should we plan on dinner tonight?" "I heard drummers might be coming, have you heard from them?" and so on, and on. If our host for that Gathering is Wabanaki, I typically receive patient looks and indefinite answers: "I'm not sure." "We'll see." "We'll/they'll figure it out."

It always takes a while for me to get my bearings, to remember that things will happen without, or maybe in spite of, my fretting. Circles will begin, and end, when the time is right. Meals get prepared, dishes washed. The days take on a dreamlike quality and, usually after the first day, I feel myself begin to relax into a rhythm. As I relax, I start to take some risks. I walk up to a Native woman I've not met and introduce myself, although I'm aware I've never had a Native person do this to me. Because this is my way, I'm trying to learn to act naturally in hopes that the intention, at least, will be understood.

The leadership of the Gatherings is now shared between gkisedtanamoogk and me – my role being logistical, his role rooted in his ceremonial responsibilities. He is the one who lights the Sacred Fire at the beginning of each weekend. He conducts the ceremonies and opens the Talking Circles. We consult on the planning involved in every Gathering and, during Gatherings, often debrief at the end of each day. After a time, I feel I can ask him anything, check out assumptions, make mistakes and apologize.

On a few occasions, I crawl into my tent on the first evening aware that he has not yet arrived. I lie in my sleeping bag anxiously wondering how we will proceed the next day if he doesn't show. On these nights, I review all my doubts about this improbable undertaking and finally fall asleep only from the fatigue of traveling. Without fail, we are all awakened, much too soon, by gkisedtanamoogk's voice outside the tents, "time to get up" – a gentle call with the hint of a grin at rousing us at such an outlandish hour. His presence means that he has driven through the night in order to reach us, possibly catching only a couple of hours' sleep in his truck before getting up to prepare himself for First Light.

For me, it is in the First Light ceremony each morning where I can feel the bond among us being woven: our Circle around the Fire growing as, one by one, we creep from our tents to stand patiently waiting to be smudged as a smoldering sweetgrass braid slowly makes its way around; hearing the different timbres of voices as prayers are offered to the Fire, prayers that are accompanied with pinches of tobacco to aid their transit to the Creator; the mingling of Mi'kmaq and Passamaquoddy, Penobscot, Maliseet, and Wampanoag with English; the final sipping from a common bowl of water – our Mother – and the spiral of hugs at the end that gets fairly boisterous, with much teasing and laughter, as we relax after such prolonged concentration.

That sense of unity carries over to our first Talking Circle of the day. After breakfast, and a little time for a short nap, since First Light is so early, we gather. gkisedtanamoogk opens with prayers in his language. He greets the Ancestors and the Spirits from the Four

Directions, asking for their support and guidance in our deliberations. He picks up the Talking Stick from beside the Fire and begins
to speak to us about the protocol of being in the Circle, about how
a Council such as this one is traditionally conducted. This is not a
debate or dialogue where one speaks directly to, or contradicts, someone else in the Circle. Rather, it is a sacred sharing into the Circle of
what is deepest in one's heart or uppermost on one's mind. There are
no rules or expectations about what to say. The message can be personal or political, or both. One may speak or pass. If one chooses to
pass, the Stick will come around again for another chance. He looks
around for an indication from someone that they would like to begin.

I am surprised by the depth of the personal revelations that are
offered right away, even in the first Talking Circle of the weekend,
by many of the Native participants – family troubles, past struggles
with addiction, testimonies about how they came to follow the "Red
Road." The level of trust that this degree of sharing assumes in a
group that has yet to gel, and in which there are still many strangers, is touching, and I attribute this ease of personal revelation to the
comfort they must feel speaking in a format they are used to. It takes
a while, and more revolutions of the Talking Stick, for more pointed
remarks to be made. gkisedtanamoogk, possibly more aware than
others that he is among friends, often takes the lead in bringing up
our peoples' past history and ongoing injustices – a more political
view. Once he does, others test the waters. Anger emerges as stories
of discrimination and humiliation are shared. None of the non-
Natives defend themselves, or leave. We stay, and listen.

Because of the sense of reverence established in the Circles, over
time it begins to feel safe to say anything. Initially, many of us non-
Natives hold back, not wanting to take up space as we usually do.

Slowly, our stories begin to find voice – reflections on our privileges in this culture, as well as our own experiences of oppression. There has been a lot of talk from the Wabanaki participants about "the system" – that amalgamation of US and Canadian policy and capitalism that, in their analysis, serves to keep their communities dependent and make economic development and sovereignty such elusive goals. What is not so evident in the beginning of the Gatherings, but begins to reveal itself over time, is how we non-Natives are impacted by the system as well. The effects of these impacts are subtler, less tangible perhaps, but their acknowledgment becomes increasingly painful.

We non-Natives begin to view the realities of our modern lives – how distanced most of us are from friends and extended family, how rigidly our lives are run by job expectations and schedules – in contrast to the sustaining and nurturing elements of traditional Indigenous culture. Perhaps most significant and painful is that many of us long for a deeper connection to the Earth and to a sense of spiritual presence in our lives. Our Wabanaki friends, in spite of five hundred years of colonization, decimation, poverty, and all manner of attempts to annihilate their culture, seem to have retained a community life that still supports them, strong family networks, and a sense of the importance of the present over endless future planning and schedules. Their traditions, in spite of everything, seem to provide them with a spiritual awareness and depth, rooted in a strong personal relationship to the Earth, that many of us envy. Standing in this gap between longing for a deeper spiritual life, especially in relationship to the Earth, while not wanting to appropriate their culture leaves me with many conflicting emotions and unsatisfactory solutions.

It is now thirty years later, and fourteen of us – seven Wabanaki and seven non-Native – have come together to share our experiences of those Gatherings all those years ago – how we were changed, what we learned, how our lives have been impacted since. Each of our stories is unique, yet we believe that, collectively, they contain lessons relevant to the issues that confront us all today, and help us to envision a shared, mutually beneficial future. We invite you to join us in the Circle as we each, once again, pick up the Talking Stick.

The Talking Circle

In our Talking Circles, especially in the beginning, our need for familiarity and security was embodied in our seating arrangements. Wabanaki participants tended to sit in close proximity to one another; non-Native participants did the same.

We mirror that configuration here, beginning with the Wabanaki participants who are members of the four tribal nations currently recognized in Maine and the Maritimes – Penobscot, Passamaquoddy, Micmac/Mi'kmaq, and Maliseet – as well as Wampanoag from Massachusetts. In addition to reflecting on the Gatherings, Native participants' stories also offer a window into the day-to-day political, social, and economic realities of their lives.

MIIGAM'AGAN

I used to get upset with my partner gkisedtanamoogk when he would go to these Gatherings. I'd say, "Why do you invest time out there, when there is so much work to be done at home?" He would talk about the importance of building alliances and he would say, "Not everyone is arrogant, not everybody's a racist. There are friends out there and they need our support too. If we educate them, they'll do the work in their own communities." One of the things he would say was, "This is important for our future, this is for our children." But for me, at the time, life was about survival. Men aren't as focused on those things, but as women we have to make sure there's three meals a day on the table. One thing that helped during that time was, because of the way our families are structured, decisions about running the house and food and so on would have occurred among my sisters and me anyway. I know my sisters' kitchens like my own – not only my sisters' but other women's too. That's how it works in our communities.

I asked gkisedtanamoogk, "What do you talk about at these Gatherings? What do you do?" That was on my good days, when I was curious. On my bad days, I continued on like I was not interested, like my life was much better than going out and working with non-Natives who've got everything already. That's how I felt. I didn't understand much about alliances or alliance building. He would bring that up and I would be really cynical. I realize that attitude comes from my history – my experience as a child with non-Native teachers, and with the priest, and the nuns, and others. They weren't people you could make friends with because they wouldn't be open to it.

I also felt a lot of anger. Our community was still living in poverty and I remembered how my mother and my grandmother had struggled. Sometimes they had to go out and ask the White grocers for food. That's what my relations with non-Natives had been like.

When I was a child, if a White person drove into our community the women and the children would take off running. Some would run into the woods, or if they were in the house they would run upstairs, go into a room, and close the door tight. We'd stay in there – my mom and her sisters and their children too, maybe twelve or thirteen people – while that White person was visiting my grandfather and asking questions. We would be in that room for hours and we wouldn't have food; or there might still be food cooking on the stove while we were upstairs hiding. At the time, I couldn't understand why we would hide like that, but when I grew up I realized that those were the years when the children were being removed from our communities. The residential schools were still open, and also the Indian Agent was removing children and taking them to foster homes, so you never knew when strangers entered the community if they were there to pick up your children or not.

As a young girl I had already internalized the stereotypes about my people. I remember thinking my family must be really inadequate or weak to be hiding from strangers, but I understand now they were protecting me.

Before attending the Gatherings, I never had a non-Native friend. gkisedtanamoogk had White friends because he didn't grow up on the reserve, but when I went off the reserve I would sometimes take friends or relatives with me because I would panic thinking about leaving the security of my community and not knowing what I might encounter in the White world. And then going out with a young child was an extra challenge because I felt I needed to protect her too. I also worried about what she might witness; it's a double trauma to have your child see her mom being taunted or humiliated.

Eventually I did start to go to the Gatherings. gkisedtanamoogk would always invite me, and the times that I did go I would say, "But don't expect me to get involved; don't put me on the spot and invite me over to sit in a Circle or to be part of things. I'll go and I'll take care of the baby." And I would mostly stay in the tent. A lot of my behavior was about fear, and also my English wasn't that good. That was a barrier for me, the communication; I felt I couldn't participate very well.

But even though I was on the outskirts at the Gatherings, I was observing. I listened to the conversations and to people being truthful and speaking about their feelings. I saw that the non-Native participants were listening to the hurts and the anger of the Native people, my people. And when my people spoke, they were expressing *my* fears, my emotions, my thoughts. So that helped.

I remember, at our last Gathering, JoAnn (whose story follows later) shared a story in the Circle about the privilege of White people. She explained why men have their buttons on one side of their shirts and women's buttons are on the other side. Historically, she said, the privileged White women did not have to dress themselves – their servants did that – and the buttons were placed to make it easier for the servants. When she shared that story, it was so important to me. I felt she recognized how things have been. The White people benefited here on the backs of people of color and, she said, this was what she was committed to changing. I witnessed an understanding, an awareness. It was such a validation. I had never heard our differences described in that way, but that's how we've felt for a long time. I remember my grandfather going to work, being picked up by a White farmer to go and harvest for him, and after a while the rest of us, when we were old enough, we got picked up too.

It's funny now, but when I would go home after attending one of the Gatherings, my sisters would ask me, "So how was it?" And I would say, "My God, they've got a lot of good food!" There were things I'd never eaten before, and I would try them. Sometimes I wouldn't pick something up, but I would ask gkisedtanamoogk to put it on his plate so I could taste it. I wasn't used to some vegetables, like greens, but I tried them and I liked them.

What was interesting too was the size of the Circle – seeing that many White people sitting there and listening to our people, and we can be very long-winded. I had always seen it the other way around – our people sitting in big groups and listening to non-Native people. Sometimes it got extremely hot in the sun, and I would get on gkisedtanamoogk's case saying, "How could you make people sit there for so long?" I'd see him perspiring too and I'd say, "Gee, think about it!" But seeing all those people willing to sit there, listening in the heat, that was one of the things that impressed me the most.

At first, I thought it was important to have our voices heard by the non-Natives because I was thinking, "These are the people that give the governments their power. They tell their governments how to make policies." Then, when I got to spend more time with them, I heard White people complaining about their government and their complaints were the same as ours. I thought, "What? Oh my God. You guys are critical of your own government, and I was counting on you!" That's how naive I was. It was such an awakening for me.

I thought non-Natives had the perfect life. I only knew the good things written about White people in Canadian history and American history. Up to that time, I'd mostly seen White families in the movies or on TV or in nursery books. We've lived side by side for so many generations but not known one another. We've had only secondhand information. When I met all the non-Natives at the Gatherings I assumed they lived the same way we do – I thought they were all from the same community. Then I found out that Shirley lived in Portland and JoAnn lived in Massachusetts and they did not see each other every day. My mind got a little disoriented. How I perceived the world then was based on my understanding of how our community was, or how our family was.

I don't romanticize the White culture anymore. What I learned in the Gatherings is that we are all people. That's not to say there's not injustice because there is, but not every non-Native is privileged … not everyone is … we're all part of the same system. Before, I had a fixed image of every White person; I would put on layers and layers to protect myself, and wear a "face," a false face. Just like any hockey player, you protect yourself when you face your opponent. But in witnessing the commitment from those people in the Gatherings, somehow my heart started to open. And with the shattering of my stereotypes about who White people are, other pathways opened for me.

The Gatherings were my springboard. Since then, I've had a lot more experience in the White world or in mixed groups. I take classes and work at the university now, for example. And it gets easier. But racism still exists. It's like being in the schoolyard – if the bullies are there, you know who they're going to bully. We still understand that we're the prey, and they are the predators, but at least now I know that not everyone is like that.

We've been so misrepresented by the media and by institutions and the educational system. In the history books, we were always the savages, the warring people. We were the ugly side of life. And as a Native child of course you hate that, and you gravitate to the Western world and look to model yourself after that, but at what cost? You walk around feeling like you're not a whole person. You feel wounded, like someone who needs to be fixed. That's why building those relationships – those friendships – in our Circles was so important because we see ourselves through others. I remember being confused when I was young because I felt love from the people around me and I would think, "If people in my family and my community love me so much, then why are we not good people?"

At the Gatherings, I felt that people really began to see us. I've always downplayed my intelligence because I wasn't fluent in English. And now I'm proud that as a young person I was fluent in my own language. I remember it was an eye-opener when gkisedtanamoogk said to me, "You know, think about some of the French teachers in Neguac, or other French people who barely speak English, it doesn't mean they're not intelligent. They are experts in their own culture and in their own language. You don't look at them like they're not intelligent, so why feel that way about yourself? English is not your first language. It doesn't have anything to do with intelligence."

In my community, the majority of our older leaders are fluent in their language and they're very intelligent, but because they're not able to speak English well, they judge themselves. They feel that they're looked at as stupid, so they downplay their own culture or they say it's of no value. That's what we're up against in our communities. We have members in key positions who are fluent in their language but who aren't open to our culture and don't support the Native language in the community. These people want our community to advance by becoming better White people, but that's the wrong message to send to our children. I think our young people have been very angry with us because they weren't speaking their language and no one was teaching them.

It was good when non-Natives from the Gatherings came up to my community of Esgenoôpetitj and spent time there. We were working on creating a Wabanaki Resource Center to address some of the issues in our community, and the center was going to be in our home. There was a team from the Gatherings that came up to help us renovate the basement. We were sheet rocking and all covered in dust, and I remember thinking at the time, "My God, they can do anything." I learned later that, for some of them, it was their first time doing something like that too. We all just figured it out together.

The last Gathering ended nearly thirty years ago but the relationships have continued. That's been a wonderful experience for me – the friendships that we've developed. By the end, I knew the importance of what we'd done and I knew some genuine, sincere people. It was a rare thing, you know.

What's important is making connections among the members of both communities – the White community and us. This can't happen unless you have a place, or a forum, to meet. We wouldn't have become friends if it hadn't been for the Gatherings. Back then our communities always had other people representing us. We had representatives who were our elected leadership to women's organizations like the New Brunswick Native Women's Council – people like Barb Martin, and Gwen Bear and Alma Brooks. If there needed to be a meeting with a White organization they would go, so they were the ones with the experience of working with White people. And when they came home, we would ask them the same thing that my sisters would ask me when I came back from the Gatherings, "How was it?"

Creating relationships is simply making that effort to get to know one another in small steps. But every step is really a big step because each one of us represents our families, and communities too. Now we count on our contacts in the White community to help people learn about us. Before, we've always been alone in doing damage control over how we were portrayed in the media. Now, we have friends out there who know we're not what the history books have made us out to be.

Because of the Gatherings, and also because of what the ceremonies have taught me, now in my thanksgiving prayers I include everyone. Before, I limited myself to just Native people, but I never felt right about that. It didn't feel authentic. I couldn't put my whole self into those prayers, and so I was denying myself in denying others.

WAYNE

In my own personal life there is a lot of diversity. The lady I married is not of my race, but we have managed to scratch out over fifty years together. It has not always been easy, but somehow or other we have transcended our differences. We have a family and a community, and we're always growing.

After finishing my degree at Harvard, I decided that my community, Motahkomikuk, was the place I wanted to be. At that time, there were a lot of job opportunities in the Native agencies in Washington, but I didn't want to live in Washington, DC. I tried it for six months. It wasn't for me. Motahkomikuk is the place for me; working within the community on the many things that we have to work on, and there's still a lot of work ahead of us.

I'm not exactly sure how I heard about the Gatherings; it may have been through friends and mutual acquaintances. But once I started participating, it became evident to me what the relationship was becoming. It's as if one day the lights went on. I woke up in the middle of the process and thought, "Wow, this is worth my time. It's worth investing myself."

I liked the people and I liked that, if nothing else, we were trying to clear the air. Each of us brings our personal history to any conversation. Native people bring a particular history in terms of what happened to us in the past and how things came to be as they are now.

My experience prior to the Gatherings had been that whenever we tried to raise some of these issues non-Natives were largely unwilling to deal with them. Instead they would talk about the superficial stuff. We'd hear "I like you people," or "I like your costumes," those sorts of things. Non-Natives were fascinated with our outerwear, but nobody wanted to talk about what was inside of us.

So all of a sudden I was with a group of people who were trying to understand one another and to be inclusive. Meeting in the Talking Circle was a major selling point because we were using a process that was very familiar to me. One of the dynamics of the Circle is that you take whatever time is needed to process something; you don't rush things. Once people "have the floor" they know they can speak about their concerns in whatever way they want, however long they want, and the rest of us are obligated to listen. As soon as you give up the Talking Stick, or whatever object you're using, the process gets reversed. Someone else starts speaking and you become part of the bigger Circle again, with an obligation to listen as others did to you. It's a sacred responsibility as far as I'm concerned. It's what makes the Circle special.

I've had experiences, particularly when I was younger, when it seemed that if non-Natives invited you "to the table" it was always to receive something. Very seldom did non-Natives acknowledge that you brought something. The Gatherings were different; there was a willingness to exchange. I didn't feel the old apprehensions: "Oh, God, am I going to be good enough?" or "What do I have to offer?" In the Gatherings, there was a mutual desire to understand one another, to reach out to one another in all ways. Even in the social times, when we ate together, there was an "above and beyond" effort to please, to help, and to share. All those positives were different from what I had previously experienced in my life.

High school is a good example. We Passamaquoddies seldom social-
ized with our classmates except in the context of school. Back then, not
only did they not invite us into their homes or to their social functions,
we didn't invite them either, though maybe for different reasons. I think
some of the Native reticence had to do with shame because we lived in
shacks, in housing that was twenty years behind or more; no indoor
facilities, for example. And the non-Natives' houses and facilities
seemed so superior. In those days, when I was a kid and we were fighting for acceptance, all those things were giant. Now, as adults, when
Natives and non-Natives experience the Circle together, all of those
things seem so trivial and unimportant – the material aspect of things.

One thing that stood out for me in the Gatherings was that there
was no talk of your educational level. It was assumed that you knew
something, but there was no labeling it, as in, "I'm from Harvard
and I've got this great degree" or "I'm a doctor" and so on. Also,
Indigenous knowledge was elevated to a status that I was greatly
unfamiliar with. That's what made the Circle so powerful for a lot of
the Natives; all of a sudden somebody was listening to what we had
to say and validating it. Very few people had ever taken advantage
of the wisdom in our experiences and in our traditional knowledge.
And boy, didn't we pick up on that, at least I did. I could feel it and
it felt awful good. I felt calm.

It might seem that the way I was brought up was paradoxical
in that I went through the public education system but was also
educated by my own people. We have a word for that – when two
things appear to be in conflict but they're not. Our word is *unci skat
keq kisesinuhk*. My grandmother was very traditional and a very
Catholic woman. It seems that the two don't align but somehow she
made it work. She taught me a lot about our stories, and to believe

in the things that have been handed down. For example, we have the Rock People, and these Rock People are very benevolent. They do a lot of good things for us if you understand what the signs are. One of the things my grandmother taught me was that any time people hear unexplained drums it means someone's going to get married, and the drums are the Rock People having a pre-celebration. Although I never saw them myself I believed what she said.

I was telling this story to a colleague once and he said, "You don't really believe that, do you?" I said, "Of course I do! Number one, my grandma wouldn't lie to me, and number two, I believe it in the same sense that you believe the things you were brought up with. There's nothing different here." I think that put him on tilt for a while; he'd never heard a response like that. He was challenging how I was brought up and I challenged him equally, as if to say, "What's good for the goose is good for the gander."

What made it easy for me to participate in the Gatherings was that our differences were not a big factor. Right away, you felt you were able to contribute your best. Feeling accepted allowed me to start acknowledging what others brought to the Circle, their own cultural or spiritual influences.

There was a time in my life when I didn't care too much for White people because of all they had done to us, but now, while I recognize those feelings, I've also grown past them. One thing the Gatherings taught me is that I didn't know as much as I thought I did. At the time we were meeting, I still had a lot to learn about working with people from different backgrounds. What I learned in the Gatherings was how to manage and articulate my feelings in a healthy way. I won't let anger be my overriding reaction, while I acknowledge that anger is still part of who I am.

For example, a few years ago, my son's best friend died in our community, and the family wanted my son, J.D., to smudge the body before they put it into the ground. Those two guys were really close – they were both hunters – and so J.D. agreed to do the smudge, which was really something because he tends to shy away from that sort of thing. He will participate in ceremonies but he doesn't necessarily take the leadership. But I'll never forget the minister, who was also participating in the funeral; he came up to J.D. and me and said, "Well, you guys do your stuff and then I'll wrap it up." "Well, that 'stuff,'" I replied, "we call it prayer." I was instantly angry at his attitude, but I thought, "Should I show anger, or is this a teachable moment?" So right in front of everybody I started chanting, then J.D. began, and you could tell by looking at the entire community gathered there that the chants and the smudging were reaching deep into their souls – you could sense it. I remember that day especially because of that minister's lack of respect, and his lack of understanding that something other than what he had to offer could be known as prayer, or could be legitimate in the eyes of the Creator. Somehow I was able to keep a check on my anger and say what I needed to say to him. I think he was instantly sorry that he said the words because he saw my reaction, but we didn't make any more of it. I just said to myself, "Well, let's hope he learned something from it." I still get angry at people's intolerance. It's something I don't tolerate!

If a person in the Gatherings was spending their time on negative energy, because they hadn't yet processed some of their issues, then somehow the group took the time to assist that person. Sometimes a Native person would come with such horrific issues in their own life that no matter what a White person said it wouldn't make much difference; that person would still be overwhelmed by his or her own unprocessed and un-dealt-with issues, and that can be as much of a block as anything I know. There's powerful stuff going on in that Circle, and if you're not ready for it you can get damn nervous seeing your issues that close up. That's the reality of the situation. But those of us, both Native and non-Native, who stayed on, and who were willing to do the work that was necessary, were able to go to another level of relationship. It was no longer Whites versus Indians, or Natives versus non-Natives; it was friends.

The people who stayed with the process are the ones who now enjoy getting together after all these years. We enjoy socializing, enjoy talking about world events, enjoy the fact that we're not afraid to talk about issues, even when we don't see eye to eye. We've actually built a "sacred circle of learning." That's not my term – I got it from another Native educator, Dr. Sandra Fox – but that's what I call it. That's what I call the space where we're not afraid to bring who we are and what we represent. It's a sacred space because it is a place of trust and safety, free from intimidation. I hold these places in the highest esteem because they deserve that.

What we received from the Gatherings was much more than we hoped for. I don't think any of us ever bargained for such a big prize. When we met together at my home to work on this book, the first thing I noticed was that now I am comfortable about sharing, about being me. I feel free to talk about things I haven't figured out yet, or about my declining health. We're all growing older, there's no escaping that, and it was good to be able to talk about it. We spend a lot of time protecting our vulnerability, but as I grow older I understand that it's in vulnerability that we learn the most. By letting our shields down, we leave ourselves open to new thinking, new teachings, new relationships.

And even though it had been thirty years since some of us had seen one another, it felt as if we had been together just the week before. It's as if we've all been in the same canoe. We know how each one leans in that canoe so that it doesn't spill, and there's a certain rhythm that we have with each other.

And we're never done. I become more self-aware every time I listen to those who have been in the Circle with me. Even though you might hear the same story from someone, you're hearing it from a different place, and that's the magic of it all. When you look at the world as a "cycle" it looks different than when you look at it in blocks – blocks one on top of the other. The world isn't like that. Just look at the natural movement of the Earth, of our moon, our sun, the life cycle of the plants, our life cycle. Everything moves in cycles, and the more we start looking at things that way the easier it becomes to understand what it is we're reaching for. Look at what happens after we pass, for example. We no longer have use for our body but the Spirit is still there. An Elder once said, "When somebody goes, a part of their Spirit is shared with us. They leave a part of themselves with us."

The other thing he said is that we can't go to that next place until we've learned all that we need to, or were supposed to learn, in this place. I'm not sure I fully understand that yet. That's probably why I'm still here.

GWEN

I've had a lot of experience in my life with non-Natives. Years ago, I began teaching Native culture and arts, and originally all my students were Native, but I knew the program had to expand in order to continue. As a result, I began to include non-Native students until my classes were about half and half. I still kept the classes small though, normally around twelve students. I like small classes. That's the way to teach because you get really close to the students. Then you know them not only as minds but also as human beings with spirits.

I married a non-Native and I've had non-Native friends my whole life, even in high school, so it was never hard for me to relate to them. I even had pen pals in my youth who were non-Native, and of course they sometimes asked dumb questions. I still get those. You meet people who walk on eggshells around you; you also meet people who want to walk all over you, usually government officials. They like power, or perceived power as I call it. But as for the Gatherings, I can't think of any awkward moments that I experienced.

I got involved with the Gatherings because I believed at the time that there were groups of people within all races that were working toward fulfilling a prophecy of a new world to come. The prophecies were calling them the Warriors of the Rainbow – people who unite to work together in a good way. By that time, I had come to understand what prophecy really is. Initially I suppose, like anyone else, I thought of prophecy as a prediction of something that would happen in the future. My understanding changed when I went to an annual Assembly of First Nations in Manitoba. Elders there said that by meeting together we were fulfilling a prophecy. I had never seen myself *within* prophecy; I had always thought it was something outside of me.

One particular prophecy described by the Elders was that Native women were going to bring the Nations up again through the teaching of traditional ways. The symbol for traditional ways is a bear, and since I was a Bear, and also a Native woman, I knew I was one of those women. Sometimes there are those moments when everything changes, and you know you're not just an observer of life anymore, you're part of it; this was one of those moments. At the time, my life included other groups that I thought were part of these unfolding prophecies, and that is what I decided about this group – the Gatherings – and the people who were participating in them. That was the reason for my continuing with them and working with them; it was as if, after my first Gathering, I knew these people were for real. Also I knew gkisedtanamoogk, and I trusted his judgment about who he became involved with.

My involvement with the Gatherings began with gkisedtanamoogk. I believe he needed a ride to one of the weekends and I was his driver. I got to meet everyone at that time. It seemed that the non-Natives there had an interest in not walking all over Native people. They weren't only interested in supporting us; they took it to the personal level. They were open to learning and they were changed by the experience. They were probably more changed by those Circles than I was.

One time, it was so hot in the Circle that we were burning up out there in the sun but people wouldn't get up and move! These were huge Circles that took hours to complete. I think it was the non-Natives' patience that impressed me, or their persistence, that they would sit in a Circle and listen to everyone for that long. It's not as if they were prisoners; they wanted to be there. I call it "Spirit feeding"; your Spirit wants it, whether it's hot or not.

Once when I was in British Columbia, one of the teachings I heard there was, "When an Elder starts speaking, you sit down and listen." So when one of the Elders began to speak, I sat down and listened until almost two o'clock in the morning. He just kept talking and sharing his teachings. There was a young woman there and afterward she said to me, "I couldn't understand a word that man said." I was amazed because I had understood him. He had the kind of power that when he spoke, he spoke to your heart. He also had a sort of lisp, and I think it filtered out those who weren't going to learn from him. That's kind of how it works.

I had the patience to sit and listen for what that Elder had to teach me, and you recognize that quality in someone else. I remember one winter Wesley, Shirley H. (whose stories are to come), and another woman traveled to Halifax, Nova Scotia, to attend an environmental conference. They must have driven a long way, and it was snowing. They came, in part, because they knew a number of us Native people from the region would be attending and they wanted to talk to us about the Gatherings. There was one evening when the Native people were going to meet separately from the others, and I had told Wesley that they could talk to us when this meeting was over. Well, the Native people's meeting went on well into the night. We kept talking because we had business to attend to, and these folks – Wesley, Shirley, and this other person – just waited. They waited on the outside of the door to the room where we were meeting until almost midnight. I remember coming out and saying, "You're still here!" They did not come in to interrupt us, which is what impatient people would have done. It was that action, that they waited until we finished talking before they came in to introduce themselves, that told me these people were honorable and worth giving my time to. There are certain qualities in other people that you recognize, and really appreciate, that are like our ways.

Another reason I stayed involved in the Gatherings was to help my people, and for that you have to look for outside support. We Native people who have good hearts and want to do things don't necessarily have the whole picture. We need outside support, people who will help us access money or access others who can help. Some of the non-Natives I met were like trainers in this area, as in, "This is how you get money," and "This is how you do things" – activism, in other words. And although they supported us in those particular ways, it was really for the benefit of both, because when you work together you are also developing personal relationships with one another. You're all in it together, whatever "it" is. It's so nice when you can trust someone and can say, "I count that person on my side." Then if something negative occurs elsewhere, it balances that out.

When people are together like that, it's a higher level of being. A Native's life is very political but we need a broader definition of "politics" before it has meaning for us. "Politics" as it's usually understood is very competitive and adversarial, and when you're not an adversarial kind of person it is hard to work within that system, so politics is not enough for us. We need a definition that includes the spiritual. We know that whatever we do we need the help of the Spirit, the Creator, the Grandmothers and Grandfathers, however you want to name it.

I see the whole world through my Native language. I was brought up speaking Maliseet; English is my second language. Although I teach in English, and live in it, my perception of the world still comes from the words that I first learned – the Native words. There are four colors in my language – white, red, black, and yellow. These colors are treated uniquely, as if they are the only four colors that exist in the world. We can express other colors like "blue" or "green" for example, but we describe these colors by saying "the color of sky" or "the color of grass." But white, red, black, and yellow stand on their own. We knew that there were Yellow people, we knew there were White people and Black people, and we knew that we were the Red ones. By portraying these colors in a wheel, the Medicine

Wheel, we also knew which direction each group occupied. It came as no surprise, for instance, when I saw my first Black person or my first White person. It wasn't surprising because I already knew those colors. And from the Native perspective I was born with, the reason you meet together is because there is nothing more important to do. Each of the races is supposed to do something. You're supposed to give something to each of the other races and they are supposed to give something to you. In this way the world comes to a place of unity, a place of peace, through working together, not working separately. That is our message.

What I have come to understand is that everyone is a Light. The skin is only a blanket, and underneath that blanket is Light. When a Circle is made, it makes all the Lights brighter, and that gets the attention of the Spirits – the Grandmothers and Grandfathers. It doesn't matter who is in that Circle; at that point we're the human family.

When all of us, Native and non-Native, came together through CVP and the Gatherings, what we created still lives. When I think about some of those people, I may not know what they are doing right now but I trust implicitly that, whatever it is, it's right. And I believe that's the way they think about me too. We still care for each other. If you didn't care for each other you wouldn't want to continue in your mission. It's the caring that makes someone want to continue. That's the spiritual element.

When the White people came to this continent they wanted something from us. I know there are many stories about all the bad things that happened, but that time is gone. We still have tomorrow. We can begin again tomorrow. Of course we can look at our history, and maybe there are still lessons there to be learned, but we can't dwell on that. What is more important is what we do now, in this time.

There is an Elder from Mexico who comes to my home every once in a while. I just love him. One time, a White woman went up to him and said, "I am so sorry for all the things my people did." And he responded, "But you didn't do that. What you can do is love my people now." As in, "Don't worry about what happened, love my people now." That is the message, I think. Yes, all that happened. Let's make things better now.*

DANA

My interest in the Gatherings was because I saw an opportunity to get our story – the real story – out there to non-Natives. Also, it seemed the group wasn't confrontational. That was an important element for me because prior to that time I'd had major involvement with my peoples' land claims process, as an opponent to the settlement that was negotiated, and I had spent a long time in warrior mode. By the time the process was over, I was not a nice guy to be around. I was pretty angry. The way I saw it, the deal we were offered would totally abrogate our rights, and would negate our autonomy and our inherent title to the land. I felt my own people were compromising our integrity and repeating history by giving away our rights to our land just for the sake of greed, for the bucks.

Involvement on behalf of our people goes back a long way in my family. When my grandfather – my step-grandfather – was our chief, he went to the United Nations, along with two of our other leaders,

* Portions of Gwen's message were taken from an interview about the Gatherings that she gave to Peace Talks Radio, a program distributed by Public Radio International, 2002.

and petitioned for nationhood. Because the US representative to the UN refused to support us, the UN said to them, "We can't receive you. We have no way to receive you," so they returned home. Of course the State of Maine heard about this, and the state said to us, in essence, "Well, you little Indians better go home now and sit down and be quiet." But that action on the part of our leaders created an awareness at the state level that we might still have a valid claim to our lands. My uncle was involved in doing some of the preliminary research on the issues, and he found that historically we never gave up our rights. I took his work further and did my own research. I found evidence that our people have never been defeated in war, that we still live on our ancestral lands, and that our government has been intact since prior to the time that the Europeans came here. In other words, we still live in our territory, and our lands never were a reservation. That means that we have the right to be here. We have the right to the air, the right to the land, and the right to the water, everything. We have a valid claim.

To substantiate my position, I spent a tremendous amount of time and energy researching our history and our culture. And I started to have experiences speaking on these issues to non-Native audiences. To prepare myself to speak in public, I went to the university and took a class on "oral interpretation of literature," where the students put on theatrical interpretations of written works. Our teacher was a young professor, and every day she would come in with a whole armful of books. She'd throw them on the table and say, "There's your homework, pick one." You had to go through a book and the next day you presented the book. You didn't just pick out a little phrase from it, you had to pick out the significant parts of the book and then get up and present the whole thing to the class. I had to give myself that kind of experience because at the time I was being put in situations where I had to talk spontaneously on topics related to the land claims, and I had to respond quickly. Most of my work in the military and in industry didn't require verbal skills. When I worked in electronics there was very little need for conversation; you kept your head down and did your work. So when I had to get up and speak, I was kind of shy. You wouldn't think I am shy today, but I am – I'm still a shy guy.

I felt I had to accept this task that was being presented to me on behalf of my people. At some of these meetings I had to really "get down" on some issues, and I learned to do it. It doesn't bother me anymore to come forward and speak, even if it's controversial. Recently at one of my public talks a man came up to me afterward and said, "Well, what's wrong with living with us, and being like us?" I said, "Well, the way I understand it, we should have a right to decide how we want to live. We should have that opportunity. And I don't think your society has been a good example of what we want to be." I guess I was kind of hostile in my response to him.

So to meet the people at the Gatherings, different kinds of people that you could be comfortable with, and who could be a sounding board for you, was really good. The Gatherings were the first place where I could speak with non-Native people and not have someone get "in my face" about things. That experience brought things out of me that I didn't know were there. It was a feeling that I wanted. We shared a lot of things, and we developed into a community for the time we were there. I brought some of my friends, and I made new friends. It was an experience that was spiritually connected, a collective spirituality that we created together.

What I remember most was the respect that was given to an Indigenous person, whether man or woman, and having people accept and acknowledge you as a Native person. It's very important to know you're going to be accepted, and where you're going to be accepted, because there's still so much negativity and racism in the world that you don't always know how someone is going to respond to you. You might be at a Gathering, and feeling really good, and the next day go into town where someone could be in your face about something. So those Gatherings, for me, were a step away from my warrior mode. They gave me a chance to be sociable. I've always felt that I'm a fairly social person, and that I can interact well with people. I'm still very guarded with women, I realize, but dealing with those feelings is part of my own learning that continues.

You have to learn to handle things in your life. There's much I had to unlearn once I left home after everything I saw in my community, and the negative impact of certain things that were done to me as a child. You have to do your own introspection, and outline everything about yourself that you see and want to change.

When I was growing up we were so poor that you couldn't even pay attention. What I mean is that we were so concerned with day-to-day survival that we didn't have time to think about the outside world and how our lives were impacted by what others might be doing to us. One time I still remember vividly: I was a kid, coming through the door of my grandmother's house, the house where I live now. I always visited there because there was food. We lived in the house next door where there were only two rooms for the fourteen of us; well, thirteen of us, because my grandmother had taken my eldest sister to stay with her. I came through that door and all I remember was her big hand coming at me; my grandmother was going to hit me. I grabbed her hand and I said, "Meme, don't ever hit me again, don't ever try to hit me. If I have done something wrong, let's sit down and talk about it, but don't try to hit me." And she said, "Why?" I said, "Because I'm not going to be responsible for my actions. I might hit you back." I think I was trying to say to her, "I'm taking back my power."

When I was young I visited regularly in every house in my community. I was in all of them at one time or another – two-hundred-some homes. So seven days a week I would see all the things that went on. I remember how people would start "sporting" – drinking – on Wednesday or Thursday. They'd work hard all week for their money and then go into town and when they'd come back you'd meet them down at the ferry landing and grab an arm, let them hug you, and you'd help them home so they wouldn't fall all over the road.

I'm one of those people who was robbed of my language. My mother spoke Passamaquoddy but she only spoke it with her mother and some of the other women in the community, she never talked Passamaquoddy with us. When we went to church we weren't allowed to speak it. In school we weren't allowed to speak it. When I think back to primary school, I was already revolting against the nuns. I could not tolerate them. One of the things that happened that was most significant to me was that, for punishment, I would always get put underneath the nun's desk – the desk where she sat. Those desks were those big old oak ones that have the drawers on both sides and solid wood across the back, so that space is closed in. There I was under that desk sitting right in front of that nun. Even now, once in a while, I get a smell of those women. I can smell those women from being underneath there. By the time I left that school, I'd see those big rulers coming at me – those big, thick yardsticks – and I'd look right at them and say, "Go ahead, you can't hurt me anymore."

I was fortunate in that my parents didn't drink. Not only that, but my own experience of going into the military taught me professionalism. I couldn't indulge in drinking and those kinds of things because if I'd messed up in my work, or in my schooling, I wouldn't be where I am today. I joined the military after high school, and then worked in the electronics industry; I worked on equipment for NASA and the Atomic Energy Commission. I married a non-Native woman. But when I came back to Maine with all my technical training I could not apply my skills because I was the wrong color. I had a huge dossier of all my classes and work experiences but no one in the electronics or technology fields would hire a Native person. What opened up was an opportunity to go into the building trades because that industry at the time was under pressure from equal opportunity and affirmative action, so I went back to school for three years in construction and got that experience as well.

I came back to Maine to be with my daughters and to be part of their lives. Our children are our future and I wanted to be there to help guide them. I had hoped that there might be something positive for our people in the land claims process that was underway and I wanted to be part of that too, though, as I said, it didn't turn out well at all in my opinion. In spite of that, I had a distinct feeling that the Spirits wanted me to return. Once I was home, back on my land, I started to become more and more aware of my connection with my ancestors, and my life began to take an entirely different path. I set out on what we call the "Red Road." I had to seek out that road – my culture's spiritual tradition – on my own because when I was growing up we were never exposed to that. My father didn't teach me. My grandfather didn't teach me that either, although there were a lot of things that I learned from him culturally. I would hunt with him, and fish with him, and watch him work and do things; I remember a lot that he shared. But when it came to the spiritual aspect, we weren't given instructions; we didn't have that opportunity.

I recently had a talk with my daughter. I was describing things I saw in our community growing up, and explaining some of the effects of that on my life. I've researched and spoken a lot about the topic of generational trauma, but at an event a few years ago I witnessed a great way to explain it. I was at an Elders and Youth conference at Onondaga where I had been speaking about trauma and how it gets passed down. Two women at my talk, who were presenters there also, jumped right on that concept. After my presentation, they went to a nearby stream and collected a whole bunch of rocks in bags, and the next day they brought all these rocks into their session.

They asked five women to sit, each one right behind the other, representing a great-grandmother, a grandmother, a mother, her daughter and the daughter's daughter – five generations. Then they had five men stand right by each of the women – right by their shoulders. They gave each of the women a bag of rocks to hold, representing their trauma. Then one of the presenters started a story. She started with the great-grandmother. She talked about this woman's trauma and how she didn't know that she was passing that trauma on to her daughter. She handed the great-grandmother's bag of rocks to the next woman in line so now this woman had two bags of trauma. She continued to talk about trauma and how it's passed down, giving those two bags to the next woman in line, who now has three. Finally, five generations down the road, here is this young girl. She's got her arms full of historical, generational, trauma – five bags of it. And the presenter said, "That's the cycle that needs to be broken."

Then she went over to the men, and she said, "And what did the men do? The men did nothing, because they were disempowered. The whole social structure of the men had been disrupted – they couldn't work, they didn't have the value of the men's role, and so they were disempowered." And there the women were, having had all this stuff dumped on them. They're the life givers, they're the carriers of the future, and yet they're not able to move out from under this burden. The trauma might be from the church, or from alcohol, or from abuse, sexual abuse. Whatever the source, it keeps being passed down.

I decided a long time ago, when my kids were younger, that I was not going to pass on the trauma that was given to me by my father and by others like my grandmother. They say "You can't erase history"; well, I disagree with that. If you don't know why you act certain ways, and you want to grow and change, then look at things that have happened in your life, negative things. You start to understand what you might be doing because of that negative thing. Then take one step further: go back into the history of that event and ask how that event happened. And once you go back, keep going back, and back, and all at once you see, "Oh, that's how that happened," or "That's who caused that." That's when you change history, because then you send that event back to the person who did those things. You say, "This doesn't belong to me, I don't want this in my life anymore." You send it back and all of a sudden you can feel the change, you realize the change. You've taken a negative thing and you've sent it back to whoever gave it to you, saying, "I don't want this."

So, in talking to my daughter, I told her, "You were born with a strong history. Because you were born in your community, and you were born in the house of your ancestors, you've got a long, strong history. The room you were born in was your great-great-great grandmother's; she was one of our medicine women. An old, very powerful medicine woman was in that room." My daughter's placenta is buried out underneath the blue spruce in my yard. That's the tree of life. This history is what we're nurturing today in our children.

What Native people are focusing on in the communities today is healing for tomorrow. The mind of the Native person is getting stronger; it's growing healthier. The mind of the White people who came here to this land and possessed this land was very sick. Their way of life was not healthy and they were carrying a lot of their own historical trauma with them. If you look at their actions and what they did to us historically, those were the actions of a sick mind. The prophecies say that they, the White people, will someday come to the Native people for help and to understand what's going on. The fact that we are still here, that we're still carrying our stories and still know the history of who we are, is testimony to our strength. When I go to Micmac country, I see it in their community too. I see the pride. I see the beauty of the people. I see the health. They're very strong people – the Micmacs – and powerful. Indigenous people have been able to persevere through our own strength and our own willingness to maintain ourselves. White people can do a lot of things to us, but there are a lot of things they can't do. They can't take away what we feel and what we believe.

I talked with the students in a local school a little while ago. I spoke to them about all of the important things that are happening today, and how we need to think about the seven generations to come. One of the teachers said, "Seven generations, my goodness, that's a long time!" I said, "Yes, imagine if you always had to think about seven generations to come, what would you change in your decision-making processes today? You wouldn't do the same things, would you?" And then I said, "If you think about what's going on today in the world, don't you think we should have started thinking about these things seven generations ago?"

The prophecies say that this is a time when we are all to come together. The Gatherings were an opportunity and a "coming out" for me, a chance to speak about my culture and to learn about other cultures, a chance to find the heart connection that can exist among us. The Gatherings showed me the importance of our connection. They set me on my path. In recent years, I have traveled all over the world as a member of an international group of Native spiritual Elders. I've seen the value in what we can share together. We need each other. We can't pick up and leave this place. We're here. We're all here for the long run.

ALMA

I became involved in the Gatherings because, at the time, there was quite a large gap between non-Native and Aboriginal people. We didn't know one another. We'd been living on this land together for five hundred years and still we didn't know one another. So my involvement was to try to understand where people were coming from in terms of issues. There are still today a lot of issues between our peoples that have not been resolved.

What surprised me right away was how much information non-Natives lacked. They didn't know what was going on in their own society in terms of what the government was doing to Aboriginal people. Their focus seemed very narrow, that was one of the things I noticed. A lot of them talked about their children or their house or cooking a meal, that sort of thing, whereas our people were involved in politics. Our people were involved; they knew what was going on in the world. I think those initial Gatherings were life-changing for the non-Natives who "got it," but others had blinders on; there were things they just didn't want to see.

I've gone to events that started out being led by Aboriginal people and the next thing you know the non-Natives took over, so I just backed out the door. If I go somewhere and I feel there is no place for me, or no involvement for me, I don't go back. In the Gatherings, people were trying more. People wanted to learn and a lot of respect was shown. There were also attempts on the part of non-Native people to meet among themselves in order to teach one another how to address Aboriginal people – where the boundaries are, for example – because there are times when non-Natives are offensive and don't even know it. For instance, when we invite someone to share in something of ours, like a ceremony, that doesn't mean that we're giving it to them, especially if it has to do with our culture or our identity. A lot of people are so taken with us that all of a sudden they want to be an Indian, and so they search in the archives until they can find, say, a distant relative who they think makes them Native.

For a lot of non-Native people, their own identity has been watered down so badly that they don't feel they have one. I've heard people say, "I'm a fireman" or "I'm a policeman" or "I'm a teacher," but when that job comes to an end, who are you? It's very shallow if you base your identity on a job or a title. I think the non-Native people had a sense that we had something, and they didn't know quite what it was, but it was something they didn't have and they longed for it. In sitting and talking to us, and participating in various ways with us, I think they began to realize it was the spiritual component.

Ministers and priests are having a hard time these days because for a long time they've been saying all these words, words, words; yet people are leaving the church. You can't only talk about Spirit. You can't put spirituality in a book. A good example is the Bible. Those are powerful words – it's probably one of the most powerful books in the world – but the Bible is only words unless there's a connection spiritually. And you have to think that the people at the top of these church hierarchies don't believe in what they're saying because look at what they've been doing all over the world – abusing children and all that. It's all coming out now. That's what can happen if intentions are not good and if hearts are not pure. That's how it works. You have to have a pure, clean, honest heart.

Imagine all of those Native children in residential schools, and fifty thousand of them killed and buried around these schools. Now the survivors are trying to get through a horrific retelling with the Truth and Reconciliation Commission here in Canada. They have to go through everything again; everything they experienced as children they've gone through again as they retell their stories in an effort to try to heal themselves and address the pain. But the shroud of secrecy has been torn, and the light is shining in on these atrocities. And the church, I believe, is now starting to say, "Maybe we did something wrong ... maybe there is something lacking in what we've been teaching people."

I work with a group of ministers – retired ministers – who are very open to seeing the church's failings, but the church is a huge machine. A lot of things that they're dealing with here in Canada, and working to expose, are still going on in South America and in other poor countries. They're still going on.

I have worked with medicine people from the South, and have gone into many ceremonies with them. Those ceremonies gave me an opportunity to meet myself, to get to know my real Self. Now I know that my Self, my Soul, is very special; considerate, respectful and generous, I would say. I can trust that it will never steer me wrong. That's a good place to be. It's not the ego I'm talking about; I mean the Self, the real Self. I know this Self not because someone told me about it but because I experienced it. I experienced it in a ceremony.

Many, many years ago, there were Wabanaki families who left the East and migrated west. They did this to protect our traditional knowledge. They had to protect the ceremonies, and the songs and the teachings. They took these things underground because they knew that what was coming would destroy them. Now the teachings are returning. These are things that are kept strictly secret because they're so powerful; and there is a certain process that has to happen for people to access this knowledge because it is so powerful. That goes for all Native people, because a lot of us have taken on the Western ways, through no fault of our own. So you learn along the way, and the teachers know when you're ready for the next step.

As a result of what I've been taught, I see it as our job – Aboriginal peoples' job – to take care of this land that we call Turtle Island. It's our job to help non-Natives see the error of their ways and to help them reconnect with Creation. We're willing to do this because now some non-Natives are beginning to see what they have done. They have come to the horrific realization that they are destroying the land that they took, and they haven't respected any of it. Now the lives of their own children and grandchildren, the survival of their own people, is wrapped up in whether or not they take care of the land. My people have been saying for a hundred years that if you destroy the land, if you poison the water, you are going to die! Everything will. Nothing can live without water. So we feel it's *that* urgent, that maybe we need to open the door and try to help people reconnect spiritually with the land.

And, once non-Natives make that connection, they'll be like little beavers! They'll work and work and work themselves to the bone because that's their nature. They'll work to put things back right. There are many now who are close to making this connection. I meet many non-Native people, more than I ever have, who are "Earth people." They're connected to their trees; it might be on their own little bit of land, but still. Still. They're not looking "up" so much, they're starting to look "around" and see that everything is here. It's right here. It's all right here.

So I think the more people that come, and listen, and participate in our ceremonies the better. What we teach and share with non-Natives when we invite them is just the very surface of what the ceremonies mean, but in a sense we're not telling people anything they don't already know. At one time, all peoples were spiritually connected to the land they lived on. People in Europe had Earth-based spiritual beliefs but the European people roamed all over, and over time their beliefs were turned on their head. Women were stripped of any kind of value or authority. Something replaced the women's role and their society went into a tailspin. Institutions replaced traditional knowledge and then the institutions began to interpret and to determine what spirituality meant, and their interpretations were not for the benefit of the people. Institutions went to great extremes during the "burning times"* to get control of traditional knowledge, and what did they do with it? They turned it into something that is

---

* "Burning times" refers to the period of witch trials in Europe during the fifteenth to eighteenth centuries, in which the charge of witchcraft could result in capital punishment, including being burnt at the stake.

not recognizable. They took what they wanted, which benefited only themselves, not Spirit, not God, just themselves.

Now people have come to a place where they don't know who they are. They don't know what they're supposed to be doing, and they are destroying everything. And the ones doing the most damage are the few at the top of the heap who have a lot of power. Those people are the ones who are gaining from all of this, and the rest of the people have become like sheep – mindless. Mindless.

A few years ago, I organized the Wabanaki Confederacy conference, which was held at St. Mary's, my home community. The conference is a week long, but for the first time, on the last two days of the conference, we opened it up to the public for the purpose of establishing and building "peace and friendship alliances" with people who are like minded, people who have "come the distance." The model was based on the Peace and Friendship Treaties signed in my territory in the 1760s, which are still among the strongest treaties that we have. At the Confederacy conference we talked about issues and about what kinds of things we need to be doing together. Right now, the priority is protecting the land and the water from irreversible damage by mining companies. In our conversations relationships were built, and education went both ways, between our people and the non-Natives. There was a lot of sharing back and forth.

Also, here on the Wolastoq – the St. John River – we recently had a Water Ceremony that was led by our people, the Pipe Carriers. Twelve pipes were lit. There were 350 people – including non-Native people – there. It was the first time that sort of thing had been opened to the public, and it went so well. We didn't try to control anything, we didn't try to manage anything, we just let the Spirit flow. Everyone was participating and I believe that everyone, when they went away, felt they had contributed. People were very respectful. The only thing we should have done differently was to have a tipi or a structure where the Elders could do individual healing. They did do it, but it was right there in public sight. They tried to secure a little private spot for themselves but it would've been better if we'd had a special place and lit a sacred fire and had a bit of a private area for them. But even with that going on, people respected their space; they just seemed to know what to do. And we fed everyone, which is something in our culture that is very important. When people come, we feed them.

In New Brunswick, you have the environmental agencies trying to manage the Earth, manage the rivers. The Wolastoq River is so polluted and still they want to manage it. "Well, my goodness," I say, "You've been managing it already, why don't you leave it alone? It'll clean itself. Stop doing what you're doing. If you want to manage something, manage yourself." That's basically what I tell these government people, "Manage yourself." And say, "Thank you." People want to go where it's pure but it doesn't take long for them to destroy what they came for. The first thing they want to do is to start controlling and managing it, and owning it.

Our people didn't have all these systems to "manage this" and "control that," and it was like a paradise here when Europeans came. In the beginning of time, when the Earth was created, there was nothing more beautiful. Everything was in perfect harmony and balance, and provided everything we needed to live a good life. All life thrived. And when the sacred colors of humankind were placed at the four corners of the Earth, each was given a path to walk on and each was given a Sacred Bundle with instructions to live a good and happy life right here on this planet. They were to share with one another their purpose and gifts so that there would be harmony and balance within the human families on Earth. Somewhere along the way, someone felt they could ignore the Sacred Instructions, and they told the world that we come here to Earth to suffer, then we die and go to a better place. Our Elders say this is not true: the reason we have suffered here on Earth is because those things that the Creator gave us to live a good and happy life were taken away from us. Reconciliation can only happen if there is restoration of all those things.

But my people keep reaching out and reaching out ... and we're still reaching out. I think it's what the Spirit wants right now. And wherever it goes, that's where it's going to go.

BARB

I was born in Boston, Massachusetts, but as a baby my grandparents brought me to live in our home community of Esgenoôpetitj/Burnt Church. My mother meanwhile moved to New Haven, Connecticut, because she had relatives there and could find work. I lived in Esgenoôpetitj until the age of ten when my mother, in an effort to reunite our family, moved my brothers and me to New Haven, where I lived until I was sixteen.

Being Native in New Haven was a whole different kettle of fish from being Native in New Brunswick. In New Haven it was exotic. There, the racism was between White people and Black people, or between Whites and Hispanics, especially Mexican-Americans. The White people didn't know what to do with me, and the Black people didn't either, so I was in a kind of neutral zone. Neither group could hate me, because I wasn't Black and I wasn't White, so that made me think it wasn't necessarily bad to be Native. Sometimes they thought

I was Asian. At that time the TV series *Kung Fu* was popular, and some thought I must know kung fu so they didn't bother me.

In New Haven, I grew up between the ghetto and a sort of pre-yuppie neighborhood where the people who went to Yale University, or who worked there, lived. I could go one block down and be in the ghetto and go one block up and see the yuppies – well, they weren't called yuppies at the time – but I could see two different worlds right there in front of me, with all the disparities. And when I went to school my friends were diverse. I had friends who were Black. I had friends who were Spanish, both Puerto Rican and Mexican-American, and of course those two groups were different from one another as well. I had White friends whose parents had just come up from the South to find work. So I got to see all sorts of differences. That was the era of the civil rights movement. I'd go downtown and see protests against the war, and for women's rights and so on. As a little ten year old you don't necessarily understand what you're seeing, but it makes an impression. I saw the Black Panthers in the street below our tenement, busting windows and chanting and marching. All my sisters were excited, saying, "Wow, look at that, cool!"

When I moved back to New Brunswick as a sixteen year old and went into high school at Miramichi Valley High, near my Mi'kmaq home community, I looked around and said, "Well, this is different." I started to understand what the Blacks felt like, the American Blacks, in the New England states. I discovered that we, the Natives, were the "Blacks" of Canada. I hate to say it but somebody called us "the n— of the North." "So okay," I said, "all right, I know how to handle that. I know how to respond to that." I had watched my Black friends in the ghetto school, so I responded accordingly. But I also had a deeper appreciation for what my friends had gone through.

Even though, as a child, I was aware of all these differences I observed among people, I didn't understand them. My partner, Reni, is the one who introduced me to the concepts of race, class, and gender, and she has been able to explain them in a way that I could understand. Before, I didn't have what you might call a "race, class, and gender analysis," even though as an Aboriginal person I was aware of issues around poverty and race and so on. I was also aware of women's issues because of the discriminatory sections of the Indian Act* that we worked on at the Native Women's Council, but I didn't necessarily understand that even among White people there were class and gender issues, although their issues are different from ours.

With us, if we were poor we were all poor. We looked around and everyone else's clothes had patches too, so we didn't feel poor. Poverty wasn't something that defined us as a person. We didn't think anything of it except when a White person came into the rez, because they had nicer clothes and they looked like they'd had a bath. They smelled different! You'd get in their cars and the cars smelled different too. But we didn't think we were "less than" them. That poverty mentality wasn't in our heads and in our spirits like it is now. It's definitely there now among the kids because of television and radio and everything else around them – the mass media.

As I got older and started seeing the racism around me, it was kind of freaky. The "chip on my shoulder" became the "boulder on my shoulder" because I was a little feisty. I was like, "What do you mean you think I'm less than you?!" I'd look White people up and down thinking, "Who the hell are you?" My response to racism was a different response

---

* The Indian Act is the principal statute through which the Canadian government administers Indian status, local First Nations governments, and the management of reserve land and communal monies.

than maybe my grandparents had. They became meek and submissive, whereas my response to racism was to become aggressive.

So I was in a major learning mode thirty years ago when the Gatherings began. I recall that gkisedtanamoogk, who was a good friend of mine, was getting together with these people from Maine. For me it's important who is introducing me to a group. gkisedtanamoogk and Miigam'agan were the ones introducing me, and since I have great respect for them, these people must be all right, right? For me, it's more about the people than the issues. There were a number of nice people involved, and I was more curious than anything. Also, given my background, I had a predisposition for trying to build bridges among people, to see how we could work together across differences, so that's why I went.

At these Gatherings, I was more of an observer than an active participant. I remember I didn't hear as much laughter as in the Talking Circles that I was used to. I said to myself, "It's going to take a while before they get it," or maybe "It may take us a while before we get them." It has to be a two-way street.

I'm used to being in Talking Circles with Native people, with a bunch of traumatized Native people. When we're together in that Circle, it's full. It's full of pain. It's full of joy. It's full of love. It's very serious, but then we laugh. And we go around again and maybe there's quiet weeping, and then we all cry together. But we understand that what's happening there is very sacred. When I'm in a Native Talking Circle, there is Spirit there. We're "in the zone" and we become one. We feel like we're one. I feel people's pain. I relate to what they say even if I haven't had that experience. I can hear it, and feel it.

From what I understand of White people – and I'm going to say "White people" here because I can't say "non-Native" or "non-Aboriginal" because there's all sorts of differences among them too – from what I understand of White people there is a kind of separation between heart and mind. When I'm with a group of White people, I don't necessarily feel that sense of spirituality in the beginning. The inklings are there, but it seems it's all new for them. They're not used to talking with the heart and the head together. When they're in a Talking Circle, they start out talking from the head, but then, when they get into the heart stuff, it's *really* emotional for them, but it's a different kind of emotion than what we feel. It comes from a different place. I think it comes from emptiness. I think the root of all that emotion that White people feel in the Circle is their wanting to belong. You can see that they crave something; you can sense that craving in them. That's where I think a lot of the tears come from; it's when somebody suddenly becomes whole. You watch this transformation happen and you feel a little bit better toward them. You say to yourself, "Oh my God ... they're in pain."

When you separate the heart and the mind you create a wound. And that wound feels like emptiness. Now, you're literally insane if you split the heart and mind, and you can't live like that unless you're in a state of denial, so the culture has to find ways to support that denial. Insane people always try to justify their craziness. So the culture creates institutions to support that split – that insanity – and then the craziness is passed down through generations, and throughout society. Eventually all the connections are broken because the basic connection was first broken – the connection between the heart and the mind – and so you start to disconnect from other things, from the land, the family, from everything.

So it seemed that the pain of the White people in those Circles came from a place of great emptiness and a desire to become whole again, to make reconnections. And you could see that, by the end, they were so moved. They were all flying high. It's like the Grinch. His heart grew ten sizes that day! Sometimes it was funny to me, but I felt sorry for laughing. I had to learn how to respond to that difference between us, and I saw that there was a need for them to be able to do more of that. Then I asked myself, "What is it that we need to do more of that they can teach us?" We were teaching them things about Spirit, things that are second nature to us. We were comfortable in our bodies, unless of course we'd been sexually abused, as many of us have. But I asked myself, "What is it that we can learn from them?" There has to be something, right? So that's what I was wondering about a lot of the time. But this group was a good group. I could see they had done a lot of work. They were really genuine in their desire to go beyond themselves.

My usual experience with White people is they look at you, and deep down they don't take you seriously. Deep down they're looking at you as if you were some kind of a thing. It's not like they can hide it. The bottom line is they don't think of you as their equal, and I think to myself, "All right, I know where you're coming from." They're what I would call the bleeding-heart liberal people. I'd rather deal with a person who's honest, one who looks you up and down when they see you and you know they don't like you. I get that. That's honest. But I don't trust people who want to help you – the missionaries, the teachers, the social workers, and so on – because they want to help you to not be who you are. Either that or they want you to be an "authentic Indian" with the feathers. That's why we find it hard to work with most non-Native agencies.

It helped me to spend time growing up next to the ghetto; I got to see the pure form of what I'm talking about. The agencies working in the ghetto are part of the "system," and the workers understand the system and they understand how to work the system. It's second nature to them because it was built for their needs. But even within that system you can see the patriarchy. There's a pecking order, and if you try to go beyond your station you're going to get knocked down. Women are told how they're supposed to behave in this system. I always know that at the top of the pecking order there's going to be a White guy from a particular family, or someone who's been able to ruthlessly make it to the top. When we are working with those agencies, we have to find a way to work the system so as to help our people, and try to find allies in that system. It's always been a challenge to work effectively in the White culture without us being at the bottom of the proverbial totem pole, because we're told that's our station and that we should be grateful for whatever we get. I don't have any use for that. I'd rather not work in that system unless it's in running a business, and that's what we've been doing, Reni and I, for twenty years. Our business is about trying to build bridges among people.

I've been involved for years in the women's movement and that's where I learned a lot of my theory too – my race, class, and gender analysis. A lot of that work was related to violence against women, and we all oppose that of course, but for different reasons. We were fighting as Aboriginal women to address violence against women because of our understanding of ourselves, and all of life, as one. Our understanding is that if you harm women you harm the Earth; you harm something very basic – the life-giver. For the non-Aboriginal women, their fight was individualistic, an individual orientation versus a collective orientation. I couldn't understand that distinction for a while. For them, violence against women was about violating individual human rights, just individual. It's as if those individual rights are sacred to them. It's embedded in both of their constitutions, in the US and Canada.

In the women's movement, when we looked at the issue of domestic violence, we looked at the dynamic between the abuser and the abused. They each play a role in their relationship; the two roles are interlinked and both know what the expectations are. And when I looked at that dynamic I saw that the way White people – the Europeans – and Native people relate to one another is very similar. We Native people know what to expect; we know how to play the victim when it pays, and so on. We've played the game for hundreds of years. So what I'd like to see is for us to get out of these roles, to get out of these roles that are so dehumanizing. It's as dehumanizing for White people to be the abusers as it is dehumanizing for us to play the victim. It's not respectful; it's not based on anything healthy. And if we can step out of these roles, what other way can we relate to one another? It's as human beings. It's not as abuser/victim and it's not about switching roles either. That's what White people are terrified of; they're terrified we're going to become the abuser. The abuser always is terrified because they were once victims too, and they're afraid that they're going to be in the role of victim again. That's why they want to keep the victim down; it's about power and control.

So we need to break out of these roles and relate to each other as human beings because in the end that's what we are. You have to look in the mirror and see yourself, and see what you're afraid of. That's what has to be done. Sadly, under the Indian Act system, we Indigenous people are starting to adopt the ways of the abuser when it comes to our own communities and families. We've been groomed to act that way, which is horrendous in itself, but it means we'd better stop pointing fingers at the other guy.

We have a lot to learn from one another, but we have to step out of these roles, because in the end it's going to kill us, if not in body, then in Spirit.

GKISEDTANAMOOGK

The first time I learned about the Center for Vision and Policy was in the mid-1980s when I was speaking to a gathering of Quakers. It was actually my first public-speaking engagement. I never thought I'd be able to speak publicly, but I had been encouraged by one of my Elders, Slow Turtle. I was spending a lot of time with Slow Turtle then, as part of a quest to get back to my own traditions and my own people.

Growing up, I never quite made the connection with my traditions. I mean, I knew where I came from and I knew I was Wampanoag, and as a child I had spent most of my summers in my home community of Mashpee with my grandparents, but at that time I was probably like everybody else, so focused on being part of the larger society. My culture didn't have much meaning to me until Wounded Knee, when I started to search for my own identity as a Native man. I returned to my home community and found other young people like myself who were coming together on their own to learn the songs and to learn about ceremony.

My connection with these young people changed my whole orientation. At one point, several of us hosted a group of Elders who were traveling across the United States. They were visiting different Native American communities and we invited them to come to Mashpee. During that visit, they needed people to watch the Fire and, although none of us had actually had a ceremonial initiation as Firekeepers, they accepted us as volunteers. I was really drawn to the duty of Firekeeper, and I stayed with it. I didn't know it back then, but it is probably one of the most important aspects of community responsibility – to keep the Fire. Fire, I've come to understand, is the center of everything. In a sense I see myself as staff of the Fire.

It was Slow Turtle who told me about the invitation to spend the weekend with Quakers at Amherst College and to speak about Native spirituality. I already knew about the Quakers because the Wampanoag people and the Quakers have a long history in Massachusetts. Quakers were actually executed for their beliefs right on Boston Commons, and some sought refuge among Native Americans in the area, including among the Wampanoag people. That was in the mid-seventeenth century, so we've had a long relationship. Then during the Wampanoag's land claims case in the 1970s, the Quakers, in a non-partisan way, decided to investigate some of the hysteria that was coming out of the "White" town of Mashpee, and also from the state. Both the town and the state were saying there would be "economic oppression" resulting from the Wampanoag land claims. They even said we were attempting a takeover of their homeland, their community.

After their investigation, the Quakers filed a report saying that the assertions of the town were false, that there would be no economic burden, and that these accusations were only serving to bring racism and hysteria to the land claims. When they did that, when the Quakers did that, it opened my heart to the idea that we can be friends and that this group of people deserves our respect. Their statement was confirmation of what the Wampanoag people had been saying all along – that we were not out to displace anybody. We only wanted to settle these land claims in an honorable and just way, but we weren't getting any support anywhere until the Quakers stepped in.

Because of this history I was more than willing to accept their invitation to speak at Amherst, although I was just coming into my own understanding of my culture, just starting to learn. It was after one of my sessions that Shirley Hager walked up to me, introduced herself, and explained that she was representing an organization, the Center for Vision and Policy. She said the center wanted to have a conversation with Indigenous people – a conversation with the cultures belonging to the land, this land, the Gulf of Maine bioregion. That was really intriguing. I'd heard ecologists and environmentalists talk about reconnecting with the land but never with the cultures of the land.

One of the fundamental differences in philosophies between White and Indigenous cultures is that one culture says the land belongs to them and the other culture talks about belonging to the land. These are two completely different constructs, but I had only heard Indian people talk about that before. And here was the Center for Vision and Policy and this young woman wanting to have a conversation with Indigenous people about what it means to be in right relationship with the land. That was the key for me.

Bringing our views together, Native and non-Native, and acknowledging the "view from the shore" was how we started on this journey. We constructed the Fire, brought out the Sacred, and sat in that space where we, both Native and non-Native, were opened up. One of the myths in North America is that Indigenous people are hostile and that we want to get rid of the invaders, but that misconception comes from not knowing the other and what's in our hearts.

We can't know one another's hearts until we make ourselves vulnerable. I remember one particular Gathering where I needed to share something in order for my participation to continue. I wanted to know that we could talk about substantial matters – current, crucial issues – that were affecting Native communities. Were we willing to investigate those and include those in the conversation about what this relationship would mean? I remember that particular moment, and wondering, "If I put this out there, will they respond or will this be the end of my participation?" As it turned out, people were open to having those difficult conversations. They were open to looking at contemporary issues and what we might do to respond to them together. It seemed at that moment that the dialogue became transformed. We became more specific in terms of the issues that were raised, and it went from "Native people educating the White people" to "what could we do together."

As long as we wanted to have those kinds of Gatherings I was committed to the Fire, and to the dialogue, and to getting the word out to other community members. Through people I met at the Gatherings, opportunities to make connections with other non-Natives opened up at places like the University of New England and the [then-named] Portland School of Art, where I visited and spoke in classes. Because of my contacts with Quaker and other faith communities, I also began to work with church groups that wanted to reach out to Native peoples.

I saw that I was making a contribution to my people and to building connections with others, but all of this activity came at a cost too. I didn't spend much time with my children in their early years, and didn't often think about the sacrifices my family was making to enable me to assume these roles. At the time, I always said "yes" to requests for presentations or to provide ceremonial leadership because I was aware that there weren't many other Native resources.

These requests came from my own people as well as from non-Native groups. Looking back, I realize I was operating with youthful notions of sacrifice. As I understood my traditional culture, young men were supposed to put the needs of the people first, whatever those needs were. In hindsight I might have encouraged other people to take up some of the responsibilities asked of me, as I do now.

Still, I believed that the work I was doing was for my three children, to help create a better future for them and for my people. For many, many generations, Indigenous peoples have been invisible – "out of sight, out of mind" – and this invisibility generates all the myths about us, exemplified by the "Thanksgiving" story and others.* In the Gatherings, in our Circles, it was a new experience for me that we actually had a voice, a voice that was recognized, and I thought, "Not only do we have a voice here, but that voice is confirmed." It was acknowledged that something was clearly wrong with our current social structures and it wasn't just in our heads. In fact, Native and non-Native were all on the same page. That's something Miigam'agan once said too, that she needed the confirmation from the Gatherings. She needed to hear that the system as it exists is wrong – that the basis on which our mutually shared history was founded was wrong – and that it wasn't just us saying this; that changing things was a challenge belonging to all of us.

---

* There are so many inaccuracies connected with the Thanksgiving story as told in the United States. There is evidence that the Wampanoag helped early settlers to survive by sharing their knowledge of planting and fishing. There is no evidence, however, to show that the "Pilgrims" (they didn't call themselves Pilgrims) invited the Wampanoag to dinner, and while it appears there was at one time some kind of gathering and sharing of food that occurred, deadly conflicts between the settlers and the Wampanoag shortly followed. (See Debbie's story, which appears later, to see how she explains Thanksgiving to her grandkids.)

Presenting this challenge was my mission when I taught at the university and had an opportunity to spend a semester with the young people in my classes. I not only talked about Indian people and our history, I also asked, "What do we intend to do as members of a society in which we perpetually do harm to one another? How do we address that together?" We have to see ourselves as part of the solution.

There was a time when I might have said that the only real issue is our estrangement from the land, which, in and of itself, becomes a separation from one another. But I'd say now the deeper issue is our estrangement from the Sacred. We've created a pretense of boundaries, saying, "This is mine, I own this," but for Indigenous peoples to say, "We own the land" is to see ourselves outside of the Sacred. In Wampanoag country we know the land as *Kautanitouwit*. Freely translated, it means "the Creator's House." How can we own the Creator's House? We were given the privilege of taking care of this House; we don't own it. We have another expression, *Naiyantaqt*, meaning essentially "the life above our heads and the life below our feet." In between these two realms we are all connected. In between these realms, the Divine Feminine and the Divine Masculine support us and we're all related, we're all family. It doesn't matter if we're the two-legged human species, or if we have wings, or fur, or fins; we're all connected.

I've never forgotten an experience I once had when I was fasting. It was during the time when I returned as a young man to my home community on "Cape Cod." As part of my reconnection with my territory and my traditions, I decided to fast for several weeks at a sheltered spot in a cedar swamp near my home. These cedar swamps are very special places to my people; they offered refuge during the colonial wars when we were hiding from the English, and in this spot you could see that others had camped there before. Early one morning

I started to fast, and at some point in the afternoon I was overcome by an immense feeling of being embraced. In that moment I knew I was being embraced by Grandma. I distinctly remember feeling that She was saying to me, "Welcome, Grandson!" But that moment also was the beginning of my transformation from racism, because I realized that when She said, "Welcome, Grandson," She didn't say, "Welcome, my Wampanoag grandson" but simply, "Welcome, Grandson." It occurred to me then that if anyone – any White person, any African-American or Asian-American – went to sit with Grandma, She would embrace them too. She knows no difference among us. We're all Her children – no different from Ant, no different from Bee. She's there to nurture everything – the great Divine Mother.

That memory came back to me one morning at the Gatherings when I was bringing the smudge around to people and seeing the different shades of hands reaching out. I was used to seeing only brown, being with my own people, but here now were all these different shades, all mingled together, all doing the same thing. That moment for me says it all. It doesn't matter what color we are, or what ethnicity we come from, we're all children of Earth. And this is where we start, right here in the House of the Creator, to begin the process of unraveling all of the mindless stuff that we've done to each other. I know we didn't create the Gatherings with such a lofty goal in mind, but by the end we certainly had a glimpse of what is possible. That's the power we're working with. That's why we need to come together.

My hope is that those who read this book, Native and non-Native, see that people like themselves came away from this process inspired in ways that have changed their lives. I hope this book enables people to say, "OK, others have been here before, so we know it's possible. It's possible, because they did it."

SHIRLEY H.

I've come a long way since the Gatherings all those years ago. In the early days especially, I was tremendously nervous that I would do or say something that would be offensive to the Native participants. I was so careful in my interactions; partly in awe, partly afraid, and also, to be honest, there was some false pride associated with my role as coordinator. As a non-Native person, you can feel such guilt about what has happened in the past, so that if a Native person befriends you, or will even give you the time of day, there's a kind of self-satisfaction as in, "I'm not one of them," meaning I'm not a racist. You can feel, "That must mean I'm a good person." All these thoughts and feelings get in the way of acting normally.

As a child, I had a lot of romantic ideas about Native people. Of course, everyone watched Westerns back then, but when I watched Westerns I always sided with the Indians. I remember being fascinated by the tipis and the Indian "villages." That's how I wanted to live – the way they lived.

I grew up in North Carolina during segregation. My mother was from the South and had stayed close to home most of her life. My father, however, grew up in Missouri, then joined the Navy and was stationed in Colorado; and when he got out of the Navy he went to college on the GI Bill. So he had seen a lot more of the world, as well as being a very compassionate man. Once, when I was about eight years old, I saw a Black person being mistreated and, although I don't recall the details, it must have bothered me. I remember being home that evening and looking up at my dad and asking, "Why? Why was this person treated this way?" I'll never forget his response. He said, "I think it must be that some people put others down to make themselves feel big." And then he said, "When I was out West they treated the Indians just the way we treat – he would have said "colored people" back then – colored people here." A light came on for me. Since I had such romantic notions about Indians, if they were treated badly too then all of a sudden the whole system didn't make sense. Suddenly it all seemed wrong.

But, of course, I still had my romantic notions. During my college years, I lived in Utah and always wanted to meet some of the Ute Indians who lived there, but there were very few Ute students on campus and I never had an opportunity. So there was a lot of ignorance and fascination on my part, while also wanting to make a connection. The opportunity for that connection came with my introduction to the Center for Vision and Policy, when my involvement grew to include coordinating the Gatherings.

During the year after our first Gathering, when we were planning the second one, gkisedtanamoogk offered to build a Fire and to have a First Light ceremony there. This was before our decision to hold all of our meetings around the Fire, and so his suggestion caught me by surprise. I was tremendously excited because I had wanted to experience something like that my whole life.

Native women had already told me that when women were menstruating they didn't participate in these ceremonies. Sure enough, that's what happened to me and, after all the anticipation, I was crushed. While the ceremony was going on, I left the group and climbed one of the little hills overlooking the retreat center. I lay down between a couple of big boulders on the hillside and dissolved into tears. I had worked all year to put this event together and I wasn't going to experience the very thing I had looked forward to the most. I remember praying up there among the rocks and asking for answers, or at least a way to cope with my disappointment, and what came to me was … this was a test of my commitment. We didn't create this event so I could take part in a ceremony. This was about something much bigger, and I needed to accept things as they were, even though I didn't fully understand them or necessarily agree with them. I think I grew up a little that day. I came to a realization of the seriousness of what we were doing, and that it was important to stay with it, no matter what.

I did of course get to experience the ceremonies, and the Circle, many times over the years. gkisedtanamoogk says that he felt "confirmed" in our Circles. I remember a distinct feeling of "filling up" as the Talking Stick would go around and the stories would be shared. Another way I describe it is, it felt like a wound healing that, until then, I didn't know was there. I think that we White people carry around the wounds of the separations that we've created, whether it's our separation from Native Americans or African-Americans, or from the land itself. Oppressed peoples feel the brunt of the system we've created, but we feel it too. We suffer from the separation without being aware of it most of the time. Being in those Circles was a spiritual experience, I don't know any other name for it; as if we were doing something so right with Creation that you could feel it.

One of the subtle but growing realizations for me was the way in which meeting in a Circle was key to the success of the Gatherings. An obvious advantage of meeting in a Circle is that every person can see everyone else, and also there is no visual hierarchy. As gkisedtanamoogk's Elder, Slow Turtle, says, "In a Circle, no one is taller than anyone else." But I came to understand that the power of the Circle was much greater than its physical qualities.

In the Circle, with the Fire at the center, I could envision us as planets around the sun, held in our places by an invisible force that

I came to trust and depend on. Every morning, we gravitated to the Fire for the First Light ceremony, preparing ourselves for the new day. Each day, as we once again arranged ourselves in the Circle, the Talking Stick went around and around, taking us deeper with each revolution, day after day, weekend after weekend, year after year.

Conversations outside the Circle were often awkward for me as I worked at being natural with the Wabanaki participants. More than once I came away from an exchange with a Native person inwardly wincing and thinking, "Why did I *say* that?" I began to hear my words in conversation as they might sound to an Indigenous person, words like "owner" and "property." I started to hear the subtle violence in my language, so different from the typical Native way of speaking. I once offered some food to gkisedtanamoogk that I had brought from the communal lunch table, saying, "Here you go, I stole this for you." In his usual light way he said, "You need to rethink your assumptions ..."

gkisedtanamoogk tells a story that, to me, is a metaphor for all the ways my culture typically relates to Indigenous peoples. Back in the 1980s, his interest in his culture led him to work with the Wampanoag Program at Plimoth [sic] Plantation, which is only a half hour's drive from his community of Mashpee. Plimoth Plantation is a living museum where you walk back in time; there are contemporary actors role-playing members of the original Plimoth colony, and also a historically accurate Wampanoag homesite from the 1600s staffed by local Wampanoag. But Plimoth Plantation didn't start out having a Wampanoag program with actual Wampanoag people. Originally, they held a stereotypical Thanksgiving event there with only the "Pilgrims," and people started to ask, "Where are the Indians?" The plantation's response to the public's question was to set up cardboard cutouts of Indians, with information on the cut-outs that people would read. But, as gkisedtanamoogk says, "There's only so much conversation you can have with a cardboard cutout"; the people wanted a little more dialogue.

The plantation's next response was to have White actors portraying the Wampanoag. The public began to object to that too, so eventually they hired Native people from *other* places. That situation existed for a while, but ultimately it wasn't enough to satisfy the public; the plantation had to hire Wampanoags, and most came from gkised-tanamoogk's community of Mashpee. The process took them quite a while; Plimoth Plantation opened in the 1940s and the Wampanoag program as it exists today finally came into being in 1975.

If non-Natives want a connection with Native people, often our first step is to create a romanticized image – a cardboard cutout. We want to become Indian, or "play Indian," but what we do may have no connection to actual Native culture. Or we may have a genuine desire to learn about the culture, but we do that through books or even from an actual teacher, but that teacher may not be from, or connected with, a local Indigenous community. The teacher might be Lakota or Hopi, but (if you live in the East) the point is they're not from where you live. To have a relationship with the Indigenous peo-ple close to home can be a little too real; you can't romanticize people once you get to know them as neighbors. It's scary too, because if you get too close you might have to open the Pandora's box of your common history. Plimoth Plantation went through a long process before doing the obvious. The real people were right there, literally next door, and they were the last ones they turned to in creating a Wampanoag program. It shows how hard it is to break through our culture's denial of the actual people who live right here with us.

As the Gatherings continued over the years, I remember thinking, "Well, this is great, but what are we going to do together? What are we going to *do*?" At some point I started to realize that the relationship – building the relationship – was enough, and it was actually very big, because to even say that we had a relationship meant that we had actually begun to heal some of our history together. It was okay not to know where it was going; it would evolve.

The time spent together in our Circles seemed to enable us, slowly, to turn from looking at one another to facing outward together. I felt a subtle shift from seeing myself as primarily a listener and learner in relation to the Wabanaki participants, to feeling that we were partners in something larger than ourselves – our shared concern for the Earth and for one another's well-being.

Being in relationship with Native people means that you will inevitably be drawn into the political dimension of their world and must choose whether to take on a particular cause as your own. One aspect of "White privilege" is having the choice of whether to become involved, whereas in most cases they do not, but I came to understand over time that their issues are my issues, and not only because of my love for specific individuals. Our social and economic policies have made Native communities most vulnerable, but they are simply the "canary in the coal mine," perhaps especially when it comes to environmental concerns. What is impacting their communities will soon impact all of us.

My experience in those Circles changed the way I look at everything: news events, historical accounts, politicians' promises, scientific claims; I could go on. Everywhere I see the absence of the Indigenous perspective, the lack of which means we are all poorer, even in peril. What the dominant culture knows and values, even our ways of knowing, seem clearly deficient in terms of sustaining our life here on this planet. We need the Indigenous perspective, but that perspective has to be honorably earned, and freely given.

DEBBIE

Like many of the people involved in the Gatherings, I was also a member of the Center for Vision and Policy. My partner, Elly Haney, was the founder of CVP. It was her background working with Indigenous people in Minnesota that made us aware that we needed to work with local Native people if we were going to create a vision for a just future. We knew there were issues of great importance to discuss, but how to do this – that was the question. In my career in social policy, I had done a lot of coalition building, but Elly kept talking about alliances, building alliances. That was a different concept for me. To create an alliance, you first have to address the relationship between the groups. We wanted to find out if establishing a different kind of relationship would enable us to work together, Native and non-Native, on peace and justice issues.

The Gathering where we first met around the Fire was the most powerful for me; that's where my personal journey started. One image is still vivid in my mind. We were in the still-dark morning, about ten or twelve of us wrapped up in blankets. It was so cold. You could see across the water to where the sun would come up, where "First Light" was just emerging on the horizon. But it is the Fire that I remember most – the special Fire; and knowing it had been nurtured, for all of us, through the night. We were each given a pinch of tobacco to place into the Fire as we said our prayers. The

Native people said their prayers and then we were invited to say ours. I didn't know exactly what was appropriate, but I mumbled my own particular words and then made my offering. Although there were a number of people I knew there – White people – I knew none of the Native people. Everything was new to me. I couldn't believe I was having this experience.

That was the Gathering where I began to learn the difference between the "White" way of having a workshop and how the Native people would meet together. I guess "tense" is the word I would use to describe how I felt. My own need was to have an agenda for everything, yet the Native people were uncomfortable with the format that had been set up by the Whites. I understood their point. They were saying, "This is your way of doing things, and we want to have more say." Subsequently, the Native people had far more input, and we shifted from the "White" way of meeting to the traditional Native concept of coming together.

That Gathering too was my first experience being face to face with the anger of Native people toward Whites. I had been in places where African-Americans confronted me with anger, but somehow it didn't hurt me as much. I had done a lot of work and self-reflection on racism toward African-Americans, so maybe I was more prepared for their anger. The oppressions of African-Americans and Native Americans are totally different – they come out of different contexts; and for me, I think there is less *personal* guilt where African-Americans are concerned. Maybe it's because my family didn't participate in slavery. In fact, some in my family were abolitionists. But I was blown away by the Native people's anger because my family was part of the founding of the colony of Massachusetts. My relatives were John Cotton, the first minister of the Congregational Church, and Cotton Mather – all colonial leaders at the time that Native oppression began in this country. I had been very proud of my ancestors' role in creating a colony that survived and grew, yet here I was confronted with the violence of my own people toward the Native people during that time. It was an emotional shock that stayed with me all through the Gatherings, and has stayed with me since, along with feelings of guilt and sadness. As a result, I had difficulty participating. It was hard for me to speak and to ask questions – especially to ask questions – although I always felt welcomed in the Circles.

I knew something about Native spirituality but I also felt conflicted about participating in it. In my church, the United Church of Christ, we welcomed anyone to take part in the service with us. I understood that Native people had had their ceremonies stolen, and money made from them, and so they were often reluctant to include Whites in their practices. I felt simultaneously welcomed and guilty about being there. When I took part in the First Light ceremony, it was the first time I felt that I could be part of an Indigenous ceremony in the same way I experienced rituals in my church. I couldn't understand what was happening exactly, but the experience of standing there, and seeing the first light of the morning, and the Fire – the Sacred Fire – was so moving. Being a mystical kind of person, that whole aspect was very important to me.

But really, the whole process was overwhelming at times. There was so much I didn't know. There was limited outreach toward me from the Native people, but after a while I began to think, "Maybe they are having some of the same kinds of feelings that I'm having." I didn't reach out to anyone either – I couldn't find people to hook up to. I'm normally someone who participates easily in groups, so it was difficult for me to be in that situation.

I wanted to connect with a Native person particularly, to have an ongoing relationship – a friend – and for me that didn't happen during the course of the Gatherings. Since then, I've learned much and gained much in my relationship with gkisedtanamoogk, and ultimately with Miigam'agan, but during the Gatherings I felt very much alone … and really, very much afraid. I can remember being in the kitchen, maybe with Miigam'agan or Alma, and they were cooking a whole fish. I had never cooked a whole fish, and I was fascinated to see how they were doing it. I thought I could make a connection then, but it was mainly they who were doing the cooking and I was trying to learn, so it didn't happen.

I felt a simpatico connection with Alma, yet she was not there all the time. One of the images I treasure is of a small group of us – all women – sitting together one evening in a tiny upstairs room. It was my first experience with the concept of the women's lodge. Alma talked to us about the women's lodge being a time away from men and family for a few days each month – a time for sharing stories, for sharing pain and joy, for being together during menstruation and childbirth. It was a place where women, young and old, could find support. The conversation that resulted in that "mini women's lodge" that night was so powerful.

I "hung in there" in the Gatherings because I wanted this experience very much. Our goal was important and what I was learning was important. Also, I could see that relationships were forming among others; I could see it happening in the group. And I was very interested in some of the political issues – the issues of land, and particularly the issues around fishing rights. Also, there was the distressing story, one that continues to this day, of gkisedtanamoogk and his difficulties in being able to move freely across the border because the treaties aren't being honored; and also the fascinating story of gkisedtanamoogk coming from a tribe on Cape Cod to marry a woman from Burnt Church, New Brunswick, and raising their children in their traditional language, and building the school – the Wabanaki Resource Center – on the reserve. Building the school was one of the things I thought was really wonderful, and it was a joyous time for me when several of us went there for a work weekend. That was more like a "Western" type of experience for me. In my world, if we have a camp that needs to be cleaned up we have a work weekend, we come together. It makes relationships easier because everyone has a role to play.

What came out of the Gatherings for me was a commitment to the Indigenous cause, or causes. Elly and I had a publishing business at the time, Astarte Shell Press, and we published a book by gkisedtanamoogk and Frances Hancock on ceremony that included a chapter on non-Natives' relationship to it. When Elly passed, she left a bequest that has funded several projects related to Indigenous concerns, and I serve on the board that administers those funds. My experience in the Gatherings has made me look at so many things differently. For example, I was once on the board of the Natural Resources Council of Maine (NRCM), and we were talking about trying to bring the salmon back, and the impact of the dams and so on. I made the point that we were talking about land that was once Native land, or was Native land now, and no one on the board was Native – no Passamaquoddies, no Penobscots, no Maliseets, no one! While I don't know if there is yet a Native person on their board, I believe there is now more collaboration between NRCM and the tribes.

It gets personal too. I have three grandchildren, and I want to make sure they understand the whole story – the whole foolish story, from the Native perspective – of the Thanksgiving celebrations that we have, and also Columbus Day. I've described to them how this land was before our ancestors came here. I've told them that when our people came they thought they had a right to the land because their culture said it was okay, but that it was really someone else's home. I asked them how they would feel if someone came into their home and took it over. At Thanksgiving, I've told them that the colonists wouldn't have survived unless the Wampanoag had brought food and taught us how to grow vegetables and live here. I want them to know we wouldn't even be here if we hadn't had the help of the Native people.

Participating in this book project has brought up a lot of those old feelings of guilt and anxiety, and pushed me to work through them again. Being an older person, you realize the usefulness of memories; they provide you an opportunity to move through something you haven't resolved yet, and relieve you of the burden. I can forgive myself and start over.

And the work never stops, really. Sometimes I can still be very cautious in my relationships with Native people. For example, at one of our planning meetings for this project, I brought along a book, *Grandmothers Counsel the World*. It's a collection of thirteen Indigenous grandmothers' perspectives in which they offer a collective vision for our planet. As I brought this book to our group and started to talk about it, I realized that no one there had heard about it, and suddenly I felt very tentative. I was thinking, here I am, a White woman, bringing a book about Native women and their philosophies to Native people. I had hoped that it might be a contribution to what we were doing, but at that point I stopped and withdrew the book from our conversation. I thought I wasn't being sensitive to how they might feel about a White woman talking about something they probably all knew about – not that book particularly – but about the concepts. That was maybe an example of being overly cautious, because they might not have been thinking those things at all; they might have been really interested.

It's important that I share my story because my experience in the Gatherings would probably be much like that of other White people. So I've girded my loins and gone forward because it's what I'm about, and what I love – being with people who are, in a very spiritual and loving way, trying to find ways to be together; people of different cultures, and races, and gender and class. I still have a lot to learn; but I feel very good about how I'm progressing.

SHIRLEY B.

I first heard about the Gatherings when I was working in Student Affairs at the University of New England (UNE). Elly Haney was teaching at UNE at the time and we collaborated together on a couple of things. As part of our programming, Elly brought gkised-tanamoogk to campus. He spoke in several classes, and we held a campus-wide forum where he presented. As I listened to him, I was astonished at the stories I had never been told of the Native experience, and I was a history major! It really bothered me that I didn't know these stories, and I wanted to know more. I talked to Elly and she told me about the Gatherings and invited me to attend. I saw a chance to broaden my understanding and get to know Indigenous people here in Maine, but what grabbed me was when she said that it was Native and non-Native people sitting together, and honoring the

Native perspective. Elly was so great about the orientation; she said, "We're not 'playing Indian,' we're being invited into a relationship."

At my first Gathering I didn't have a lot of expectations; it was all new to me. I don't enter groups very easily, so it took me a while to get my bearings. It was evident that a lot of the people there already knew each other, not that it was unwelcoming. I just did a lot of watching and listening at first.

I loved the slow pace of our weekends. Because of the work I did on campus, I was very regulated by time. You have your next appointment, and your next appointment, and the next. So when I went to a Gathering, before I left the house I would take off my watch because Elly had said, "Shirley, you are just going to have to go with the flow." So I took my watch off and simply showed up and tried to be open and without an agenda. It's possible to do that when you're out camping. Back then we didn't carry cell phones everywhere, so you were completely out of touch and it was fabulous.

I loved the organic movement of the days. Sometimes I wasn't quite sure what was going to happen next but I trusted that I would hear from somebody when it was time to move. I loved everyone cooking together; you brought food and then groups of people said, "I'll cook lunch." You took from what was there and made things. I loved that community kind of feeling.

They say that smell is one of the strongest senses we have, and though I don't have access to sweetgrass now, I can still smell it. I still know that smell. And the drums; I can still hear the sound of the drums. I've done some Celtic rituals, and drums are very important in Celtic spirituality – it's that connection with the primal sounds, the heartbeat – but that was the first time I had heard Native drumming.

I did have a difficult experience in the Circle once where I almost felt attacked. It was at my first Gathering, and almost stopped me from going back. I don't think I've ever used the word "pacifist" to describe myself, but I would say that probably I am one. It's very uncomfortable for me when people use "war" language; as in, there is a war going on against Indigenous people. I felt I was hearing that kind of language a lot over the weekend, and in one of the Circles I expressed how uncomfortable it was to hear so much of it. I said I understood that people had been hurt badly and that we had a responsibility to acknowledge that, but I said I hoped we could find a way to express it differently. So when the Talking Stick came around to a particular person in the Circle – who was White by the way, not Native – that person looked at me and said, "It is a war," and everything she said after that was directed at my comments. I was mortified. I wondered if I had now offended the very people I wanted to understand.

The next morning, in what would be our final Circle of the weekend, gkisedtanamoogk began by saying, "In the Circle we don't make direct comments to each other. We speak our own thoughts and feelings." I felt he was trying to moderate what had happened the day before. Even so, when the Talking Stick came to me, I was pretty emotional. I said I was sorry if anything I said the previous day had been hurtful, and that I was only speaking from my own experience. At that point I had decided I probably wasn't coming back. But when we were doing the big group hug we always do at the end, gkisedtanamoogk came up to me and said, "There is a place for your peaceful voice in this Circle." I thought, "Okay … okay … I can do this."

My learning from that experience was that when we are invited into a process that's not culturally ours it will be messy. Our Western culture, the dominant culture, tends to be very "in your face, come back at you." It was a culture clash between what the expectations in the Circle were and how we non-Natives typically behave. But when gkisedtanamoogk said there was a place for me, I said to myself, "All right, I guess I can come back. I didn't completely screw up." Though I was still wary for a while.

The Gatherings changed my perspective on a lot of things. One evening a group of us women were meeting, and Alma was talking to us about the Moon Lodge. At that time I had some health issues going on, and for a year and a half I hadn't had a period. My doctor, who I now believe was a quack, had said to me, "Hey, if you're not trying to get pregnant, enjoy it," so I was going along being complacent about not having a menstrual cycle. But sitting in that room and hearing about the Moon Lodge made me think, "I'm missing something." I realized I was missing something that is part of a woman's identity. What Alma was saying made me think for the first time, "This might not be normal and maybe I should do something about it." So I went to see another doctor and he said, "You don't just let your body stop working and enjoy it!" I had to rethink what it means to have our natural bodily cycles, and even though sometimes they're a real pain there's also a blessing in them. At that time, I was a young woman who wasn't in a relationship and wasn't looking at having kids, so I couldn't have cared less whether I had a period, but I realized that our natural world, myself included, needs to operate like it's supposed to.

It took several Gatherings for me to start hearing the deeper pain of the Native people. Early on I heard a certain level of frustration, but over time I think I changed. Maybe my hearing got more fine-tuned so I could hear more deeply the oppression that Indigenous people felt. I started to be more aware of the different ways that my people – those of us from the dominant culture – take for granted and don't even recognize how privileged we are. And how, in our privilege, other people continue to be oppressed. Being at the Gatherings sometimes broke my heart, but in that breaking, my heart opened and enabled me to hear more and understand more.

I remember a Native woman standing and speaking in the Circle and she was angry. I don't remember now what she spoke about, but it seemed to be clearly righteous anger; it was appropriate anger. After that Circle, a few of us took a walk and we talked about learning to sit with people's anger, to experience it but not to "take it on," and to know that the anger was not necessarily about us personally. What we were hearing was Indigenous people's experience of the dominant culture's continuing oppression. But you have a visceral response when you hear that much candid, raw emotion, and we were taking a walk to catch our breath and remember that it's a privilege to be trusted enough to hear it. It's still a struggle for me to hear anger and not want to turn into a "fixer," but in the Circle, it's your job to just sit and *acknowledge*. In that Circle there's nothing you can do but to be with the person speaking. It's later, in our own lives, that we can do something.

An experience that stands out for me was the long weekend when we went up to Miigam'agan and gkisedtanamoogk's home in Burnt Church. Several of us went to help work on the Wabanaki Resource Center they were trying to start on the reserve. That wasn't an official Gathering, but it's where we got to be with each other more informally for an extended period of time. I mean, the Gatherings were wonderful but they *were* manufactured. Our work weekend didn't feel manufactured; it felt like friends simply coming to help friends. One of my most poignant memories comes from our time there. It was evening, and we were all sitting around the living room talking. People were starting to go off to bed but I wasn't quite sleepy yet. I was watching gkisedtanamoogk sitting with their son, Goptjaoeta, teaching him words in his Native language. It was a sweet little scene, like any parent teaching their kid to read – just family life. Then the phone rang. Miigam'agan, at that time, was running for tribal office in her community against some of the established leadership, and that ring turned out to be a threatening phone call.

We non-Natives want to romanticize the Indigenous experience, and it could've been easy to do that night, watching this "nice little family" up there in the north woods, but then Miigam'agan got this call that shattered all our peace. What I took from that experience was, this is the cost of being an activist. This is the cost – to have a threat intrude into your home. I remember thinking, "This is serious business." This isn't just – and I don't mean "just" in a diminishing way – but this Wabanaki Center isn't just a school to teach children their Native language, this is part of fighting corruption and oppression, really taking a stand, which then puts you in the bullseye. That night was a major shift for me. It was after that I started to look for ways to be an *active* ally – not only to be someone who shares my experience with others and contradicts stereotypes that I hear, but to try to more actively make a difference in the world.

Since the Gatherings, I have become an Episcopal priest. During the time when we were meeting in the Gatherings, I began to feel a strong call to return to the church. I had dabbled in what's referred to as New Age spirituality – though never in terms of trying to practice Native American ceremonies – but I came to realize that in order to access the sacred I had to be in community. My home church, all my life, had been Episcopalian. There the service is liturgical, meaning it's the same every Sunday; readings change, but the service itself doesn't change. At some point, gkisedtanamoogk and I were talking about expressions of spirituality, and I said that I wasn't sure I wanted to return to something that was so rote. "Whatever you do," he said, "do what feels right, but let me give you another way to think about doing the same thing every time"; and he shared his experience of ceremony, saying there was something about the consistency of the rituals that made him ready to be in a sacred space.

That conversation got me to go back to the Episcopal Church, to see if my experience could be different from what it had been before, and after a time I came to really appreciate the service. When I went to seminary I learned why the service is put together as it is, and why it builds as it does, and I thought, "Okay, I get it now." I realized the structure wasn't arbitrary; every step has meaning. I now see so much power in the preparations that happened prior to the ceremonies in the Gatherings. I didn't necessarily understand what those preparations were, but I always noticed gkisedtanamoogk doing things before we got started and it seemed as if there was a "building up to," which I recognize now in my own tradition as being intentional and a way to invite us all into a different kind of experience.

One thing in the Gatherings that was very familiar to me was the use of fire; our weekends began and ended with the lighting and extinguishing of the Sacred Fire. In the Episcopal tradition, it's when the candles are lit that the service begins. That's a signal to say, "We've moved into a sacred place," and when the candles are extinguished, that's when the service is over.

I would equate our time in the Circle with the church's sermon. In my tradition, the sermon is where we attempt to discern, having read the scriptures, the message that God wants to give us that particular day. That's how I would describe the Circle; the "sermon" is whatever is moving in people's hearts on any given day to share with the group, and the purpose is to elevate all of our understanding. The purpose of the message, just as in my tradition, is always corporate; it's not about the individual. There are some within the Christian tradition whose sole emphasis is personal salvation. That's not true in the Episcopal Church; the purpose there is always corporate, to raise all of us to a new understanding. The Talking Circle was the same. It wasn't about personal agendas. I felt God, Spirit – the Holy Spirit – in that Circle.

At the Gatherings I had an intense several years of hearing people's stories that were very unlike mine, and it certainly changed me. You can't witness people's suffering and stay the same person, you just can't. Currently I am the executive director and chaplain at the Seeds of Hope Neighborhood Center, which provides programs and services to poor and oppressed people in the Biddeford area. The people who come to our doors have lived lives that I've never experienced, but I've been taught to listen. I believe that my ability to do the work at the center is because of the willingness of the attendees at the Gatherings all those years ago, especially the Native attendees, to share their vulnerability so deeply. I think it was St. Benedict who said, "Listen with the ears of your heart." I'm able to listen to our neighbors more completely, to try to understand their experience and to be more compassionate about what their needs are, as a result of my experience in the Gatherings.

I think the most important thing I've learned is that those of us in the dominant culture have so much responsibility to understand the experience of people who don't stand in our shoes, and to do what we can. Not to do *for* other people but to work *alongside* people, to work alongside people to change the story.

WESLEY

I grew up in central Pennsylvania – conservative country – and as a young man I shared those values too. I remember a trip I took to Washington, DC, right after college where I saw people protesting the Vietnam War and being arrested. I thought at the time, "Well, they're breaking the law, they deserve to be arrested."

But in leaving home, and seeing what was going on in the world, I started to reject some of the ideas I had grown up with. In my early twenties, I moved to Florida to start my career as an accountant. It was there I heard people talking about a book, *Bury My Heart at Wounded Knee*, by Dee Brown. I had always been interested in history and I decided to pick it up. Prior to that, I hardly knew anything of Indian people or what had gone on in the past, but something drew me to this book. What I read enraged me; I couldn't put it down. I couldn't believe we had never been taught this in school.

In those days, I carried a lot of anger inside. The relationship between my parents was not good, and it made for a lot of turmoil in my family. As a child you see something that's not right and you get angry, but you don't know what to do. Somehow that book brought out my anger.

It affected me so much that I started reading anything I could find on our history with Native peoples. I got so immersed in my research that I started looking at graduate schools. I decided to go to State University of New York (SUNY) at Buffalo because of its Native Studies program, but at the time a White person couldn't enroll in Native Studies, so I majored in US studies and then took courses on topics like the Wounded Knee massacre. It was at SUNY-Buffalo that I met John Mohawk. John was a well-known Seneca scholar there, and he became my mentor.

While I was at SUNY-Buffalo I had an experience that left a big impression. I was living in a suburb of Buffalo, a conservative Catholic town where I stood out because of my appearance. By that time, I had long hair and drove a van covered with bumper stickers. One day I went into a jewelry store in town to get my watch repaired. When I returned to the store several weeks later, the shop owner asked me what I was doing there. Apparently since my last visit she had noticed that a diamond ring was missing. She called the police right then and described *me* and said that I was the thief. I left the store but was later picked up by a couple of officers who put me in the police car, read me my rights, and took me to the station. After three hours of interrogation, I was released. It was a terrifying experience. Later, the police did arrest a man who supposedly looked like me. I felt I had been identified as the thief purely because of my appearance, because I looked "different." Since that time, I identify with the stories I hear from Native people who are continually harassed by law enforcement just because they look "suspicious."

Eventually I left New York and moved to Portland, Maine, where I enrolled at the University of Southern Maine to finish my degree. I wanted to continue my involvement with Native issues, and I must have read something about the Center for Vision and Policy and decided to go to a meeting. The meeting was at Shirley Hager's home, and I remember sitting in her living room and talking about possible Native speakers for an upcoming "gathering." "I know who would be good," I said, "John Mohawk," and I offered to contact him. John agreed to attend, and of course I went too.

That was the group's second Gathering, and my first experience of such an event. Not knowing what was going to happen, I was very curious. I remember one tense moment. We were in a meeting room at the retreat center where the Gathering was being held, and several Native people – John Mohawk and others – were sitting up front in a row of chairs facing us. At one point, one of the Native speakers said that she didn't like this arrangement. She said she didn't want to be up in front of White people talking about Indians, or talking about herself and her issues. She didn't want to be separated from us. That comment was the beginning of the change; the change from a format in which Native people were the presenters to a traditional Council Circle where we all met around the Fire for the whole weekend and used the Talking Stick.

It made a big impact on me to sit in those Circles. It was hard for me, as a White man, to keep my mouth shut, to just sit there and listen. But that's the purpose of having the Talking Stick, so you listen.

Also, there was the Fire. It is traditionally the men's role to keep the Fire, and it burns twenty-four hours a day. I'll never forget sitting around the Fire with gkisedtanamoogk, just the two of us through the night, and what we talked about. We talked about football, but about other things too. I remember him saying you have to be careful with joy because you can become arrogant. I don't know if he was intentionally speaking to me but I took it that way.

Once, during the years in which we were meeting, we were invited up to gkisedtanamoogk and Miigam'agan's home in New Brunswick for their annual Mid-Winter Gathering. The Fire had been lit, and I was asked to do a shift at two in the morning. It was so cold that, at one point, I got in my car and turned on the heater so I didn't freeze to death. I was determined to stay with it though; it was my responsibility at that point to keep the Fire going. I was being trusted to do what I was asked, and I knew the trust arose from a relationship that had taken a long time to develop. I think that 2 a.m. shift was some kind of test.

Some people I met at the Gatherings stay in my mind even though I haven't seen them since. I remember a Maliseet man I met once. We were all waiting for a meal to be served and he was standing next to me, so I introduced myself. He had a button on his chest that said, "It's too bad that ignorance isn't painful." I'll never forget that button; I tell people about it all the time.

I remember also a Native man from Nova Scotia. I first met him one winter at an environmental conference near Halifax. We were going in the front door of the conference center and we introduced ourselves. He said he was on release from prison to come to this conference. The next time I saw him was at one of our Gatherings. As with the previous event, someone had "sponsored" him so he could leave the prison for the weekend. We had a chance to talk again, and I remember him saying that he was afraid to come out of prison. He was afraid he was going to end up doing the same thing that he had done before, though he didn't tell me what that was. Somehow, over the years, he kept attending the Gatherings; and, after a few times in the Circle, he eventually did tell us about himself and why he was in jail and so forth. That was a significant experience for me, to sit and listen to him and realize that, in many ways, he was just like me. I could relate to his fears and anxieties about going out into an unfamiliar world, knowing he would have things to deal with and not wanting to. I can't be sure, but he seemed to draw strength from being in those Circles.

Those kinds of encounters had a big effect on me, and on my view of the world. Most people want the same things: family, health, shelter, safety.

I kept returning to the Gatherings all those years simply because I became friends with the people I met there. I never anticipated becoming friends with Native people until it happened. I never thought it *could* happen. But because we were meeting twice a year, year after year, over long weekends, sharing food and housing, that's what happens – you become friends. I learned a lot about their lives. Some were barely surviving financially, sometimes lacking even food and housing. I never realized that before – the hardship of their day-to-day lives.

I knew that "the system" was oppressive to them, but I came to realize that it's oppressive to me too. It was an awakening for me to realize that, yes, it's more obvious with people of color, and there's no comparison, but even myself – a White man – I'm oppressed also. I started to understand that it wasn't only their issues that we were talking about. When I look at our government, and at our economic system – the way it's set up – there's a lot of injustice. A lot of people don't have choices. If you feel you have choices you can accept the system, or live with it, even thrive in it, but some people don't have choices and that makes them angry, or frightened, even paralyzed. I'm part of the system because of the financial obligations I have to my family and what I've had to do to earn a living over the years, and that to me is oppressive – to go along with something I don't agree with in order to survive. So it was good to get together with like-minded people and talk about issues that faced Native people but that also face all of us, and look for ways we could support one another.

When I came home after these weekends I had no one to share my experience with. Friends typically didn't ask me about it. Sometimes I would try to talk about it but people didn't understand – it was hard for them to understand – what I was doing. I have a brother-in-law who would ask why I wanted to "work with Indians." "Why are you doing this?" he'd say, and I'd try to explain to him, but it didn't seem to make an impact. Sometimes when I tried to describe my experience, I would break down because it meant so much to me.

I only knew this was what I was supposed to be doing; that it was the right thing to do. Particular moments confirmed this for me. I remember one Gathering where, looking around the Circle, I realized that all four races were there. I think that only happened once, where there were not only Indigenous and White people but also African-American and Asian people as well – the whole Medicine Circle. Lots of people noticed it, and I remember several commenting on it. That's what needs to happen to save the world – the coming together of all the races, reconciling our differences and supporting one another. I'll never forget that Circle.

I remember clearly when Miigam'agan joined us for the first time. That seemed significant to me. I respected her very much and was aware that she had held back for a long time. To me she had always been part of the group, but always on the periphery. I felt it gave a lot of credence to what we were doing the day she entered the Circle.

Several years after the Gatherings ended, in Miigam'agan's community of Burnt Church, the Mi'kmaq started lobster fishing as a result of the Canadian Supreme Court affirming their right to fish for subsistence. I was in Burnt Church at the time, and witnessed the fishing activities and the violent reactions of the White fishermen and Royal Canadian Mounted Police (RCMP) against the Mi'kmaq. I wanted to help, and asked what I could do. My task was to stand on the shore and watch as signals were sent from the fishermen in their boats to their supporters on land. I felt frustrated because I wanted to do more, but I was taking my cues from the Mi'kmaq people. To me, being an ally means being willing to stand with Native people, sometimes to simply be present, and to be willing to take instructions.

For the past ten years, I have worked in "Indian Country." As a certified public accountant, I wanted to offer my skills where they were needed. My most recent position, and where I stayed the longest, was in Arizona working for the Tohono O'odham Nation. It took a long time for me to be trusted by the people there.

Even though you might visit a reservation, until you live or work there you don't really know what it's like. Being so close to the US/Mexican border in southern Arizona, I continually encountered the US Border Patrol. They have checkpoints all over the area, not only on the border but in the vicinity as well, and one of these checkpoints was located between where I lived and the reservation where I drove to work every day. Becaue I'm a White guy, the Border Patrol never bothered me – I passed through with no problem – but I regularly saw them stop cars with Native and Hispanic passengers. Dogs were brought out, cars were searched – an intimidating process that could take fifteen minutes or more. I would talk about this with my Tohono O'odham co-workers and with other White people from the area, and they would all say they noticed it too, but everyone seemed resigned to the situation.

In addition to my financial duties, I taught several courses at the community college on the reservation. The Native students there were very quiet, and it was hard for me to know if they understood the material or if there were other reasons for their silence. I tried to draw them out, though I often thought I was too aggressive and asked too many questions.

I began to ask, "Why are you here, and what do you want to learn?" Some of the students had to be there because their degree program required accounting, but I began to realize the textbook made very little sense to them. A White person wrote it, of course, and accounting is a different and unfamiliar language at best. I started to relate the work in class to real-life experiences; to use *their* work experiences to help them understand the content I was teaching. As the class went along, we got more comfortable with one another.

It was my experience in the Gatherings that helped me to hang in and continue to work in Indian Country. Even though I have moved back to Pennsylvania to be near my family, I still want to be connected with Indigenous people or to assist in whatever way I can. I know there's work I'm meant to be doing as an ally, one way or the other. I'm not sure exactly what that work will look like in the future, but there is still that desire.

Being an ally means being a supporter. That's one reason I opened the art gallery that I ran for a while. I feel that one of the ways to be an ally to Native Americans is to buy their art so that they can support themselves and their families. I wear Native jewelry to support those artists.

I have a responsibility as a White person to educate other White people about what my experience has been. White men often think we have all the answers and know what's best. I once met a Native man in Albuquerque who said he believed most of the world's problems were the result of White men being on top. "Go home," he said, "and work with White men." One time, I actually asked five or six of my male friends to get together and talk about our White privilege. I talked about what I had learned from this man in Albuquerque, who said that White people need to give up some of their wealth. I tried to convince them that they have to give up something. We only met twice. White men aren't willing to give up their power because they perceive they will lose something that matters to them.

I'm not afraid to lose my privilege, because for me I'm not losing anything. When I have shared my knowledge and my privilege with Native people, in return I have gained friendship. It's all been positive, even the difficult moments. The relationships I have with

Native friends I've made through the Gatherings are deep; they exemplify respect. If any one of them asked me to do something I would do it. It's been nearly thirty years since the Gatherings ended but the relationships remain as they were. We are family.

MARILYN

Prior to the Gatherings, I was used to the discomfort of cross-cultural situations because I had attended a Black Pentecostal church in my neighborhood in Philadelphia for about fifteen years. At this church, I was usually the only White person and sometimes I would not do things correctly, which was always embarrassing. That's if I even *knew* when my behavior was incorrect. Who knows how many people I offended unintentionally. Usually people were nice and would tell me what I had done, and some things you pick up. But sometimes you're left thinking, "Gosh, maybe I shouldn't go places where I get myself in these ridiculous, uncomfortable positions." But I always went back.

When we first moved to Houlton, Maine, where there is a significant Maliseet population, one of our White neighbors had some Christmas lights stolen and they said something like, "Well, it must've been the Indians." Harry and I looked at each other and said, "What? What are they talking about?" We had never encountered any prejudice against Aboriginal people before, even though we had been very involved in the civil rights movement.

Sometimes we White people don't even realize how ignorant and arrogant we are. I shudder when I think of the arrogance of my own attitude in the early days, but I wasn't educated enough to know I was arrogant. I'm thinking now about my work in archaeology. I got a master's degree in archaeology because I wanted to learn more about humans and war. My publications are on the origins of warfare. I have to say this: war is not in our genes, folks! I know that for sure.

I have done no digging or research in North America – my work had more to do with Europe, the Middle East, Africa, and so on. I assumed, however, that the archaeological research done in North America – referred to as Turtle Island by many Indigenous people – would be of interest to the Aboriginal people here. At the time, I had no awareness of the disrespect and shameful ways exhibited by many archaeologists and anthropologists over the years, particularly in the late 1800s and early 1900s. I'm talking about the removal of artifacts, putting human remains on display in museums, that sort of thing. When I think of it now I am absolutely appalled. This was before NAGPRA – that's a law that was passed in the United States in 1990. It stands for Native American Graves Protection and Repatriation Act.

In Scotland, for example, I would be happy to dig. I would dig and do my archaeology over there, but I would not dig here on Turtle Island because our cultures differ in our perceptions of our relationship with the Earth. I don't think most archaeologists understand this. I hope they will come to understand it, and I must say I think the tide is changing and that the new archaeologists are much more respectful. Aboriginal people here have a different mode of perception about the land, and that impinges on a whole range of things.

My experiences in the Gatherings, and our relationships with the Maliseet people where we live, have profoundly changed my worldview. For one thing, we no longer say that we *own* land. As gkisedtanamoogk says, we pay taxes on the land, but the land belongs to the Creator and Mother Earth. There is also the Indigenous idea that we must consider the consequence of all our decisions on the seventh generation to come; this concept was a huge gift to me and so important for all White people to learn.

I'm still learning, of course; I have to stress that a hundred times. One teaching I have had from Aboriginal people is that they are responsible for this continent because the Creator put them here first. Their "Original Instructions" are to care for this land that we call North America. Yes, we White people are the ones who have messed it up, and we can and must be important allies to Native people – vital allies because there are so many of us here – but they see it as their job to be the guardians of the health and integrity of this land.

I tried to practice this teaching a few summers ago when I participated on a Water Walk with Grandmother Josephine, who is Ojibway Anishinaabekwe. This walk was to raise awareness of all the threats to our water, and people were traveling from the four directions of Turtle Island to meet on the south shore of Lake Superior. A group from this territory was leaving from Machias, Maine, and heading westward to meet all the other walkers. Even though I was offered the water bucket to carry, I did not feel it was my job to carry the water. I chose to walk *behind* the water carriers, who were Aboriginal people, as an ally. I have tried to learn what is, and what is not, my place.

For me, being an ally to Native people means to back them up, and to help, under their direction. In working on behalf of the Earth, for example, we need to take our lead from Aboriginal people and their consensus about what should be done. What Alma is doing right now is so fantastic – organizing Native *and* non-Native communities in New Brunswick against fracking. I can't tell you how much I respect that woman. And the non-Native people who are taking their direction from Alma may be much more effective in what they achieve.

Probably one of the most impactful experiences in my life was when Alma, whom we knew from the Gatherings, asked Harry and me to go with her to visit with the Native Brotherhood at what we call Renous prison. The actual name of the prison is Atlantic Institution and it's the maximum-security facility in Renous, New Brunswick. The Native Brotherhood is an organized group of Native inmates in the prison whose purpose is to provide support for one another, especially in the practice of traditional ways, and to protect the interests of the Native inmates and ensure that their rights are being respected. In terms of support for the Brotherhood's presence in these institutions, I think Canada is ahead of Maine by about thirty years.

The Brotherhood would at times have celebrations and various events in the prison to which volunteers were invited, as well as families of the inmates and, of course, the Elders. The people in charge of the ceremonies were the Native Elders. At Renous there was at least a half-acre of land that had been set aside for ceremonies where the White staff of the prison was not allowed. There was a tipi, and picnic tables, and a storage shed for the firewood used in the sweats. When we went to these gatherings, the Native Brotherhood paid for the feast that we had there. We would be there usually six to eight hours, basically a whole Saturday. gkisedtanamoogk was often there ahead of us because, prior to the time when the families and volunteers would come in, usually an Elder would have been there already, conducting a sweat with the men who wanted that. I remember that the Inuit, some of them, could not be in a sweat because their metabolisms were so fast that they couldn't be in intense heat. There were Native inmates there from all over Canada, and some of them were very powerful Indigenous leaders who, along with others from outside the institution, had helped to bring about reforms in the

Canadian prison system. One of the reforms was that Indigenous Elders were allowed to come in on equal status with the chaplains. These Elders, I think, made a very big difference in the lives of the many, many Aboriginal people who were incarcerated. We're still trying to get that particular reform in Maine, and it was only a few years ago that a sweat was even allowed in a Maine prison.

At first, I didn't know why Alma would want White people to go with her into the prisons but we certainly wanted to volunteer, and because we were with Alma we were allowed on the ceremonial grounds. We did this for at least a dozen years, and came to care very much about some of the inmates we met. Like everywhere else, you connect with some people more than others, and when some of the men got out we tried to help. One man I particularly remember. He told the guys in the prison he was not coming back, and he did everything he could to make that a fact. He came to live in Houlton so as not to be under the watchful eye of the RCMP – the Canadian police – and because he was in our community we were able to assist in various ways. I then understood one of the assets of having non-Native volunteers. If an inmate is not returning to a reserve or reservation, in other words if they're going to be living in the general population, sometimes non-Native volunteers can help to smooth the way.

I hope that Harry and I have been good allies, but we couldn't have assisted, even in the very minor ways that we have, had we not had those experiences in the Gatherings long ago, and gotten some understanding of the current issues in Maine and New Brunswick. I remember testifying once before the Houlton town council. The Maliseets were having trouble getting additional police and fire protection from the town so that they, the Maliseets, could build more housing in their community. It was just before Christmas time. I called the town councillors "grinches" because they were holding up the housing, and pointed out that the Houlton Band of Maliseets had brought *millions* of dollars to the town.

Because of the support we offered at that time, the Maliseet chief called us once again and asked for some help when they and other Wabanaki in Maine were testifying on an issue before the Maine state legislature. That was a very sad learning experience for me. I, as a White person, was absolutely ashamed to be at some of those hearings where Aboriginal leaders were testifying and to witness the demeaning treatment they received from some of the legislators.

Being allies matters because of the huge injustices that have gone on. The United States was founded on genocide and slavery. I didn't know thirty years ago that Columbus Day was nothing to celebrate. I had no knowledge that all the Native people that Columbus came in contact with were killed or committed suicide or died of diseases. I didn't know about the smallpox blankets. This is why being an ally is important – it's a justice issue.

The Gathering I remember best of course was the one held at the camp we used to have at Eel River Lake in New Brunswick. We knew this was a special place when we bought it. It is part of Maliseet territory – on the old Maliseet trail from the St. John River down to the Penobscot. We had heard from the White people we purchased the property from that there were spirits – good spirits – down by the lake. I myself had quite an experience down there one night.

The property had five acres by the lake; then there was the house, which was on about four acres; and then there were about twenty additional acres. Even prior to the weekend when we hosted the Gathering there, one of the local Maliseet Elders had asked if it would be all right to have vision quests on the property, to which we of course agreed, and several had already been held there.

Years later, we decided that we couldn't continue to keep up the camp, and rather than sell it we approached three traditional Maliseet Elders about receiving it. The word "gift" should not be used, because at this point we did not feel that this land was ours to give. It wasn't. There had never been a land claims settlement in New Brunswick, at least nothing significant, so this land had never been ceded to the settlers. The Elders did agree to have the three various parcels transferred to them, one parcel to each. It was one of those legal arrangements where you transfer something for a dollar or whatever, and so that's what we did. As the Quakers would say, it was a "rightly ordered" thing to do, meaning that's the way it should have been.

There is one point that needs to be made about this transfer. In receiving this land, these Elders had to agree to pay taxes on it, and that is such a great injustice. This was their land to begin with, and to have to pay taxes on what they consider to be a gift from the Creator is a terrible, terrible thing. When they agreed to this transfer, they were undertaking something that at the same time was a burden, a very unjust burden. I just need to make this point – taxes on land are something that no Aboriginal person should ever have to pay.

The Gatherings gently and patiently introduced us to the issues affecting Native people, and all of us, here in Maine and New Brunswick. There are the same, or similar, issues of course across the whole of Turtle Island. But the Gatherings were safe. They were a safe place to explore these issues together. I suppose they were safe because no one was terribly judgmental. I was told by the Native participants at the Gatherings that if I did something wrong people would be honest and tell me. That was a great comfort because it can be very disconcerting to go outside the comfort zone of your own culture. I thought that the way the Center for Vision and Policy orga- nized the Gatherings helped people to overcome that discomfort so we could actually listen and learn from each other.

In those Circles, there was such a sense of appreciation from every- one involved – appreciation for one another's presence and for the effort we were making to be together. The Wabanaki people were able to speak important truths without alienating people, or in such a way that they could be absorbed slowly by White people. And of course, once you love people it doesn't matter what they tell you, you know. Once you get to know people and love them, they can say anything.

BETTY

After my husband Gunnar's death, I threw myself into activism. In those days, Halifax was a beehive of activity where many things were going on in terms of peace work – demonstrations against nuclear power, antiwar protests, and much more. I had been a Quaker since the 1940s – since the Second World War – so it was natural for me to plunge into all of these kinds of things. Soon, I was asked to repre- sent Halifax Friends Meeting at a conference of the Canadian Friends Service Committee – the national peace and justice organization of Quakers. This was a very large gathering where all the Meetings sent a delegate. Once there, we were each asked to be on a committee and I chose the one on "Native concerns" because I'd worked a long time on issues affecting Black people living in the southern US, and it seemed to me the same problems existed in Canada with Native people. I thought, "What can I do?"

After that meeting, I became involved with several Quaker groups that were trying to work with, and support, Indigenous people at various levels. I'm an organizer, and that was always my main role, getting people – non-Natives – to meetings. I tried to make the meetings interesting enough to attract an audience and then often turned the meeting over to a Native person to speak. Usually these events were around a cause – a social justice or environmental issue.

As a result of all these connections, I had a tremendous opportunity in 1985. There was a call for those who could get away from their day jobs to spend a week and fly to Labrador. The purpose of this trip was to observe and to understand more about the issue of NATO's low-flying planes and how they were impacting the Innu people. So I went, along with five or six other church people, all non-Native. I represented the Quakers.

The Innu were such a small group that hardly anyone in Canada or in the States had ever heard of them. That was the first time I had contact with Native people on their ancestral land. These were people who lived in the mountains where the caribou are. They had only come out of the bush as recently as the 1960s, and didn't speak any English at all, so we had to have translators.

A large part of my continuing motivation to work with Native people has come from that experience of being with the Innu near Goose Bay. They flew us out to one of their camps where they were shooting caribou and gathering herbs and so on. I was there only a few hours, but it didn't take long to grasp the situation. NATO had built an enormous airport on Innu land for the purpose of training, and they intended to increase that training. The NATO planes, coming mostly from Europe, flew at treetop level in order to test the planes. The women, the children, and the old people, when these planes would fly so low, would fall to the ground screaming, terrified. That scene made a lasting impression on me. When we asked, "What can we do?" they said, "Go back and tell people."

That became my mission. I made dozens of speeches, all over. I traveled as far as Toronto to speak about the issue, and I began to bring Innu people with me. Non-Natives in other places organized large interest groups and collected money for the Innu to go out speaking on their own. For ten to fifteen years I spoke to groups against this assault. Finally, others took up the cause, and gradually it grew and spread throughout the 1980s and 1990s. Eventually, sometime in the 1990s, NATO changed their plans.

A couple of years after my trip to Goose Bay, in 1988, I became involved in another issue, this time involving the Lubicon Cree and oil and gas development in their territory in Alberta. Our big Quaker yearly meeting was being held in Alberta, and I invited Chief Bernard Ominayak of the Lubicon Lake Indian Nation to come down to speak to us. He didn't have to come – it was maybe one hundred to two hundred miles for him to travel – but he did, and he was so winning, such a wonderful speaker. He described how terrible it was that these monstrous oil-drilling machines were coming in and breaking up their traps and keeping them from going out hunting. Again, we asked, "What can we do?" He said, "Come, and bring some people to the big demonstrations that we're going to have in the fall in Peace River, Alberta."

The Quakers decided to send three representatives to Peace River, I being one. We trained ourselves in non-violence because we felt this sort of experience might be needed. We didn't know whether they were going to bring in guns or whatever – we didn't think so – but we thought, "One thing we can do here is offer non-violence training."

When we arrived, Chief Bernard came over with a big smile, shook our hands, and called us the "Rambo Quakers," which broke the ice because he knew full well the Quakers were peaceful. Well, after we were there a day or two, and people kept coming in and coming in, we realized that in no way were they going to be violent. That's not how Native people are. They didn't say, "Oh, we're going to practice non-violent resistance," but they didn't have to say it. Anyway, we all ended up sitting down in front of these big machines, and we were arrested and put in jail. There were twenty-seven of us – the women in one cell and the men in another. And all night we sang and sang, just trying to cheer ourselves up.

The premier of Alberta – his name was Getty – had refused to meet with the Lubicon about their demands to be recognized, which they had been demanding for fifty years. They wanted to be an officially recognized reserve, which would mean that these monstrous machines and people coming in to drill on their land could be kept off. In the midst of this situation, with twenty-seven of us in jail, the premier finally offered to meet with the chief, and Chief Bernard said to the premier, "I will not meet with you unless you let my people go," which included us non-Natives as well. So we were released, and we decided to go home because it seemed these two men were finally going to speak to one another. We thought we might be called back to stand trial, or be fined, but we never were, and so it seemed maybe the negotiations were working out.

Around the time of these events, I began to hear of the Center for Vision and Policy in Maine and the Gatherings it was sponsoring. From what we in Canada could tell of these reports, CVP was sort of a "Native awareness" group – I think that's how we referred to it. In our minds it was different from our groups that were working with Natives on specific issues. The Gatherings didn't seem to be focused on "causes" but rather on understanding of one another, and on relationships.

The name encouraged me to get involved. Putting "vision" before "policy" interested me. As I said earlier, I'm an organizer – that's my big thing – and I'm always pinching myself to remember other kinds of things like vision, and the spiritual aspect, which is easier to do, of course, when you work with Native people.

At my first Gathering, I met gkisedtanamoogk. Shortly after, he moved to Burnt Church – Esgenoôpetitj – where Miigam'agan's family is from, and then the whole border issue came up. The Canadian government refused to recognize his right to live in Canada. They did not recognize his and Miigam'agan's traditional wedding ceremony as being legitimate, which would have granted him legal residency. Also, the Canadian government wasn't honoring the Jay Treaty (of 1794), which guarantees freedom of travel across the border for Indigenous people regardless of their status. That was a very difficult time for him and his family. Quakers in Canada worked very hard to support his case. We helped him to get a lawyer, but eventually there was not much that we could do.

Since the Gatherings, gkisedtanamoogk has been a key person in many events and activities in New Brunswick and Nova Scotia focused on Native concerns and Native/non-Native relations. For many years during and after the Gatherings, he and I worked together to help form several coalitions and organizations in the Maritimes, gkisedtanamoogk driving the long distances from Maine since he wasn't allowed to live in Canada. With the support of a number of churches, the Aboriginal Rights Coalition of Atlantic Canada was formed in 1995 along with KAIROS Canada, an ecumenical justice movement; also in the 1990s, Native awareness weekends began at the Tatamagouche Centre in Nova Scotia.

Tatamagouche was originally a retreat center of the United Church of Canada and is now used for many different purposes. At our weekends there, gkisedtanamoogk took the lead in helping non-Natives to understand Indigenous concerns and to participate appropriately in Native customs and practices, when invited, following the example of the CVP Gatherings in Maine. I represented the Quakers and encouraged many Quakers and others to attend. Over the years, the Aboriginal Rights Coalition, KAIROS, and many other Native/non-Native groups have met at Tatamagouche in peace and friendship around specific causes and to share deeply in our common humanity. More recently, Talking Circles at Tatamagouche have provided an opportunity for Natives and a few others to unburden themselves of their haunting experiences of residential schools in early childhood, and to cope with the lingering effects of these "schools" throughout the years.

My involvement with Indigenous friends and their concerns has permanently changed how I see the world, partly because of the experiences I've already described, but also because of my work in the prisons. It was through Marilyn and Harry Roper that I started traveling over to New Brunswick, where the Quakers were already well organized for this work, to visit the prisons and to support the Native inmates.

You never forget your first visit to a prison: feeling that chill; stepping up to present your documentation, which is very hard to get, to be admitted to the prison; and then having ... well, it's not exactly a strip search, but they're very thorough. In those situations, though, the point is not to worry about yourself; it's what they do to the Native people that we should worry about. When we first went in, the officers grabbed the Elders' medicine bundles, dumped the contents all over the desk, and pawed through them saying, "What's this?" It was maybe a rabbit's foot or something like a little medicine pouch. Well, of course they have to be sure it's not drugs and all that, but their attitudes were so terrible, saying, "You can't take that in there!" The first time I went in, I didn't open my mouth. I did speak up later on, but that first time I was afraid they would keep me out, that if I spoke up I wouldn't be able to go inside at all.

Once we got in, however, the attitude of the prisoners toward the Elders, and toward the ceremonies, was one of immense respect. Some were hardened criminals at the maximum-security prisons – although we never asked the men why they were there – but mostly they seemed so very shy, although open to us and even friendly. Once in a while, an inmate would hang back and give us looks like, "Who are these White people? They're the ones who put us in here in the first place." But over time, you came to know people that you would see again and again. There even were girlfriends or wives of prisoners who got my name and telephone number, and I was very free to give them rides to and from the prison so they could visit.

These days I sit and worry when I watch the news. It's now over thirty years since I visited Alberta and the Lubicon Cree and nothing has changed. The development of oil sands in their territory continues, as well as their fight for recognition. Now the machines cover the territory entirely and it's called "Oil Sands Number Two." Have you ever seen pictures of these places, gobbling up the Earth as far as you can see? They had a big spill there recently, right there on Lubicon land. There was a break in one of the oil pipes and it went all through the boggy land surrounding the Lubicon. It's terrible. That area will be devastated.

I think about the Native people in places like northern Ontario. Because of climate change, they now have to fly in all their supplies; the ground is no longer frozen and the trucks can't get through. What is this going to mean for them? They're probably going to have to leave their traditional lands to get what they need – jobs, better food, medicine. I don't know what the outcome is going to be for them. Most people haven't grasped climate change yet, haven't *begun* to grasp it. Hopefully, more non-Natives will begin to realize, as Native people surely do, that Mother Earth is our only home and we must change our habits, our values, and our society while there is still time.

I have these long thoughts as I sit here working on my files to donate to the archives here in Halifax. I am profoundly grateful for my experiences with Native friends and other community co-workers over the past thirty years. Always, I have tried to listen and learn, but when the call for action has come, I have been moved to respond.

JOANN

I first heard of the Gatherings from Frances Hancock. At that time, I was a graduate student in theology and a friend of Frances, who was a student in the program as well. Frances had come to know Shirley Hager and Elly Haney, and the Center for Vision and Policy, so she knew about the Gatherings. In our theology classes, we had been studying the -isms – classism, sexism, ageism, and racism – I guess you could say we were gaining consciousness. And so Frances invited me to go to a Gathering with her. The Gatherings had been going on for maybe two years at that point. I went, and then continued to go twice a year wherever the Gatherings were held. After a while, I found myself wanting to organize my life around attending. It became a cyclical thing, with the seasons.

My own experience of Native people up to that time was very limited, even though I lived on Cape Cod where there is a large Wampanoag community and this is their original territory. I knew there were Wampanoags on the Cape, but I was only peripherally aware of them – just what I might read in the paper. My closest contact had been at a theology conference held locally, where a Wampanoag Elder was invited to come and open the day with a ceremony. I remember my thoughts at the time were, "Wow, this makes perfect sense. Here she is, a person of this land, welcoming us here and opening this event." Sometime after that conference, I went to New Zealand, where you see the Māori people involved throughout the culture. You go to a baseball game, or to any public event, and it seems the Māori are always part of it – in the opening ceremonies, for example – so, unlike here, their presence is very much evident.

I did have a feeling for the overall devastation of the Native peoples. I knew that my people – White people – had caused this devastation. As a result, I felt that I would be, and ought to be, unwelcome in any meeting, or any conversation, with a Native person; that is, if there *were* any meetings, which of course there never were. Also, I was afraid. My shame, or my guilt, was so deep that I was afraid to encounter a Native person.

So at my first Gathering, I think I cried from the moment I got into the Circle. The sense that "I ought not to be here" or "I have no right to be here" was so great. As a result, I hardly spoke. I'd have the Talking Stick and I'd have to pass it on, because I would not be able to say anything. But I loved what I heard; I loved hearing the others speak. Their words would wash over me. I already knew some of the facts about what had happened – the people and the communities so devastated – so that wasn't new information, but what I heard increased the depth of my understanding, and my fears, about our history. It seemed as if some of the non-Natives – Elly and Debbie and Shirley for example – could hear everything and yet still speak in the Circle. They could talk about the issues, and I could see that alliances were forming among some of the people. And I wanted that. I wanted to be where they were. The idea of building an alliance – I felt that was something I could do. I thought the last thing I could hope for was to have a relationship – to be really connected – but I could be there as an ally.

It's hard to describe the separation I felt. It was a real block. I felt unworthy, and I knew I had to let go of that feeling in order to engage. I think the unworthiness had to do with … well, there is a Catholic prayer, "I am unworthy, but only say the word and I shall be healed." As in, you go to the altar with a sense of unworthiness inside, but you pray, "Just say the word and I shall be healed." I think I needed a word to come to me so that I could be there, but the word couldn't come from a non-Native person. A Native person had to welcome me, in a sense, so I could begin to feel that I belonged.

The consistency of meeting seasonally helped, having that to depend on and knowing that you were setting that time aside. I had to carve the time out, and work out all the details of being away, and then drive seven to ten hours each time. And the personal preparation that went into it, everything that you had to bring – sleeping bag, tent, food – all this was preparation for being there, so that by the time you arrived you felt it was a serious matter because you had brought so much to it already. It was an investment. You imagined everyone else coming from different directions, preparing themselves in the same way. When you bring people together who have been preparing to be together, already something has happened. So over time, on these long weekends, things began to shift for me.

At the time, I was going through such an internal shift in my own understanding of being a woman, letting go of the internalized male definitions of who I was. I felt separated from myself, and from the land. But at the Gatherings I felt, "This is the starting place." I thought, "We have to come to this place and begin all over again," meaning we have to go back and really understand what happened here in this country.

I knew we had a massive wound that needed to be cared for, and healed. I didn't know how to face it, actually, because it was so big; there were so many generations involved. But I knew that what happened when my people came to this land affected me too, because I didn't feel connected here and now. In the beginning, I didn't know how disconnected I was from myself and from the Earth, but when you stand in the presence of the Circle, then you know. The only response I had to that revelation was sadness, and sorrow, and the sorrow was for me. I remember feeling too that I didn't know how to get reconnected, but these Gatherings seemed like a path that was being offered, and I wanted to be there and accept the offering.

It happened slowly, but after a while I started to feel, "I'm part of this." I felt engaged, although it was still a long time before I felt I had anything to say in the Circle, or that I *could* say anything. The Gathering where I actually spoke turned out to be the last Gathering. We had been studying women's history and the women suffragists in school, and I can't remember exactly what I said but it sounded like a voice coming out of the women's suffrage movement. I think I quoted Julia Ward Howe. I felt really strong, as if I finally had something to offer. It was a huge breakthrough, as if a door opened and I walked through it, never to go back. I felt then that I belonged there, in that Circle. I felt accepted. I remember Dana came up to me afterward and said, "I knew there was something in you."

The First Light Ceremony, where we were always invited, was such a beautiful thing. It was beautiful, really, to have a little struggle to wake up, and not quite want to get up, and then within minutes you're there in the Circle. It felt so good; the whole concept of welcoming the day, from darkness into light, and being with people who understood what that meant. To make the welcoming of the day a ceremony – it put such value in the day, and created the atmosphere for what would come after.

Our times in the Talking Circle, though, were the most significant. The Circles were a refuge from individual conversations. You could go to the Circle and sit; you didn't have to speak; you could just listen, and it felt safe. I suppose that, in the beginning, I was hoping to gain knowledge, to learn, but really I wanted to understand something. As a therapist, I used to feel that the whole purpose of my work was to understand where this one person, my client, was coming from. If that person could communicate something, and I could fully understand it, then we'd be standing on the same ground together, and it would be a healing experience. I carried this idea into our Circles, thinking, "Can I hear, and truly understand, something in a way that puts us on equal footing and helps us to heal?"

Getting to know Miigam'agan and gkisedtanamoogk as friends was critically important in my growth. I began to realize, in addition to my affection for them as individuals, that *this* is where I begin. I thought, "This is how we start over in this country and in our history together." My personal relationship was allowing me to "go back" and stand, not only with them, but also with their people. It wasn't as if I was saying "these are my people" – it wasn't that – it was that I would always stand with them as equals. I made that commitment. That was it. It wasn't an intellectual thing; it was experiential.

And maybe the most important thing is that I stand with Miigam'agan. I say that because she's a woman – an Indigenous woman, a woman of color. When you look at the structures of race and class in this country that's where the shift has to begin. Back during my divinity school days, I remember going to a conference called "Woman Church" in Cincinnati. Elizabeth Schussler Fiorenza, who was a great biblical scholar, developed this concept of "woman church," which was a feminist critique of the established church and its patriarchal structures. She was speaking at this conference and many of us in my program went to see her. I was there with all these women who taught in universities – in women's studies and other programs – and yet even then I remember thinking, "There's an element that's missing." I thought, "We can't be developing a 'woman church' unless we go much deeper. We can't be here unless there are so many others here with us." There were no Indigenous women there, for example. Prior to going, I had thought, "This is going to be so exciting because these will be women who understand what needs to change in the church" – the racism and classism and everything – but yet when I got there I realized it was still a church of privilege; it was being built on top of the old order. I had to walk away from it.

What finally made the biggest difference in how I view myself, and my place in the world, was going to Ireland. My decision to go began in a conversation with gkisedtanamoogk. I remember saying to him that I didn't feel I had my own ground to stand on. He said, "Well, I think if I were you I would go to Ireland and walk the land." He said that to me more than twenty-five years ago, but I held onto that idea. It struck me, "That's where I need to connect. I have to connect with my own ancestry, my own family roots. Where did I come from?" So finally I went there to live, in Ireland, for five months. And it was being there, where my people came from, that deepened my sense of who I am. The idea of being *of* the land, which was spoken of in the Gatherings, had always affected me, but I knew I wasn't connected to the land where I lived. I lived on it, but not of it, not with it. I had to find my own land, not in terms of ownership, but someplace to be *of*, a place where my people came from.

Now, having had that experience in Ireland, which was profound for me, even though I'm back on Cape Cod I feel that I'm grounded because I'm connected somewhere. That feeling is mine; it lives in me. The Native people in the Gatherings had this sense of belonging, and now I understood it. They knew this was their home, and so no matter where they were, they still had a sense of belonging. Over in Ireland there's so much talk about people coming back to find their roots and it's kind of glib – almost embarrassing really. American Irish go over and visit all the places and kiss the Blarney Stone and so on. But when you understand why you're there, you see this search in a different way. You're there to find your identity; you're there to understand something really very deep – your original connection to the land. We need it; we absolutely need that sense of belonging in order to live. Once you have it, you want the environment to be healthy and you want to protect it wherever you are.

By the time the Gatherings ended, I had a whole different way of looking at the world, of looking at history. And I felt I had developed relationships that were permanent. They were solid. I was committed to and responsible to these relationships so that they felt like ...

well, they felt like family. The people were on my mind from one Gathering to the next. There was a sense of loyalty – maybe it wasn't so much loyalty as it was consistency. People kept coming, both Native and non-Native. We were creating something together, and I began to feel more and more a part of it; like, this is my work. This is my work in the world now. It was probably the biggest thing of my life. At the time, it seemed it would grow into some kind of massive thing that could spread all over the country.

The Last Gathering

But the Gatherings didn't spread all over the country. They ended abruptly.

It was May 1993. I was looking for a place to hold our next Gathering and contacted Dana, as it had been a while since we'd met in Maine. It turned out that a non-Native friend of his, a herbalist and healer, had an ideal meeting place – a small farm near Dana's home – and when approached with the idea of hosting a Gathering, she welcomed us.

That spring was also a time of peak activity in Maine by an Indigenous group, made up entirely of Wabanaki women, that had been demonstrating, boycotting, and otherwise putting pressure on activities around the state that they felt were demeaning to Native people and, most especially, co-opting or appropriating Native traditions and spirituality. They had managed to stop an eighty-five-year tradition of a "squaw party" at a University of Maine fraternity. They protested outside university classes, health fairs, and other events where they felt Indigenous practices were being inaccurately or inappropriately represented by unauthorized people. Especially egregious to them were events where Native ceremonies were shared in exchange for money. They created a list of individuals and organizations to target. We had recently heard that the Center for Vision and Policy had been placed on this list, though we had no verification. Also on this list, unbeknownst to us, was the farm of Dana's herbalist friend, where we had just agreed to hold our Gathering that year.

During one of our morning Circles at that May Gathering, Miigam'agan happened to be in the parking area when two members of the protest group arrived. She recalls the encounter:

I was just going to our car when I saw the women coming in. I knew them and we greeted, and they shared why they were there. They asked me some questions, and I responded as best I could. Then I said, "But you're welcome to come into the Circle and see for yourself." They were upset because they had heard that people had been "selling ceremony" at the place where we were meeting – in other words, conducting Native spirituality workshops for money – and they were there to break up our Circle. I told them that no one was selling ceremonies; that we were meeting to talk about partnerships. I said, "These are sincere people trying to improve relationships and support Native people." And I said, "There's a lot of sharing, and our own people are here saying the same things that you are saying, and people are supportive."

The women did stay, and we walked over to an area near where the Circle was being held. They talked to a couple of other Native people who were also standing outside the Circle listening, as I had always done. The Talking Stick came around to several of our people in the Circle and they started sharing about their hurts and anger in a way that was empowering not only for me but also, I think, for our visitors. We were observing people – our people – having a voice and being able to share their truth in a public forum.

It was then that JoAnn spoke for the first time and shared about the buttons on women's blouses and why they are on the right side, and about how White people's wealth comes on the backs of people of color. She said, "This is what White people have to carry, this is what we need to answer to." Right then her statement emboldened me to join the Circle and to speak – my first time too – about how I felt about these things. In my message, I also shared what the two women protesters had just told me – that the place where we were meeting was on their list, and that they wanted to know why we were gathering there.

It seemed that our two visitors left that day understanding that we were meeting with good intentions. They also witnessed their concerns being conveyed, but the experience was not enough to change the minds of the leaders of their group. Wesley and I, along with another non-Native participant, decided to visit one of the leaders in her home, hoping to have a dialogue about our purpose and their perceptions of us. We called ahead to make the appointment and, when we arrived, another Native woman was present as well.

Neither of these women, unfortunately, had been a visitor to the Gathering that day. At one point, as we sat talking at the kitchen table, one of the women rose, picked up a paper on a nearby bookshelf and handed it to me, saying, "Look at this." It was our invitation, the one that I reworked before every Gathering and sent to all past participants. It had found its way into her hands and, when she handed it to me, it was as if I saw it for the first time. I had created this flyer when the Gatherings first began, cutting-and-pasting images from a textbook entitled *Wabanaki of Maine and the Maritimes.* It was Indigenous art, all of it. For every Gathering, I reused this template, changing the dates and the relevant information, but I hadn't critically looked at it again. She said, "Well, look at this, it looks to me like a bunch of White people – the Center for Vision and Policy – having a Native gathering." And I saw it through her eyes.

When I created the invitation, I had thought the design was a way of honoring Native culture. It shows how far I had come that, when presented with it now, I could understand her perceptions as well as her anger. Since neither of these women had been to one of our Gatherings, they had no way of understanding the intent of our effort. To an outsider, there was no way of distinguishing our work from any other "wannabe" activity at the time. Worst of all for me, I felt that our flyer – this piece of paper that showed our face to the world – conveyed, however unintentionally, the very image we sought to dispel. We left that day chastened and thoughtful, and our hosts remained unconvinced.

Miigam'agan puts the response of the protesters in context:

I think there was just too much that had happened already around Maine, of non-Native people conducting Native-like ceremonies – some actually *were* Native ceremonies – and justifying their right to do that. At that time, there was nothing to safeguard any of our rights. And too, we couldn't even conduct ceremonies in our own communities because of the church. The church was still attacking the sweat lodges or any kind of cultural activity. So it was really insulting when we saw non-Natives doing what we couldn't do – practice our own traditions.

The Decision

After the group's visit to our Gathering that May, and our subsequent failed attempt at dialogue, several conversations ensued between gkisedtanamoogk and myself, culminating in a small meeting in Maine of those who lived close enough to attend. At the meeting, we learned that Wesley had recently attended an event where a couple of the protesters confronted him angrily about his participation in the Gatherings, and that experience, combined with our uncomfortable kitchen-table meeting, greatly distressed us.

Our dilemma was this: continue to meet, secure in our conviction that what we were doing together was important, as well as respectful and mutual, but knowing we were acting in opposition to the demands of the protesters; or cease meeting, at least for the time being, for the simple reason that we were being asked to by a group of Indigenous people who were offended by our actions. This conundrum seemed to challenge the very purpose for which we gathered – to learn how to be allies and friends across our cultural and historical divide. Continuing to meet in the face of this opposition felt, at least to some of us, like repudiating the very principles we stood for.

Miigam'agan brought a Native woman's perspective to our deliberations, saying that if a group of Native women said they didn't want these kinds of events to happen then we needed to pay attention, because it wasn't easy for them to stand up like that. She felt it took a lot for them to get to that stage of anger and wanted to take it seriously; she wanted to honor and respect the women's feelings even if we were being misunderstood.

After much deliberation among those of us in attendance that day, it was decided to discontinue the Gatherings, thinking that, when the time was right, they might re-emerge in some form. Some of us felt that we should use the time to do some work in our respective communities to educate others about our experience. We acknowledged that the sponsorship of the Gatherings by CVP, a primarily White organization, created an inherent imbalance in power. If and when the Gatherings re-emerged, perhaps their sponsorship might be a more mutual effort.

Hindsight

I think about that time, and I think, "How could we have responded to those concerns in a way that would have been more useful?" It would have been ideal, and a tremendous confirmation of the process if, the next time we met, we had met all together in a Council Circle.

gkisedtanamoogk

Creating this book has given us an opportunity to revisit our decision all those years ago. Clearly mistakes were made: the design of the flyer and the fact that only non-Natives met with the protest group's leaders, for example. We discovered that some of us had been opposed to ending the Gatherings. Sitting together again gave many of us an opportunity to express the deep sadness we felt at the time. JoAnn, for example, reflected:

Maybe it was my age and experience, or because I was so involved at the time in my education about racism and sexism and classism, but I wanted to have a conversation with those who were objecting to us, to have a continuing conversation rather than simply stopping the Gatherings. I felt we had something we could stand on, but we needed to go through some sort of passageway together. It was hard, really hard. I felt they had legitimate complaints; I also think that we could have worked with them, and talked with them, and they would have come to know us. It might have changed things, and we might still be meeting, evolving.

There is, of course, no way to know, had the protesters sat in the Circle with us, what the outcome would have been. We ended the Gatherings; we went on with our lives; yet, for many of us, the bonds woven in all those Circles have held.

Looking back, a number of us have "done some work" in our respective commssunities. Several of us have replicated aspects of the Gatherings in other settings. In recent years, non-Natives have twice been invited to sit in Circles at annual Wabanaki Confederacy gatherings. It is our sense that the Gatherings continue to seed Native/non-Native connections throughout the territory in various forms, frequently with the leadership or involvement of some of our original members. Most especially, the Gatherings live on in our coming together again to create this book and to share our experiences with you.

At the end of traditional Indigenous gatherings, there is often the laying out of a "giveaway blanket." Each person has brought a gift to the gathering – a gift that has meaning for them or that feels important to share. The gifts are placed on the blanket and then everyone is invited to come and take something – something that they need or that calls to them. It's an exchange that Miigam'agan says is fundamentally about binding relationships. In the following sections, we reflect on the lessons we learned in the Gatherings and in our connections since. We offer these lessons as our gifts for the giveaway. They are our gifts to you and to all who want to understand and confront the tragic history of Native/non-Native relationships on this continent, and who are ready to imagine how it could be different.

PHOTOS: THE GATHERINGS, MAY 1987 TO MAY 1993

Photos were not taken of First Light ceremonies nor of our Circles, these being considered sacred aspects of our weekends together. We did find a few images of our "hanging out" and in-between-Circles times.

Left to right: Shirley H., Sarah Schmidt (participant not featured in book), gkisedtanamoogk, Shirley B., Debbie. Photo by Betty Peterson.

A young gkisedtanamoogk with son Goptjaoetj. Photo by Betty Peterson.

The drummers arrived! And Barb joined in. Photo by Betty Peterson.

A spontaneous moment after a small group discussion. Photo by Debbie Leighton.

PHOTOS: CREATING THIS BOOK

Planning meetings to co-conceive and create the manuscript of this book were held beginning in 2011 at Wayne's home, again in 2013 at Dana's, and continuing in 2015 with Frances's trip to the United States during which we visited with nearly all of the contributors to gather feedback in preparation for a second draft. (See Appendix: How This Book Came to Be.)

First planning meeting, held in Wayne's home in 2011. Wayne's neighbor, Joan Dana, made a delicious supper for us one evening, and this photo was taken in her kitchen. *Left to right, standing*: Wesley, Miigam'agan, Shirley B., Joan Dana, Wayne, Dana, gkisedtanamoogk. *Left to right, seated*: Shirley H., Debbie. Photo by Sandy Newell.

Second planning meeting, held in Dana's home in 2013 on a beautiful September weekend. *Around the circle, clockwise*: a reclining Wesley, who was feeling a little tired from his travels; Harry Roper, who accompanied Marilyn; Alma; Dana; Marilyn; Miigam'agan; JoAnn; gkisedtanamoogk; Shirley H.; Debbie. Photo by Elizabeth Blaney.

Hard at work considering themes, book structure, and so on. *Left to right*: Miigam'agan, Shirley H., JoAnn, gkisedtanamoogk, Dana. Photo by Elizabeth Blaney.

Frances Hancock visits old friends in Wabanaki territory, as she and Shirley H. spend time gathering feedback on the first draft of the manuscript, 2015. *Clockwise, starting upper left*: Alma and Frances; Frances, Miigam'agan, and Shirley H.; Shirley H. and Alma.

THE GIVEAWAY BLANKET

The Circle and Ceremony

We were engaged in our conversations, but always within this parameter: we were doing so in the presence of the Sacred. We were guided by the truth of the Fire, the truth of the prayers, the truth of the ceremonies, the truth of the Circle.

gkisedtanamoogk

Non-Natives have reflected on the experience of being in the Circle, how it felt, how it enriched us, and how we came to trust in it. JoAnn described it as a place of comfort, sometimes a welcome oasis from one-on-one interactions. You could go to the Circle and sit; you didn't have to speak. Marilyn remembered the safety in feeling she wouldn't be judged. Wesley described how it taught him to listen.

The presence of the Fire and the ceremonial way in which someone, usually gkisedtanamoogk, opened the Circle seemed to hold us in a particular way, protecting and supporting us in our vulnerability with each other. We non-Natives did not need to understand how gkisedtanamoogk and others invited that protection or support, or what they said in their opening prayers uttered in Wampanoag or Mi'kmaq or Passamaquoddy, in order to feel its presence.

From the Native participants, we non-Natives learned that the secret of the Circle lies in giving oneself over to it. Alma makes a plea to allow the power of the Circle to transform us, and to resist the urge to control it:

> In the Gatherings, meeting in a Talking Circle with ceremony made all the difference. Nowadays, here in Canada we even have government departments wanting to use the Talking Circle in meetings, but they don't want to use it properly. They can't give up control, so it doesn't work for them. There will be one person who holds the stick and they decide who's going to speak next, and so they pass it to that person. And then they pass it "here" and they pass it "there." I couldn't stand being in a circle like that. I was in one once, and I had to get out of there. I couldn't stand it because Spirit is supposed to *flow*. You don't control a Circle. It will do its work. You just have to leave it alone and stop trying to manage it. That's the hardest thing for non-Natives to do, to stop managing. Stop, stop, STOP already!

The Circle and Decision Making

Generally, in our Circles, we did not need to make decisions or plans; our focus was primarily to share our life stories and to find and strengthen our sense of common ground. But in traditional Indigenous communities, the Council Circle was the format used for all discussions, all decisions, all planning. Action wasn't taken until a consensus by the people in the Circle was reached.

Wayne describes the use of Council Circles in his community:

> The Native way of conducting traditional meetings is very well organized and very deliberate. There's no chaos. I was familiar with

it because of how I was brought up. When left alone, that's what we used to decide things for ourselves. We would always use the consensus model and only secondary to that would we use the model that was imposed upon us, the so-called majority vote. I would attend council meetings when I was a little boy, and I remember how no one would leave the hall until that magic time when everybody would agree. You could sense it – that everyone is now agreed – and people would get up then and go back to their homes, and they felt good going away.

My mother said that when she was a little girl she would go to council meetings with her grandmother ... well, she wasn't actually her grandmother but the woman who raised her when her mom died. This lady was one of the respected Elders in the community, and my mother said sometimes the meetings would go all night and into the next day if people could not agree. She and the other little kids would go to sleep under the tables because her *nukomoss*, her grandmother, was so into politics that she refused to leave until the outcome was known.

I asked gkisedtanamoogk if people in his community still meet in Circles when they need to have a discussion, or make a decision, and if they use a Talking Stick or other object in speaking:

Yes, we do still meet that way, and there's always a Talking Stick. And we include ceremony so that the Sacred is brought in. I'm not talking about the band/tribal council kind of meeting, because they meet like everyone else, but most of the community likes to meet in a Circle; that would be their preference. And we know what happens when we meet like that. We might have a particular topic that we need to discuss, but it's in the sharing, in that format, that the magic happens. Something transforms us. We might have a passion about something, but even the passion is transformed.

And if a decision needs to be made, it usually comes after a very long process where everyone not only speaks their piece, but there's a time to reflect. After that time, usually one of the Elders will get up – one of the Sachems or the Clan Mothers – and they will talk. These would be people that we have the greatest confidence in, and respect for. They are the ones who guide the process. Sometimes their message is a recapitulation of what they've heard us say. They might say something like, "It seems that we've arrived at a direction." In some instances they might say, "Maybe we need to think about this some more," and that could engage us in the whole process again. But usually by the time the Sachem speaks – and they usually speak last – the direction is pretty clear.

What the Sachems or the Clan Mothers do is confirm what they hear; they are directed by the community, which is the inverse of the tribal council. The tribal councils say, "This is what we're going to do ... how do you feel about it?" as if the matter's already been settled. But the Sachems and Clan Mothers respect the will of the people and, in turn, people have a great deal of respect for their perspectives; so, after their recapping, you're less likely to have someone say something to the contrary.

I recall historic descriptions of the treaty process: the English, or the Canadians, or the French would have a conversation with our Confederacy, and both parties might even map out what they were agreeing to – the terms and so on. The North Americans would simply ratify that in their Congress, saying, "This is what we agreed to." But for us, we would take an agreement all the way back to the

communities and have a discussion about it there. And then, that discussion had to go from the communities on to the region, and then to
the Nations, and finally back to the Confederacy. So, the Confederacy
began the conversation, but then confirmation from the people was
required. It's a much longer process. That's probably why the feds
wanted to shorten the process by having tribal councils do their bid-
ding. But for us, that traditional system worked. It recognized that the
voice of the people was really the place where the sovereignty was.

In the traditional system, we can't go forward if people are opposed
to a decision, so we have to invest the time to find out where the
"happy mediums" are. Also, we might agree to something but for different reasons, so we need to acknowledge what those reasons are so
that the result takes all perspectives into consideration. And maybe
we find out there should be caution in moving forward because we
have certain parameters to consider. The idea is that we can't move
forward with a decision when there is opposition to it.

Ceremony: Protect or Share It?

At the time the Gatherings were held, it was a rare experience for
non-Natives to be part of a Sacred Circle that included traditional
Indigenous ceremony. That we non-Natives had been invited to
meet in this way spoke to a level of trust that we all held dear.

As non-Natives' understanding increased of the protocols surrounding ceremony, we took great care to pass this information on
to non-Native newcomers. Sometimes there could be disagreement
among the Native people themselves about certain protocols, and
in those instances we non-Natives took our cues from whoever was

leading the ceremony. There was no disagreement, however, about the issue of appropriation. We continually stressed to non-Natives how imperative it was that they not leave the experience and presume to have the knowledge or the permission to share these traditional ceremonies with others. The notion of adopting any of the practices in one's private life was shaky ground as well, so fearful were we that we could be perceived as just another non-Native there to "play Indian."

The protectiveness that Indigenous people all over North America felt at the time about their ceremonies was deep and well founded. Miigam'agan explains the many dimensions of this protectiveness:

If there had been a sense of balance and wellness in our relationships from the very beginning of our history together, then maybe the idea of sharing our culture wouldn't have been such an issue, but that balance wasn't there. Then you take into account Native people's economic conditions; you saw non-Native people offering ceremonies, charging for them and living well off the proceeds, while ceremony was not allowed in our own communities. And sometimes – not in our Gatherings but elsewhere – non-Natives who had mastered some aspects of Native spirituality would actually correct Native people about how to behave in a Circle, saying things like, "You don't walk around the Circle this way, you walk around the other way." I would think to myself, "Oh, my God, he's saying that to *this* woman?"

You can feel that there's a last little spark of something sacred that we have, and if we share that, it could be trampled on and not regarded – not regarded in the same way as we do. Or, will this last precious thing disappear, or get lost?

And for me – I can't speak for others – but I didn't know enough about my own culture at the time to want to share it. I didn't know enough about my history, or who I was. I felt kind of possessive, and very protective of it, because I needed to grow from it first.

Now, years later, Native contributors to this book observe that traditional Indigenous culture is experiencing a rebirth and the voices of Indigenous peoples are being heard. Efforts to underscore tribal sovereignty and to increase self-determination are at the forefront in many tribal communities. Miigam'agan and Wayne offer their more recent thoughts about sharing their culture, sentiments that have shifted over the years:

Miigam'agan: Thirty years ago, in my community, the chief and council had banned any form of Talking Circles. That's how threatened they were by their own culture because they had gained their power by observing the church, and the Western government, and using those methods to keep the people low in spirit, oppressed. You can control people who don't feel good about themselves. But over time, even they started to learn about their culture, and they started to grow and feel good about it, and to see that this is who they are. Now, I don't think we ever have to worry about losing our culture. Our people are open to it, where before many downplayed it and attacked it. Now it cannot be held back. We don't need to protect it because it has a life of its own.

And now I see that our spirituality and our connection to the land is raising a nation again – a nation that was meant to be destroyed. We weren't supposed to be alive and around in the twenty-first century. But our traditional culture has enabled us to rise, and there's no longer a fear of assimilation. We're moving out of our box, that oppressive box we were in, and we know that we have a lot to contribute to shape the future for all of us.

Another reason I feel it's important to share our culture is that, when I look at our younger generation, I see they're looking at the White culture – the Western system – and wanting that. There are a lot of contributions to be made from both sides, so it's important that they see our leaders collaborating with and sharing with non-Natives, and that the sharing occurs on an equal footing, with mutual respect.

Wayne: I'm glad to hear others talk more about sharing, because I've always been in the more liberal wing on that issue. I believe that we're too invisible, and that we have something to give. For example, we have an issue right now in my community concerning the Native medicines. There is a project going on to identify all the medicinal plants, and what they were used for, and then to make CDs out of this information and also put it on the Internet. Of course, the minute you put it on the Internet you're exposing it to the world. There are some of us who believe that we ought to support this project and there are other Passamaquoddies who don't believe we should do that. We're trying to resolve that conflict.

It used to be that when anthropologists would come, or ethnologists would come – all those "ologists" – we would talk to them but the information they gathered would never come back to us. Also, they would interpret it according to their own understanding, and we had no control over that either. We never gave away our proprietary right to that information just because we talked to somebody. Even today, some of the information that we shared a long time ago is being held by the families of those who gathered it, and the families aren't willing to give it back to us, they want to *sell* it back to us. We're really struggling with that, because we believe it was ours to begin with, and that they ought to return it to us as the rightful owners. Now we have better control over those things.

Miigam'agan speaks of a deeper need to ease the protectiveness she felt in earlier days:

As Indigenous people, we've experienced rejection and isolation, and we've learned those things well. So, we became rejecting of others, even though in our prayers and when we speak in our language, we're supposed to be inclusive. So I say now that it's necessary to share because that's how we will all continue. Like any other relationship it's about boundaries. Like any relationship, there's a time for family and there's a time for your larger extended family. I think it's just recognizing that.

I've come to understand that ceremony is a human need – a human need we all share. I used to hear gkisedtanamoogk say, "It's no coincidence that the whole world came to this continent." People came looking for trade, but they were also looking for something else. They were moving away from a place that was sick, and they were arriving in a place where there was something different, something healthy, but maybe they couldn't recognize it. We've struggled this far, and survived these many years, and we're still trying to get people to connect to the land.

These days, Indigenous leaders are being called to expanded roles as their communities experience the brunt of environmental threats. Here in the East, some Wabanaki are finding themselves at the forefront of environmental movements. As Indigenous and non-Indigenous groups join forces around various causes, it is becoming more common for non-Natives to be invited into ceremonial activities, conducted by Native Elders, as part of their work together and in the spirit of sharing. What are the responsibilities associated with non-Native participation in any ceremonies to which we are invited? Observing protocols is a matter of listening, watching, asking questions if we are uncertain, asking forgiveness – and forgiving ourselves – if we blunder, and committing to better educate ourselves before the next time.

But sometimes, in addition to being a respectful participant, we are deeply moved by these experiences. As Miigam'agan says, ceremony is a human need, and for many non-Natives, ceremony may be largely absent from our lives. We can be overtaken by a longing for more connection, for a more ceremonial relationship to others and especially to the land. What to do? For most of us, whatever Earth-based religion existed at one time in our cultural lineage is so far back in history that it seems too difficult to access, and yet we feel that a deeper connection to the land is exactly what is needed. Wherever we live in North America, we are on land that was, and is, the home of Indigenous peoples, and if we are in alliance with Native people we regularly witness the strength that they draw from their traditions that are grounded here. Is it okay to borrow, to incorporate Indigenous ceremony in our personal lives if we are not ourselves Native? I posed this question to Miigam'agan. I asked her how she felt about my people practicing ways that came from, or were very similar to, her traditions:

Well, I think there's a responsibility attached to that. If people are applying Native spirituality in their own lives, I think they are in a marriage. It's a marriage to the land, a marriage to the truth of this land. So, non-Natives practicing Native spirituality, gaining and growing from it, must be accountable. In a marriage, you don't just have a sexual relationship and leave without sharing responsibility.

Or, another way to say it, when you go and eat in someone's home you help with the dishes. If you stay there, you contribute; you learn how to support and how to live among that family. You're respectful of whose home you're in, and you're aware that it's their territory. And if you benefit from something there, you should acknowledge the people who shared it with you.

Non-Native people who benefit from our practices need to understand that we have treaties here, and part of acknowledging the People is to make sure that their rights are respected. There is a legal obligation in our relationship; people may not know that. They should make sure their government respects Indigenous peoples' rights and that it upholds its legal obligations. Back to my example, if I were living in someone's home, in addition to getting to know that family, if there were needs there I would want not only to support them but to advocate for them too.

Respect for Indigenous spirituality includes, for non-Natives, understanding that authentic Native ceremony takes place within the context of community; in other words, under the leadership and care of those who have been acknowledged by a Native community as having the training and authority to conduct that ceremony. Non-Natives who fall into this category are rare. Participating in ceremonies led by someone who does not have proper authority or experience perpetuates cultural appropriation, and also can lead to unintended consequences. Gwen describes a case in point from 2009:

> There are instances like the sweat lodge that was built in Arizona where a non-Native man killed three people by building a sweat lodge that was much too big. He had sixty people in that sweat, built a huge fire, and used plastic to cover the lodge. You can't use plastic; the covering of a lodge has to breathe. And so those people suffocated.
>
> Our philosophy is, and has always been, that you don't acquire knowledge all at once – you have to be trained. This is a perfect example to say to non-Natives that, okay, you can learn something from Native people but that does not make you an expert.

If some Native people feel more open about sharing their culture with non-Natives, that does not mean we beat a path to their door wanting to talk to them or asking them to do a ceremony for us. They don't have that kind of time or energy. Again, I asked Miigam'agan about the pressure Indigenous people can feel from non-Natives wanting to learn how to be more connected to the Earth:

> Well, I've been doing a little of my own research, learning about European history and the comparisons with our culture. And I see that our spiritual knowledge, our Original Instructions or Earth-based ways, were all the same. I think when people go to Elders – traditional Native American Elders – it's because something resonates with their own heritage. I also think the larger society – the White society – is looking for something, something beyond institutions, even if they don't know what that is. They don't want the kind of hierarchy that is in most current religions.

There are spiritual Elders in the White culture that have done a lot of research into their own heritage and are recognizing and practicing these Earth-based ways. I've been listening to Joseph Campbell, and Christiane Northrup and others. They might not have titles like "traditional Elder" but I would look at them as mystics, as spiritual mystics. These individuals all would confirm a person's inner truth, because really that's all it is. We all have the truth; we're just looking for someone to confirm it – not even confirm it really, but to support, or complement, what we already know. That's what our traditional Native spirituality does for us.

And if we had gathering places where Native and non-Native people met together, we could start to make these kinds of connections, culture to culture. I think that kind of exchange is important.

Allies, Friends, Family

There is a Passamaquoddy word, *mawiyane* – let us venture together. I kind of like that one. And a word that I used to hear from the Elders when I was a kid was *mawoqekapuwiyane* – let us stand together. We have a lot of different words for "gathering," but they all have this sense of inclusiveness: let *us, together*. When we gather we become vulnerable, and to me the lessons that we have yet to learn are hidden in that process.

Wayne

Beginnings

Our early attempts at connection were often awkward, tentative, and sometimes, thankfully, humorous. The relationships that developed among us over the years developed slowly, but they grew nonetheless through the consistency of our contact and our shared commitment to the process. Over time, the Gatherings, and opportunities that grew out of the Gatherings, provided each of us a window into the other's "ways." Sometimes even food was a revelation, as Miigam'agan relates:

I remember a time when Barb had a meeting at the university. She was representing the New Brunswick Native Women's Council, and she had to make an appearance at this particular event. She told me it was a friendly social affair, and asked if I wanted to join her. This was during the time that we were having the Gatherings, and because she knew I'd had that experience, she said I wouldn't be uncomfortable, even though these would be White people and they'd be wearing their suits and all that. So I went, and I wasn't intimidated. I was comfortable, even eating with them. That had not been my experience before. But since I'd been to the Gatherings, now I knew the food was good. Now I recognized some of the food and I was open to trying it. Can you believe it?

Likewise, we non-Natives were being introduced to foods harvested from the land that were, for many of us, a fascinating first-time experience, Debbie once declaring, "I want that recipe for moose stew!"

But when Natives and non-Natives come together, differences in cultural perspectives can lead to misunderstandings. We learned to accept, and gradually to understand, some of these differences. Looking back, Barb and Miigam'agan reflect on the tensions sometimes created around perceptions of time:

Barb: There are concepts in English that Mi'kmaq have no words for. For example, take the English word "priority"; we all understand what that means; there's a whole world of meaning there. Well, there's no such word, there's no such concept, in Mi'kmaq. No such word! Whatever is happening right here, right now, that's the priority, so there is no need for the concept "priority." If I were in a traditional Mi'kmaq state of mind I wouldn't be looking at a clock. It wouldn't matter. But in the White world if we are in that traditional state of mind then we're going to be "late," and someone's going to have a perception about us being late, and say that we're on "Indian time."

Maybe we're "late" because we're valuing the situation or the interaction that we're in, and it's not time to move on to the next thing.

Miigam'agan: For me, living by the clock is stressful, and still, to this day, it's foreign. Our Wabanaki way of life is really centered on the present, and on people, even though I know about the work world. I always corrected people when I was working in the city up near my home. They would say, "In the real world ..." and I would say, "No, that's not the real world. You mean the *work* world. The work world is not the real world." The real world is the natural world – people, life, Creation. The work world is where we step out of the real world and live in the structural, cubical, organized world. And that's stressful.

Not all differences are culturally based, however. Non-Native participants came to understand the error of interpreting behaviors as cultural that were sometimes economically driven, a result of living in uncertain financial circumstances. Wesley recalls:

I remember being at the Gatherings and not understanding why someone we were expecting didn't show up. Well, in most cases they couldn't. I began to realize that many didn't have a lot of financial resources.

In most cases we non-Natives drove long distances to attend the Gatherings and we did that on purpose. We felt we needed to go where Native people lived instead of asking them to use their resources to meet with us where we were. I think it was important for all of us that we were willing to do that.

Historic injustices, as well as current social and economic structures, have resulted in multiple and gross inequities between our peoples – inequalities in opportunities, in income, and in access to resources. We acknowledged these inequalities, attempted to compensate for them where possible, and worked hard always to meet as equals. We, both Native and non-Native, muddled our way and learned to speak up, or check things out, when something didn't feel right.

If non-Natives tended to arrive with more financial and other resources at their backs, inequality went both ways. Many of us non-Natives felt at a distinct disadvantage in terms of our culture and what it had to offer. As we experienced and absorbed the sense of community and spiritual connectedness of the Wabanaki participants, it was easy to discount our culture and put the Native participants "on a pedestal." Wayne shares what it felt like to be on that pedestal:

In the early days, there were some people – non-Natives – who came looking for something and hoping that this was the place to find it. Probably this wasn't the first place they had looked. Probably at some point they had tried to find it within their own spiritual traditions or church denominations. I'm talking about some of the people, not all non-Natives. But I generally could pick them out because, for example, after our formal sessions they would come and ask me these profound questions for which, lots of times, I had no answers because I was trying to figure them out myself! But they would ask anyway, and if I said anything they would say, "Yes, oh yes!"

I felt kind of bad for people who were like that but, on the other hand, there was a part of me that wanted to reach out in the hope that they might receive something better than what they had experienced before. But we Natives are human. We have our own issues; we just have our way of dealing with them. So, the red flags always went up when someone said, in effect, "You must be right" just because I was a

Native person; as if I could take care of their problems, or heal them, or whatever. I do think we Native people are greatly aided by the processes that we use, but that doesn't make us perfect. We're the Creator's creatures and we are limited like everyone else. I saw some Native people, myself included, trying to confront those assumptions in a loving way.

The people who stayed on, though, really grew over the years. I think they learned to be patient and to listen. They started getting as comfortable as the rest of us in the Circle, and understanding more of their obligations. I think after a while they understood more fully that the Sacred Circle would give them all the time they needed to express all they needed to express, and that the absolute truth is not in us individually; the absolute truth is in us collectively, in terms of finding those answers that we're all looking for.

Some people didn't stay, of course, because they didn't get that instant gratification. Maybe they went somewhere else and hopefully found whatever they were looking for. Sometimes people made the mistake of … they started "acting Native," I guess, is the only way I can say it – clothes, that kind of thing – trying to be as Native as they possibly could. And sometimes, the Native people got very angry with them. You wanted to say, "You know, you really don't have to do that." Those weren't the people who stayed.

Although there are acknowledged leaders, or Elders, within Native communities, their own people do not as a rule treat them differently from others. As Gwen explains, Elders are greatly respected but not exalted. Neither do these leaders typically refer to themselves as "Elders":

I went to a book launch the other day – a Native friend of mine wrote a book and I went to buy a copy from him. But we Native people don't put him on a pedestal. You acknowledge that a person has done well, but there's not any of the hierarchy you see elsewhere. I've met premiers, I've met senators – but you don't put them "up there," and it's more comfortable for them too because you don't do that. You just say, "You made a really good point there, I like that," and then they're just another human being. None of that hero worship.

We have an Elder from Nova Scotia – Murdena Marshall – who has identified the seven qualities of Elders. She talks about the gift of humility. She says you don't go around saying, "I'm an Elder." We never say we are Elders because it is for the community, or others, to put you in that category. I remember someone who kind of put me on a pedestal once and, because of that, got really disappointed when I became human and I made a mistake. My God, his world crumbled. I said to him, "Don't do that to anyone. Don't do that to anyone because they will fall eventually." We are human beings and we are going to make mistakes. That's how we progress, that's how we learn.

The Women Compare Notes

Many of us non-Native women have said we were challenged, enlightened and, in some cases, transformed by what we heard from, and observed in, the Native women who were knowledgeable in their traditions. For me it was sometimes unsettling as well, calling into question beliefs and assumptions about being a woman that I had held my whole adult life.

Native participants reminded us non-Natives that Wabanaki cultures traditionally were matriarchal, with enormous importance given to women's roles. These cultures have been viewed by modern society primarily through the lens of those who wrote the history books and who misperceived the women's roles as lesser than they were. While there were male chiefs, or sachems, the actual power of these men was limited. The power of the elder women was highly regarded and respected, and the whole community sought their counsel when decisions were called for.

The traditional role of women in Wabanaki societies still influences how things happen in those communities today, although the overlay of the federally imposed tribal government system substantially dictates policies and procedures. Miigam'agan gives an example:

When we were trying to get projects started at the Wabanaki Health and Wellness Center, where I used to work, I would say to the staff, "We can go talk to the chief and council, we can talk to the program heads – which are primarily men – but if the women in the community don't support these programs they won't last." That's really the key. I'd say, "Just because the men are out there in the forefront doesn't mean that they're the decision makers, so we need to make contact and talk to the women, the Elders." That's how we approached the workers in the blueberry fields when we were trying to reach them. We looked for the matriarchs. We talked to the matriarchs and explained our purpose, and if they felt that what we were doing was valuable then they would take the initiative to call other people and help spread the word.

Even if you get a good response from the men initially, if you only focus on those particular leaders – the men in the community – then your program won't be long term because the money will run out and they won't keep the project going. But if you get the support of the women then even when the money runs out, if the women are trained and have the knowledge, the program is going to continue naturally. It just keeps going.

Traditional Wabanaki understood the Earth as feminine. The Earth gave Life, and was therefore sacred and to be protected. It followed then, because women were the Lifegivers, that their role was sacred, to be revered. It was the sacred duty of the men to be the protectors of that Life. In role definitions that in modern society might be labeled as sexist and confining, women in traditional Wabanaki society had status and power. With the subjugation of traditional ways to Western philosophies and systems, Native communities of course were not immune to Western ways of thinking and acting toward women, but in recent years traditional views have been resurging and Native women's voices have grown stronger. In our Gatherings, a natural affinity among women took hold and led to conversations that continue to reverberate through many of our lives today. Gwen recalls:

> I remember the Circles, of course, but also the other times that the women were together. In the evening the women would gather and share the "woman thing" – their relation to the phases of the moon and so on. There's this recognition that the women are the real leaders and that we have to meet as women, and it doesn't matter what race you are. I've always found this to be true – this cooperation among women.

The Relationship Evolves

Over time, our experiences with one another, our openness to those experiences, and the sharing of our personal stories began to shift the relationship. Inequalities remained inherent in the lives we returned to each time we parted, but our connections forged in the Gatherings allowed us to see one another as individuals. We continued to speak of our time together as intentionally "building alliances," but we were also becoming friends.

Debbie: The trust builds in a step-by-step way of sharing, in that good old "break the bread" concept of being together. Not only eating together but talking together, in that simple way. I loved what Miigam'agan said once. She said that before the Gatherings, she always had to "step out of her canoe" to be with White people. That's asking a lot. In the Gatherings, I think we non-Natives stepped out of our canoes for a while, meaning out of our safe territory, and really listened for a change.

Shirley B.: I think people were willing to make themselves vulnerable, to take risks, to recognize that the process is messy. To be willing to apologize when we hurt someone and take responsibility for that; and on the other side, to be willing to forgive unintended hurts. Both have to be present – the willingness to apologize, and also to know that there will be forgiveness extended because the relationship is more important than any given thing we screw up and say or do.

Wayne: Friendships were born, true friendships, which – I'm trying to find the right English word here – were unconditional. The Passamaquoddy word would be *tan te eli wiqoki*. It's a word that means "being accepted as I am."

Offering a Native perspective, Barb pointed out that, although she'd had years of experiences working with mixed groups of

Native and non-Native people, what made the Gatherings different was a joint intention to make explicit the issue of the relationship between our peoples:

> I had worked with women's groups before, but we were very focused on an end result, to amend the Indian Act for example. That was legislative work and we were Native and non-Native women fighting together to address that. But this was the first time I had observed a group of people trying to address, to talk about anyway, the issue of the problematic relationship that existed between us – to make that the topic. The women's groups never saw that, except it popped up all the time. It really did pop up – the race, class, gender thing – but they never examined it to any significant extent.

The only way to examine the "race, class, gender thing" was to be together, to surrender to the slow process of seeing, experiencing, and understanding the effects of our tragic shared history and its consequences for our daily lives. We, both Native and non-Native, began to gain a visceral understanding of what had been lost on both sides.

Mutuality

When people of unequal societal privilege and position meet, these disparities don't go away, but being open to learning and being changed by the other can allow a sense of mutuality to still exist.[1] What seems to be key is that what each has to offer is acknowledged and valued, that there is an exchange.

Barb described the activities of a Reiki community in New Brunswick as an example of exchange between Native and non-Native communities. That community has offered its services over the years to Native-run conferences in the area:

The people involved in this community range from young to old, from mill workers to environmentalists. They differ in many ways and yet they've become a community. The majority of members are White but, as a Native person, I can say they actually relate to you. When I look in their eyes, I don't see judgment. The qualities that I see in them are honesty and sincerity and a genuine desire to understand. Not to "help," but to understand.

This group has become quite involved in assisting when we have Native conferences. They bring the crew in to the conferences and offer Reiki sessions to the people there; so, they give something back while they also gain from being at the conference. In Reiki, the concept of exchange is a key component.

Just as in our Mi'kmaq culture, if you ask a healer – an Elder – for healing, you give them tobacco; so, there is a kind of exchange – a relationship – established through the tobacco. But if you genuinely want to be part of your healing – let's say you ask for a sweat – then you help out in that sweat. You bring food and firewood and help in the construction of the lodge; then you are part of your own healing. I think this Reiki crew has got that idea down pat. There's an exchange, so no one is feeling like they're "up there" – the healer – and down here is a little lost soul that they're doing something for.

It's a central precept of Reiki that in doing Reiki you're healing yourself. To give Reiki you're also getting Reiki. That's a model for how Native and non-Native people can do things together.

During the Gatherings, moments of mutuality and exchange let us know we had come a good distance together. One Sunday morning during a Gathering, some of the Quakers decided they would like to hold a Quaker Meeting. That weekend we were gathering at the home of a Maliseet Elder, and on the land there was a tipi that he had constructed. It seemed that the tipi was the perfect place to hold the Meeting, and he offered it, so everyone was invited and a lot of the Native people came. To be sitting in that Circle, in a Quaker Meeting that wasn't very different from the Talking Circles we had been sitting in, and feeling the respect and reverence from the Native people who came, remains a tender memory among many of the non-Natives who were present that day.

Throughout the Gatherings, and in subsequent years, we watched the children of Miigam'agan and gkisedtanamoogk grow up. Over time, a few Native participants even used the word "family" to describe connections that had developed among us. Barb had some thoughts about how you know relationships have become "family," saying that the ultimate marker is when their (Native) children are comfortable with us (non-Natives) and see us as part of their extended network of support:

Kids, they see stuff. You can't fool kids. I see Miigam'agan's children as my family, but if her children start seeing a non-Native person as part of their family, then that's another thing. That really begins to change things. If, from babyhood on, a child knows a non-Native person, they see them in a different way than I as an adult could ever see that person with all my preconceived notions and baggage. When a child accepts you because they've known you all their lives, there's real trust there. That's a community.

Allies, friends, family: these words do not describe the relationship that existed between the original European settlers and the Indigenous peoples of this continent. Instead, words like "conquest," "colonization," and "genocide" apply. Still today, five hundred years after first contact, the social, economic, political, and judicial structures that so negatively impact Native communities have their origins in the beliefs and assumptions of the early colonists. Sovereignty and self-determination for Native peoples are elusive goals. Current US and Canadian policies perpetuate disparities in health and living conditions on some reserves and reservations that rival Third World countries. Perhaps the most vivid and striking statistic illustrating current realities for Native communities is the suicide rate among their youth and young adults – the highest for any race, ethnicity, or age category.[2]

How did we get here? How could it be different?

How We Got Here

Those who came here came under the pretense of eradicating everything Indigenous and substituting that with an idea – an abstract idea. And what was that abstract idea? That there's a God out there who has empowered us to own everything, and that once we own it, we can control it.

gkisedtanamoogk

The Doctrine of Discovery

To understand the current relationship between Indigenous and non-Indigenous peoples on this continent it is necessary to understand the foundational assumptions that the first explorers brought with them – a set of principles that has come to be known as the "doctrine of discovery." During the period between 1452 and 1455, a series of papal bulls (meaning letters, or decrees, issued by the pope) asserted that any "Saracens (Muslims) and pagans and any other unbelievers" encountered on voyages of discovery might be reduced to "perpetual slavery."[1] It was permissible to "invade, search out, capture, vanquish, and subdue all Saracens and pagans whatsoever, and other enemies of Christ wheresoever placed ... and [to appropriate] all moveable and immoveable goods whatsoever held and possessed by them and ... to convert them to his and their [King Alfonso's and his successors'] use and profit."[2]

Conquest and appropriation of goods were not the only goals. Conversion to Christianity was a mandate as well. In 1493, the papal bull *Inter caetera* states: "Among other works well pleasing to the Divine Majesty and cherished of our heart, this assuredly ranks highest, that in our times especially the Catholic faith and the Christian religion be exalted and be everywhere increased and spread ... and that barbarous nations be overthrown and brought to the faith itself."[3]

When explorers first arrived on this continent, the area corresponding to the current United States and Canada was the sole domain of potentially eighteen million Indigenous peoples (estimates vary widely), who spoke three hundred to five hundred different languages.[4] Topography of the land was the determinant of cultural diversity – cultures differed because the land itself differed.[5] The tragic history of disease, warfare, and outright genocide that followed early contact is well known and well documented. Shortly after Europeans arrived, Indigenous populations shrank by roughly half.[6] By the end of the nineteenth century, 90 to 98 per cent (depending upon the source) of all Indigenous peoples on the continent were wiped out. Diversity of cultures greatly suffered as well; in Maine, for example, many more tribes existed (estimates vary up to twenty) than the four that are officially recognized today.

The assault on the Native peoples of the United States was so successful and so thorough that, according to John Toland's definitive biography of Adolf Hitler, it caught Hitler's attention and provided a model for his plans to exterminate the Jews:

Hitler's concept of concentration camps as well as the practicality of genocide owed much, so he claimed, to his studies of English and

United States history. He admired the camps for Boer prisoners in South Africa and for the Indians in the wild West; and often praised to his inner circle the efficiency of America's extermination – by starvation and uneven combat – of the red savages who could not be tamed by captivity.[7]

The use of the doctrine of discovery to "justify" the taking of Indigenous homelands did not die with the early explorers, but made its way into the US judicial system. In 1823, it provided the legal foundation for the most important US Supreme Court decision ever decided affecting the Indigenous peoples of this land, Johnson v. M'Intosh. In this case, the court ruled against the plaintiff who claimed title to a piece of land by asserting that his ancestors had purchased it from a Native person. The legal decision stated that Indigenous peoples had no legal title to the land, only a mere right of occupancy, and could therefore not transfer their land by selling it.

Over a century later, in 1955, the Tee-Hit-Ton, a subgroup of the Tlingit, brought an action in United States claims court for compensation for timber taken from tribal-occupied lands in Alaska, a taking authorized by the secretary of agriculture (Tee-Hit-Ton Indians v. United States). Citing the 1823 Johnson v. M'Intosh court case described above, the eventual ruling of the US Supreme Court was:

The Government denies that petitioner [the Tee-Hit-Ton] has any compensable interest. It asserts that the Tee-Hit-Tons' property interest, if any, is merely that of the right to the use of the land at the Government's will; that Congress has never recognized any legal interest of petitioner in the land and therefore without such recognition no compensation is due the petitioner for any taking by the United States.

The ruling goes on:

> It is well settled that in all the States of the Union the tribes who inhabited the lands of the States held claim to such lands after the coming of the white man under what is sometimes termed original Indian title or permission from the whites to occupy. That description means mere possession not specifically recognized as ownership by Congress. After *conquest* [emphasis mine] they were permitted to occupy portions of territory over which they had previously exercised "sovereignty," as we use that term. This is not a property right but amounts to a right of occupancy which the sovereign grants and protects against intrusion by third parties but *which right of occupancy may be terminated and such lands fully disposed of by the sovereign itself without any legally enforceable obligation to compensate the Indians* [emphasis mine].

The doctrine continues to govern United States Indian law today and was cited as recently as 2005 in the decision City of Sherrill v. Oneida Indian Nation of New York. In this case, the US Supreme Court relied on the doctrine of discovery to limit the Oneida Nation's sovereignty.

But What about the Treaties?

US courts continue to uphold the idea that Indigenous peoples do not have title to their original lands in the legally recognized meaning of "title." But what Native people do have in their favor is the continued existence of signed treaties. There were, in fact, many treaties established; however, neither the United States nor Canada has honored the promises made in these treaties. According to the National Museum of the American Indian's exhibit "Nation to Nation: Treaties between the United States and American Indian Nations," approximately 368 treaties were negotiated, signed, and subsequently approved by the US Senate from 1777 to 1868. The very existence of these treaties meant that the tribes were being recognized as nations, "a fact that distinguishes tribal citizens from other Americans and supports contemporary Native assertions of tribal sovereignty and self-determination."[8]

Treaties are not relics of the past; they are legally binding and still in effect. This assertion is borne out by language in the US Constitution:

> This Constitution, and the Laws of the United States which shall be made in Pursuance thereof; and all Treaties made, or which shall be made, under the Authority of the United States, shall be the supreme Law of the Land; and the Judges in every State shall be bound thereby, any Thing in the Constitution or Laws of any State to the Contrary notwithstanding.[9]

And in the constitution of Canada:

> The guarantee in this Charter of certain rights and freedoms shall not be construed so as to abrogate or derogate from any aboriginal treaty or other rights or freedoms that pertain to the aboriginal peoples of Canada.[10]

In addition, part 2, section 35, item 1 reads:

> The existing aboriginal and treaty rights of the aboriginal peoples of Canada are hereby recognized and affirmed.

Most North Americans know little about the treaties, however. The late senator Daniel K. Inouye (D–Hawaii), the longtime chairperson, vice-chairperson, and member of the Senate Committee on Indian Affairs, lamented:

> Too few Americans know that the Indian nations ceded millions of acres of lands to the United States, or that ... the promises and commitments made by the United States were typically made in perpetuity. History has recorded, however, that our great nation did not keep its word to the Indian nations, and our preeminent challenge today ... is to assure the integrity of our treaty commitments and to bring an end to the era of broken promises.[11]

International law also dictates the upholding of treaties. In 1986, the Vienna Convention on the Law of Treaties between States and International Organizations or Between International Organizations, declared, in article 26, "Every treaty in force is binding upon the parties to it and must be performed by them in good faith." And from 1992 to 1999, the United Nations conducted a study on Indigenous treaties that reached the following conclusions:

> Indigenous peoples have ... not ... lost their international juridical status as nations ... (Item 270) ... Treaties and other legal instruments concluded by the European settlers ... with Indigenous nations ... continue to be instruments with international status in light of international law. (Item 275) ... Treaties without an expiration date are ... continuing in effect until all the parties to it decide to terminate them ... (Item 277).[12]

There have been a few instances in which the Canadian Supreme Court has upheld the treaty rights of Indigenous people. In practical terms, however, even affirmative court rulings have not ensured the end of violence or led governments to uphold the law. The Burnt Church fishing crisis of 1999–2002 in Miigam'agan's and Barb's community is a case in point.

In October 1999, a Supreme Court of Canada ruling (R. v. Marshall) acknowledged that prior treaties held that a Mi'kmaq man, Donald Marshall, Jr., had the legal right to fish for eels out of season. The Supreme Court emphasized Indigenous people's right to "hunt, fish and gather for the purpose of making a moderate livelihood."[13] The Burnt Church First Nation interpreted the judgment as meaning that they could catch lobster out of season, exercising their right to a "moderate livelihood," and began to put out traps. Neither the provincial nor the federal government, however, was prepared to deal with the backlash from local non-Native fishermen or to defend the Mi'kmaq's rights guaranteed in the Court's decision:

> When a few days after the Marshall ruling the people of Burnt Church First Nation (New Brunswick) set lobster traps out of season, nearby "white" communities took this to be a taunting act of lawlessness ... [and] some 3000 "Native" lobster traps were destroyed or cut loose by 150 local fishermen.[14]

Tensions built into acts of violence. In addition to the destruction of thousands of traps, non-Native fishermen sank a Mi'kmaq lobster boat and intimidated the Mi'kmaq with rifles and shotguns. Mi'kmaq were threatened and beaten, and shots were fired on several occasions. The provincial government, however, did not take the side of the Mi'kmaq. Instead, the crisis escalated into standoffs between the Mi'kmaq and the RCMP and federal government of Canada. At the peak of the conflict, Department of Fisheries and Oceans (DFO) officers resorted to using their boats to run over the Mi'kmaq fishing boats, forcing the fishermen into the water.[15] It took three years to reach an uneasy peace in which the Burnt Church Band Council eventually agreed to DFO requirements in exchange for a package of benefits, but according to Miigam'agan, dissatisfaction with the outcome remains.

Here in Maine, the Penobscot Nation (Dana's people) sued the State of Maine because of the state's 2012 legal opinion that the Penobscot Nation's territory (consisting of a chain of islands in the Penobscot River) did not include the river itself – despite the fact that the Penobscots' sustenance fishing rights in the river are guaranteed by early treaties. These treaties were referenced in 2015 correspondence between attorneys in the US Department of the Interior and the federal Environmental Protection Agency:

These statutorily-acknowledged fishing rights are rooted in treaty guarantees ... The Penobscot treaties of 1818 (with Massachusetts) and 1820 (with Maine) do not expressly mention fishing rights because they [the Penobscots] did not cede the Penobscot River, explicitly retaining islands and granting to non[tribal]-members only the right to "pass and repass" the River. The Penobscot Nation had historically relied on fishing and the islands mentioned in the Treaty would have been of little value if they were not accompanied by fishing grounds.[16]

In spite of the opinion stated in this correspondence, in June 2017 the Penobscot Nation lost its argument, in both the US District Court and in the 1st US Circuit Court of Appeals, that its reservation includes the Penobscot River. Both decisions left intact the Penobscot Nation's sustenance fishing rights within the river, but ruled that the Nation did not have jurisdiction over the river itself. The Appeals Court decision, however, was a split decision, with dissenting Circuit Judge Juan Torruella noting that treaties signed in 1796, 1818, and 1833 giving the Penobscots sustenance fishing rights "only make sense and can only be exercised" if their reservation includes at least part of the water of the river.[17]

The State of Maine has a long history of ignoring its treaty obligations. In 1820, Maine became a state by separating from Massachusetts and establishing its own constitution. Under the separation agreement with Massachusetts, Maine was required to uphold all treaty obligations that Massachusetts had entered into with "the Indians," and this requirement was written into the new state's constitution within article 10, section 5. But as Colin Woodard writes, it's difficult to find out about these obligations:

That's because in 1875 the people of Maine ratified a constitutional amendment forbidding this article to ever be published. That amendment is still in effect: Open any copy of the Maine Constitution to Article X, Section 7, which proclaims Section 5 will "remain in force" but "shall hereafter be omitted in any printed copies." Exactly why this was done remains unclear ... [but] if the constitutional commissioners who proposed the change intended to ensure the state's obligations were forgotten, it was effective.[18]

In 2015, Maliseet tribal representative to the state legislature Henry Bear succeeded in getting legislation passed to require that the text of article 10, section 5 be available on the website of the Maine state legislature's Law and Legislative Reference Library, but failed both in 2015 and again in 2017 at his goal of requiring that this section be added back into printed copies of the Maine constitution. Article 10, section 5, therefore, is accessible only if one is searching for it, which requires being aware that it exists in the first place.

Miigam'agan offers a personal reflection on treaty obligations and the costs, on both sides, of discounting them:

Federal policies deny us access to resources for us to thrive in the same way as the White people are thriving. To this day, [non-Native] people still benefit from all the resources – economic, political, social, and spiritual – that they derived from the treaties, but Native Americans are not benefiting. It's important to understand the truth of our history, the truth of our relationship. Our true relationship to each other is that we're all part of our original agreement with the Creator; so, if we want to grow and evolve as human beings, and be spiritually fulfilled, it's important that we try and correct what has happened. It's not enough to say "I'm sorry" and keep living in a certain way. When you've done wrong, you publicly make an acknowledgment of what you need to amend and start amending it. White people, especially the ones who are enjoying all the benefits of life here on this continent, need to acknowledge that these benefits are from Indian land – from Indians' home. That's hard for people to say, but acknowledging that in the courts, and in the government systems, and in schools, I think is important.

The Personal Is Political

Large-scale legal issues play out on national and international, provincial and state levels, while assumptions and enduring stereotypes
about Indigenous people are reflected daily in policies implemented
in Native communities across North America. Well-meaning initiatives, and people, can have negative consequences where there is a
lack of understanding of the actual impact of policies, or when there
is limited knowledge of Indigenous people and their cultures.

For example, many non-Native individuals live and/or work in
Indigenous communities. Certainly they marry and move there,
but non-Natives also occupy many of the jobs within the community. Those who come with an openness to understanding and
appreciating the culture, and with the intention to contribute in
ways that are desired and needed, are usually welcomed and valued. Issues arise, however, when there is a lack of understanding,
or an unwillingness to learn, on the part of non-Natives, or when
federal policies require them to perform their jobs in ways that
conflict with the community's values. Wayne and Miigam'agan
provide a Native perspective on their communities' education and
childcare systems:

> *Wayne*: I've been working in the school system in my community for
> nearly forty years, working with the non-Native teachers to get them
> to a place where they realize that they're teaching Native children and
> that they're in a Native community. They work in a Native communi-
> ty and yet they don't see it. If they do look around, what they see is the
> alcoholic behavior or the drug addiction in the community – all the
> negative things. And their conclusion is that the parents don't care

about their children. And that's not true! We love our children very much, you know, even the ones that are suffering from addiction.

A few of the teachers really had an attitude, and it was easy for me to forget about the successful experiences that I'd had with some of them because, some days, I felt like I was at war with all of them. Finally, I said to myself, "I really *am* at war, and as long as I'm at war I can't give my best to the children." That's what we're there for, the children. I kept telling myself that, and all of a sudden it became my mantra to the teachers: that the most important people are the kids we're trying to teach, without them none of us would be here. Well, that didn't go over too well with some people, but it's true.

Miigam'agan: A big reason that you can't get Native participants to come to a mixed [Native and non-Native] gathering is because non-Natives are already such a dominant force in our own communities. For example, the schools in First Nations communities are all federally operated and almost all of the teachers are White. In the past, I've said to the principal and the teachers, "Let's make our students fluent in Mi'kmaq by immersing them first in their Native language," and they got very upset with me. They said, "Well, Miigam'agan, we don't speak Mi'kmaq. If we support what you're saying, we're basically working our way out of our jobs. Where does that leave us?" And I said, "When you applied for this position was it for the best interests of the community or for a paycheck?"

A lot of the ill feelings in our community are due to White people working there and controlling some part of our programs. We keep pumping our kids into that system and they get reprogrammed and further disconnected from their culture. Then we expect them to come back into our communities and be Wabanaki, or to be human beings, but the institution isn't training human beings; it's training them to be dehumanized, to be part of the system.

We do have social workers in our community who are Native, but they have policies that are dictated by the federal government. For example, they say we cannot sleep with our babies. Sleeping with our babies is a natural way of living, but they say we can't do this. They say these ways are not going to serve us if we want to survive, or "That's the old way, we don't do that anymore, this is the right way to do it." We have all this in our communities because of federal and provincial funds; in order to be eligible for these funds we have to put our own ways aside and tell our children, "We can't do that anymore."

Alma describes the effects of Canadian federal policy on how resources are distributed within the tribal communities there. These are policies that, by their nature, create conflict and divisiveness between Native and non-Native residents within the communities:

Say that a non-Native gets a job in our community; the next thing you know they're making a career. Then, you know, they've got a boyfriend or girlfriend, and next thing you know they're getting a house. They come here and want to "help the Indians," but it ends up that they have a lifetime career in the community. And it's many, many of them, not just one or two. So, the result is that Native people are being pushed out of jobs and homes. Everything that a non-Native takes is a resource that our people have to give up. When the government provides resources for our community, they don't count the non-Natives, they only count the Natives; and there's only so much to go around.

Economic Self-Determination

Native communities are often located in rural areas, miles from commercial centers or major highways; Alma's urban community of St. Mary's, surrounded by the city of Fredericton, is an exception. This isolation makes economic development, a key to self-determination, extremely difficult. For many Indigenous leaders and community members, developing local industry that can provide jobs is fundamental to the health, well-being, and cultural identity of their people. Time and again, tribal governments feel the frustration of obstacles placed in their paths by federal policies, state or provincial laws, and the attitudes of their non-Native neighbors. Wayne reflects:

> If the Passamaquoddy ever expressed their economic power we could make some changes, but most of the money from our paychecks goes to the Walmart in Calais [a half-hour away]. We do nothing with that power; we could if we acted together, but look at what happened when we tried to get a casino. Look at the results of the state referendums. The results had nothing to do with people being in favor, or not in favor, of gambling, because when non-Natives want a casino it gets passed. When we present a referendum, it's voted down.
>
> We like to think that we've made some progress in people's attitudes, but that one saddens me an awful lot. Hopefully we can change it. Not that I believe that gambling is our economic savior; there are other things that we could do that might be better economic development, but that is one solution that's being considered at the moment.

Beginning to Make Amends

Currently, there are movements on several fronts to begin to address the wrongs perpetrated by colonial societies in North America. Significantly, these movements have originated primarily outside of the court systems and legal institutions of the United States and Canada.

A number of US, Canadian, and worldwide religious institutions, in public statements, have officially repudiated or are in the process of repudiating the doctrine of discovery. Among these institutions are the Episcopal Church of the United States; the Anglican Church of Canada; the United Church of Canada; the United Methodist Church; the United Church of Christ; the Presbyterian Church USA and Canada; a number of Monthly Meetings, Yearly Meetings, organizations, and affiliations of the Religious Society of Friends (Quakers); the Unitarian Universalist Association; the Mennonites; and the World Council of Churches. In 2014, the Leadership Conference of Women Religious, representing approximately 80 per cent of Catholic sisters, passed a resolution calling on Pope Francis to repudiate the doctrine.[19]

In 2007, the United Nations General Assembly adopted the United Nations Declaration on the Rights of Indigenous Peoples (UNDRIP). According to Tim Coulter of the Indian Law Resource Center, the declaration is "one of the most significant developments ... in decades. It recognizes that indigenous peoples throughout the world have a permanent right to exist as peoples, nations, cultures, and societies."[20] At the time of adoption, only four countries opposed the declaration – the United States, Canada, Australia, and New Zealand. It took until December 2010 for the last country, the United States, to endorse the declaration, but it is now part of international human rights law. The declaration is only the beginning of the work ahead for countries of the Americas. According to Coulter, "To see the promise of the Declaration become a reality, we must continue to fight for laws, policies, and relationships that take into account the permanent presence of indigenous nations in the U.S. and throughout the world."[21]

In Maine we have a perfect example of the work ahead that Tim Coulter describes. In 1980, after tremendous friction, tension, and suspicion on both sides, the State of Maine settled a historic land claim by the Passamaquoddy and Penobscot peoples – a settlement that the *Christian Science Monitor* called "the biggest Indian victory since Little Big Horn."[22] This out-of-court settlement, the Maine Indian Claims Settlement Act, was the result of the Passamaquoddy and Penobscot tribes suing the State of Maine for illegal sale and transfer of their Aboriginal land. What was intended to be a mechanism of justice, restitution, and economic self-determination, and which began with high hopes on the part of the tribal negotiators, soon after signing began to be interpreted by the state in ways that thwarted tribal efforts to achieve the very self-determination they thought the settlement would ensure.[23]

In April 2008, after nearly thirty years in which the State of Maine used provisions of the Settlement Act to deny, rather than support, tribal proposals, then–Penobscot Nation representative to the Maine legislature Donna Loring entered a resolution proposing that Maine enact the United Nations' newly adopted UNDRIP (two years before it was signed by the United States!). By her own admission she didn't expect it to pass, but to her surprise, members of the Maine House and Senate voted unanimously, without discussion or debate, to support the resolution.

In an interview with *Indian Country Today*, Representative Loring said, "I expected them to turn it down because of all the stuff that was going on [in the legislature]. We didn't get anything that we had worked on that year and they [the legislators] were pretty nasty about things." She added that some legislators were supportive of the tribes but didn't have the political will to make the changes that were needed. She continued:

> I was very frustrated, so I put in that Declaration resolution because I really wanted the legislators' true colors to come out. I wanted to see a debate on the floor. I wanted to see someone say, "No, we shouldn't adopt this." I wanted to hold a mirror up to them and say, "Hey, look, this is what's going on in the world globally." I wanted them to have some kind of consciousness about how they treat Native people in this state.

What she got instead was a unanimous vote to pass her resolution without any debate. But nothing changed. She continued:

> The adoption of the resolution has had absolutely no impact on anything. When you look even at what happened this year in the gambling industry – everybody and his brother have gambling rights in this state now except for the tribes. They [the legislature] just approved gambling for the veterans' organizations. When it comes to economic equality, we haven't reached that mark; we're not even close.[24]

Some Progress … and a Long Way to Go

There is some progress, however slow and arduous, in bridging the gaps of understanding between our peoples, and combating longstanding prejudices and racism. For example, after years of discussions, presentations, and lobbying by Wabanaki people and allies, in 2019 the Maine legislature banned racist "Indian mascots" in all public schools and universities.[25] During that same legislative session, Maine joined a number of states, cities, and towns in declaring the second Monday in October to be Indigenous People's Day.[26]

In 2001, Donna Loring, as Penobscot tribal representative to the Maine state legislature, sponsored a bill, LD 291, stating that Maine Native American history and culture must be taught in all elementary and secondary schools, both public and private. Against tremendous odds, the bill passed and was signed into law that year, the first of its kind in the United States.[27] Many people, both Native and allies, who put much effort into the bill's passage had high hopes for its potential to correct stereotypes, misinformation, and lack of information in Maine's school curricula. Its implementation in the beginning, however, was a bit rocky. Wayne, who served on the committee that shaped the legislation, shares his experience:

The Maine legislature passed LD 291, and what happened was they tried to dump it on the Natives. They tried to say it was the Natives' responsibility, and it clearly wasn't. We could assist, but it was up to the Department of Education to provide the curriculum and train the teachers, and they didn't provide for that. So Native people started getting phone calls. At first we responded, but then we said, "Wait a minute, we can't keep up with this, we've got jobs!" Someone would call and say, "Hey, would you come speak to my class for twenty-five minutes up in Kittery?" That's a whole day's drive – at least five hours one way – for us to get to Kittery for a twenty-five-minute presentation, and they would think nothing of asking. Then they'd say, "We don't have any money in our budget so we really can't pay you an honorarium." I'd think, "Somebody's missing the boat here." Finally, the Department started doing something.

Currently in Maine, resources for Wabanaki studies are made available to teachers, and voluntary trainings in curricula are offered in summer institutes, but with Maine's policy of "local control," local school districts are in charge of the standards that guide their teaching.[28] Expectations for what is to be taught in Wabanaki studies are outlined in the state's Learning Results for "social studies," but there are presently no guidelines for how it is to be taught or the time to be devoted, and the state Department of Education does not collect specific information regarding implementation. There also is no official statewide assessment in place.[29] In spite of its less-than-perfect implementation, the original sponsor of LD 291, Donna Loring, takes the optimistic view: "[Implementation] still has a long way to go ... The fact that not all public schools have complied still is an issue, but some do, and the children are learning. We had nothing in place before this ... So yes, there is still much work to do, but the seed has been planted and the groundwork has been laid."[30]

Notable in terms of progress are the Truth and Reconciliation Commissions (TRCs) that operated recently both in Canada (nationwide) and in Maine. These commissions investigated decades-old child welfare policies that removed Native children from their homes in disproportionate numbers and placed them in residential schools and foster homes outside of their communities. These policies had devastating effects on the children, their families, and their communities. Both TRCs completed their work, which sought "truth, healing and change" – the motto of the TRC in Maine – and released their findings in 2015.

The education and development of allies in non-Native communities has been a goal and an outcome of both TRC processes. Shepherding this process in Maine is the organization Maine-Wabanaki REACH, which originally evolved to support the TRC process. REACH has continued as a cross-cultural collaboration to implement the commission's recommendations, to foster healing in Wabanaki communities, and to educate and prepare non-Natives to advocate for the TRC process and for improved Native/non-Native relationships in general. Maine-Wabanaki REACH now provides educational experiences for over two thousand individuals a year, and in 2019 presented eighty-five programs statewide that include developing an awareness of "White privilege" and creating a historical context for understanding ongoing societal attitudes and structures that negatively impact Wabanaki people in Maine.[31] In Canada, as part of the TRC's education mandate, close to fifteen thousand young people across the country participated in various Education Days to learn about the residential schools and to think about their own role and responsibility in reconciliation,[32] and the National Centre for Truth and Reconciliation carries on the TRC's work as a "living legacy" and "a teaching and learning place" to promote understanding and reconciliation.[33] At the centre, in addition to housing the archives from the TRC process, they host groups from across the country, offering ongoing educational experiences for youth, university students, and adults.[34]

In December 2015, the TRC of Canada issued ninety-four "Calls to Action" to address the devastating impact of Canada's residential school system on Indigenous peoples, and to promote reconciliation. This is a nation-wide effort reaching into all aspects of government, health care, education, religious institutions, media, and so on.[35]

A June 2019 Human Rights Watch dispatch noted, however, that "four years later, monitoring indicates that only ten of these recommendations have been completed."[36]

Notable are the Circles for Reconciliation, an outgrowth of the TRC process in Canada, in which groups of ten individuals, with an equal number of Indigenous and non-Indigenous participants, meet weekly or biweekly for ten gatherings of seventy-five minutes in length: "These ten meetings allow for the beginnings of respectful relationships, which the TRC stresses is the basis of reconciliation. The participants sit in a circle, providing greater opportunities for consensus and being respectful of traditional Indigenous values and customs." At the beginning of 2020, two active groups were in process, with thirty upcoming groups listed and sixty-seven completed.[37]

While signs of progress are to be celebrated, substantive and more immediate progress in the daily lives of Wabanaki peoples will be achieved only when the barriers to economic self-determination and self-governance are removed. For example, Wabanaki tribes in Maine are unique in the United States because of a provision in the (federal) Maine Indian Claims Settlement Act (MICSA) that excludes them from benefiting from any federal laws relating to tribes passed since the act was signed in 1980 (unless they are specifically named in the law).[38] Likewise, the companion law to MICSA that implemented the law in Maine, commonly known as the Maine Implementing Act, has led to a steady decline in opportunities and resources available to Wabanaki communities, and placed them at a distinct disadvantage when compared to tribes in any other state in the United States. In particular, they have been disadvantaged in economic development opportunities and in the ability to self-govern and to address unique and urgent needs in their communities. Currently there is an effort underway in the Maine legislature to remove the obstacles created by both the federal and state Settlement Acts and to ensure that the tribes in Maine "enjoy the same rights, privileges, powers and immunities as other federally recognized Indian tribes within the United States."[39] It is hoped that this effort gains traction and ultimately succeeds, but it will take a concerted effort by Wabanaki tribal leadership and allies to win legislative support.

In Canada, the above-mentioned Human Rights Watch dispatch went on to say that since 2015, when the TRC issued its report, "Indigenous communities continue to suffer systemic discrimination and violence. Indigenous women and girls are far more likely to be victims of abuse and homicide – including at the hands of law enforcement. Indigenous people are significantly overrepresented in the prison system and many communities don't have access to clean drinking water in one of the most water-rich countries in the world." A key call made in 2015 was to fully implement the United Nations Declaration on the Rights of Indigenous Peoples. On this matter, the Human Rights Watch report states, "Successive governments have been hesitant to bring Canadian legislation in line with the UNDRIP, in part because of the requirement of free, prior and informed consent from Indigenous communities in regard to any policies or decisions that would impact their lands, resources or rights. There is no accepted definition of this clause, which has raised the issue of whether or not it provides Indigenous communities a veto over government projects."[40]

Since first contact with settlers, and subsequent near annihilation, Indigenous peoples within the borders of the United States and Canada have been struggling to assert their right to existence, to hold on to their cultural identities and their lifeways, and to travel the long road of healing themselves and their communities. Entrenched state and provincial legislatures, administrations, and judicial systems seem to resist giving an inch, perhaps out of fear – conscious or unconscious – that admission of tribal sovereignty, or right to self-determination, is a "slippery slope" that could lead ... who knows where? To non-Natives giving up their homes and land? To being evicted?

Since this continent was taken by force and deceit, it could certainly be said that we non-Natives have no inherent right to be here, an "inconvenient truth" that our governments and judicial systems seem determined not to acknowledge or address, hoping that such an uncomfortable notion will simply fade away. gkisedtanamoogk told me he once had a conversation with John Mohawk, the Seneca scholar, who said the real issue between Indian Country and North America is that, deep down, North Americans realize they aren't here legitimately, and that's why they don't want to talk about Indigenous issues or want to pretend that these issues are in the past. He said that North Americans suffer from not knowing that it's okay for them to be here. "Why else," Mohawk said, "would it create such hostility, fear, and anger whenever we raise the specter of Indians being Indians in their own context?" gkisedtanamoogk continued:

When Indian people sit with government officials, be it state or federal, and we talk about sovereignty, there's an angry response. They say, "This is not on the table for discussion, we're talking about [specific] programs here." People become defensive because they don't want to talk about that "dark matter" – they're scared that "this might mean something."

And Walter Echo-Hawk, in his book *In the Light of Justice*, notes:

> The real problem in according collective relief for collective wrongs
> is not a legal one, but the deep psychological barrier ... [that] arises
> because we cannot confront our inner demons from the legacy of
> conquest and bring ourselves to face the collective wrongs committed
> against Native Americans, because their claims implicate the legiti-
> macy of a nation built upon the taking of tribal land, undermining of
> sovereignty, and the historical mistreatment inflicted upon American
> Indians.[41]

The practice of avoiding, or denying, the truth of our past, and
an unwillingness to engage with Indigenous peoples as sovereign
and equal partners, defines present-day Native/non-Native relations
and prevents our shaping a just, peaceful, and mutually beneficial
future together.

But it could be different.

How It Could Be Different

Being Here Legitimately

It's not about building the great ark and shipping everyone back to Europe or wherever they came from. It's about how we live together in this shared space. For me, the ideal is for people to have the same love for the land, and for being part of the land, as we have. It's on that basis that one can be here legitimately.

gkisedtanamoogk

As gkisedtanamoogk says, no one is busy building an ark to ship non-Natives back to their ancestral lands. Since we non-Natives are here to stay, perhaps it's time to explore this idea of being here legitimately. What would that look like? Non-Natives' experience in the Gatherings taught us that one path can be as simple, and as profound, as seeking our own unique relationship to this land, to relearn what it has to teach us. gkisedtanamoogk reflects:

I remember a woman at one of our Gatherings; we were having a lunch break and she wanted to talk to me about something, an issue that was heavy on her mind. At one time she had lived in South

Dakota, and in the place where she lived she developed a relationship with a particular plant. This plant completely enthralled her, and she honored it; it became a sort of saving grace for her, and it turned out to be sage. Not having any contact with the Indigenous people there, she didn't know at the time how important this plant was to the Lakota. Since learning that it was sacred to another culture, she was having trouble maintaining her relationship to this plant, wondering if she was "appropriating" their culture. But the only thing I could say to her was, "That was *your* relationship with this plant. This plant and you had a conversation, so it's for you to honor the conversation."

Spend enough time with the Earth and She will tell you what you need to know. She already knows you, no matter where you are.

Given the current threats to our water, our climate, in fact to our entire ecosystem, how we relate to, and protect, the precious gift of this planet is the most important issue that any generation will ponder for a long time. There are numerous opportunities for activism in the protection of our planet in which we non-Natives can engage on our own, as well as join with Indigenous peoples in the spirit of mutual endeavor and exchange.

Acknowledging First Peoples / Honoring the Treaties

As the original inhabitants of this continent for many thousands of years, Indigenous peoples' knowledge of, and relationship to, this land we call North America is vaster and deeper than the rest of us can conceive. Acknowledging and honoring their deep attachment to and right to thrive in this place is a first step in righting the wrongs of the past and moving forward together.

Acknowledging Native peoples' unique status in no way negates or diminishes the value or the rights of any other cultures now living in North America. It does remind us new arrivals who live and work on this continent that we derive our wealth – however we define that wealth – from and within the home of the people who are indigenous here.

The existence of numerous treaties, still constitutionally in force, between the nations of the United States and Canada and this continent's Indigenous peoples confirms the unique status of the tribes as nations as well. As the beneficiaries of these treaties, we should insist that our governments honor their promises. The treaties are the documentation of the inherent right of First Nations to self-governance, self-determination, and preservation of their cultures, regardless of who else might live in their territory. Miigam'agan explains:

The nations were all supposed to coexist, to work together, and the United States and Canada were bound by the treaties as well. If this were a reality, then our nations would have our own institutions where people go to get accreditation and other credentials. We have to step out of our culture and go into the White culture to get our credentials, or to celebrate our achievements; it's only through that avenue that we are currently recognized.

The notion of coexisting, of working together nation to nation as equals, enables us to envision a mutual respect and exchange between our cultures in which Indigenous knowledge, philosophy, and lifeways are regarded as containing information of great value concerning how to live rightly and sustainably in this place we all now call "home," as gkisedtanamoogk describes:

> I participated in a series at the university with seven other Wabanaki scholars. In my presentation, I introduced the idea of "indigenizing the academy," meaning having Indigenous views become part of the *entire* curriculum, not only in "Native American" programs. What we really need, in my view, is a place in the general curriculum for Indigenous philosophy, Indigenous science, Indigenous law, Indigenous spirituality. All we get now is one perspective. The United States, by virtue of establishing the treaties, implied that such a nation-to-nation exchange would be the ideal. What I'm suggesting is that a nation-to-nation format needs to be reflected at the university as well as at the federal and state levels. Indigenizing the academy means that we create a partnership.

An Indigenous Worldview

Native contributors confirmed that, while there can be significant differences in the multitude of Indigenous perspectives, there are also strong commonalities among them. Foremost, they are Earth based, and rooted in a particular place. Those who grow up in present-day Native communities absorb aspects of this worldview even amidst the overlay of Catholic or public school educations and the influences of modern technology and mass media. Barb explains:

> I have lived off-reserve for many, many years now. Someone like Miigam'agan, who has lived in a reserve community most of her life,

still has the language and a better understanding of what it means to live as a collective. But still I've come to know that, as a Mi'kmaq woman, I can't conceive of or understand myself as separate from the land. My identity as Mi'kmaq, or even as Barbara Martin, is inseparable from my connection to the land. When I look outside in nature, even though I'm not out there hunting or trapping or fishing, I see myself in it.

I pray every day to the Earth Mother, in English. I'm hoping that one day I can pray in Mi'kmaq. And when I pray, I say to Her, "Thank you, thank you so much for all your blessings." I look at the environment and it's not the same as it was five hundred years ago. There are different species out there. We've put pesticides and poisons in it as well. But look at us; we're not the same Mi'kmaq as we were five hundred years ago. We are a reflection of our environment. Things have changed. Yet we are still the land and the land is us. It's still very much a part of our spirits.

Years ago, when participating in the Gatherings, I remember the moment I realized that to understand the language indigenous to a place was to understand how to live there. It was as simple as that. Language evolves as the people learn to survive within a particular watershed or territory, and so it contains everything you need to know to find food, water, shelter, and to be safe. Significantly, Indigenous language also places this knowledge within a cosmology that is entirely different from our Western worldview. Barb continues:

I still have a connection to the land, and yet someone like Miigam'agan is even closer to the land because she has the language. The language comes from the land. The land and the language are one. More than that, Miigam'agan has the Spirit of the language, and she is a caretaker of that Spirit. She can hear and speak the language and also understand the form and the spirit of what is meant underneath it. The language is rich and complex, and so full of meaning. There are words – old words – that say so much, but it's only someone like Miigam'agan who can take those words and – I hate to use this term – deconstruct them, for others to understand. If you went down to the New England states, to Maine, you'd be hard-pressed to find any of our people who still have that understanding, whereas there are people here in New Brunswick who still do.

Dana describes how his people are sustained by their connection to the river that bears their name, and how the river is central to their emotional and spiritual life. He speaks of the river as a conduit to the Grandmother, the "Great Mother" of all life:

We carry the name of the river, the Panawahpskek/Penobscot. We're the People of the River. It is our highway, our lifeline and our blood-line. One of the teachings I give is that if you have a need you can go to the water and immerse your hands above your wrists – because that is where some of your neuron centers are – and make your offering to the water and pray. You put that need into the water and send it to the Grandmother. We were all brought up with the idea that if there was a real problem that needed to be solved, or some-thing needed to make you well, you could go see your grandmother. Praying in this way is also offering up respect and honoring the Grandmother of all life. And we should honor that water and not turn it into a trash dump.

Fundamental to an Indigenous worldview is the idea of taking no more than you need and sharing what you have, as Miigam'agan demonstrates:

> We know what will happen if we just keep taking. We're going to destroy ourselves. We know that. If I take more than I need I might be okay within my lifetime, but my children will not be okay. So if you see me filling up my plate at a buffet, you know I'm going to share it!

Central concepts that have always been part of Indigenous cultures are now being understood and appreciated by environmentalists and scientists in the Western world as essential for our survival in an increasingly threatened ecosystem. Non-Natives have much to gain by understanding and incorporating Indigenous knowledge and perspectives as we seek to renew our relationship to the Earth. Miigam'agan continues:

> We've played around with fire long enough – everything we've done to the environment, everything we've taken – but this is not just a White person's problem anymore, this problem belongs to all of us. Native people may feel that we didn't benefit that much from the "candy store" but we wanted to! I have to say – and I'm being really honest here – sometimes you feel like, "Gee, how come we didn't get a nice house? How come we didn't get this or that?" We realize now that we can't have all that, but it would've been nice to benefit a little from it, to experience the comfort and enjoyment of that part of life while it was here.
>
> Now we have to collect all that longing and put it away in a box because this way of being has hurt all of us, and it has hurt the Earth.

On the other hand, I feel like, well, I don't have to make that many changes in my life. On the reserve, we already know how to live with the bare minimum. But the best part is that we're all going to be learning together how to live with the bare minimum, in a good way.

The Need for Gathering Spaces

Miigam'agan once said, "You know, Shirley, without the Gatherings, I never would have met you or any of the other non-Native people." She pointed out that in the "White community," or dominant culture, all kinds of networking opportunities exist – forums, committees, councils, and so on – spaces where people interact. There are typically no spaces, however, where Native and non-Native people routinely come together to know one another and find shared interests. This lack of regular, everyday connection contributes to misperceptions and misunderstandings of one another, to conflict, and even to violence.

Miigam'agan referenced the fishing crisis, previously described, that occurred in her community and resulted in three years of violence between the Mi'kmaq fishermen, local non-Native fishermen, and the provincial and federal governments. These events were the culmination of years of misunderstandings and tensions between the Mi'kmaq community and their surrounding neighbors. Miigam'agan reflects:

In my community of Esgenoôpetitj/Burnt Church, the White community is all around us but there was never any space to come together. If there had been a place where people were already talking and learning about each other, I don't think the fishing wars would have taken place.

In the midst of the crisis, a group of local non-Natives decided to do something about the rifts that were being created between the Mi'kmaq and their neighbors. A community forum, initiated by church leaders and the Aboriginal Rights Coalition–Atlantic, was created to bring people together. The effort, which lasted about six months, even attracted a few representatives from the RCMP (Canada's national police force) and the DFO (federal Department of Fisheries and Oceans). Miigam'agan describes:

They sent people to speak with the French and English communities, and to the Mi'kmaq, to get people talking about what was happening and how they felt about it. They would ask, in the non-Native communities, "Is there an interest to hear the voices of the Natives?" And to us, they'd say, "Not everybody feels that way in the French and English communities ... would you like to hear what they have to say?" And everywhere they asked, "Would you like to get together?"

The meetings were held in neutral areas, and gkisedtanamoogk and I went. At first, there was a good handful of people from Esgenoôpetitj who went with us, but they didn't stay long because it was a little too hard. Soon there were only three of us from my community – myself, gkisedtanamoogk, and another friend of mine – and even she didn't stay after a while, because she hadn't had the experience we'd had in the Gatherings. It was that experience that made it possible to know there are stages to this process. I knew we weren't going to say the right things right away. People were going to make mistakes and not know how to talk to us, and that would trigger us. I felt triggered in the Gatherings too sometimes, like when someone would say, "You know, I have so much respect for your people and for your culture," or "I had such a wonderful experience at the ceremony," and in my mind I would be thinking, "Yeah, that's right, but there's a lot of issues here. What about those? Are you willing to talk about those?"

But now I knew there was a process to this. I knew the simple fact that everyone was there, sitting through the discussion, said a lot. These talks were all held in the winter, but we stayed with it no matter the weather, and I would go back and share what I heard with some of the key players in my community.

It was this effort that made a big difference in how people related to one another after the crisis was over. But I still say, if we had built those kinds of relationships with our neighbor communities in the first place, the fishing crisis never would have escalated.

JoAnn explains, from a non-Native perspective, the importance of formalizing a time and place to gather:

I felt that institutional support of the alliance was critical. I knew that independently, individually, I couldn't do this sort of thing; but together, with others, I could. Because of how the Gatherings were organized, through the Center for Vision and Policy, I felt that everything didn't depend on me. I could be part of the process without taking full responsibility for it. I mean, there were necessary instructions given before people could even attend the Gatherings. We practically had to be taught how to behave. And appropriation was an issue ... so many things. So, to have the protection of that kind of organization was critical.

Creating a Gathering Space

For me, the hope is that we can create forums where we get together in friendship and mutual regard for each other ... and love, as Wayne would put it. Where we can be open and frank, where we can bring topics that have great merit to us and we can have a discussion about them.

gkisedtanamoogk

In recent years, some non-Native groups have begun to understand that forming alliances with Indigenous peoples can provide great strength to their cause. For example, an environmental group and a tribal government may join together, utilizing a treaty or trust obligation on the part of the United States or Canada as a defense against a particular environmental threat. But without a prior relationship, alliances between Native and non-Native entities are usually temporary. When the issue is resolved, the relationship dissolves.

Wayne offers a Native perspective:

We've made some progress in terms of alliances, but we have a long way to go. Sometimes the alliance has been for economic reasons; people have entered into it to get something for themselves. The casino issue is a good example, or the LNG [liquefied natural gas] issue. People reached out to us because there was something in it for them. If I had a magic wand, I would wish for us to be more visible in the state, and for people to be more interested in wanting to help ... not to "do for" us, but to stand with us ... to want to get to know us because it is the right thing to do, for all of us. That's a powerful alliance.

Additionally, if the non-Native group does not honor and support tribal sovereignty – the tribe's right to self-determination – then when conflicts occur over purpose or objectives, the non-Native group may balk at tribal leadership, damaging the alliance.

Shirley B. describes the importance of the prior relationship in anticipating and understanding differences:

> We should always be cultivating relationships with people who are different from ourselves; number one, because they enrich us; number two, because we have a responsibility to know what other peoples' experiences are like. Then, if we have a notion to do something together, that impulse is not the first point at which we encounter each other, and if they say "no" to the project it doesn't mean we're not in relationship. If you try to work with someone who is a stranger to you, then if the project doesn't work out, that's all there is.

If there is a desire, or need, to create a space where Indigenous and non-Indigenous people can come together, it can be difficult to know how and where to start, especially if there has been no prior connection or relationship to draw upon. It is best, almost necessary, to start small. It can begin with two people. Get to know one person, or find out what relationships, either individual or institutional, might already be in place. Holding the vision and looking for opportunities to connect in small ways may ultimately bear more fruit than trying to create a larger meeting or event right from the start.

The process of building trust takes time. And if the situation is such that conflict is already present, if Native and non-Native parties are already at odds, it can feel that there is no time for getting to know one another. Shirley B. puts into perspective why taking that time may be the most important thing we can do in service to our shared future:

> The first thing I would say is, I hope you're not in a hurry, because you will need to build a relationship first in order to do anything. The relationship work that you do now is more important than the immediate outcome, because there may be other times when you butt up against each other; so do the work now, and do it right. One of the things that I've learned from my Native friends, and that I carry with me all the time now, is the concept of keeping in mind the "seventh unborn generation" in any decisions we make. This means that what we're doing isn't about you and me right now, it's about our children and grandchildren and great-grandchildren. So let's fix our relationship now so we don't continue in this awful mess that's based on animosity and distrust.

Both opportunities and challenges exist in established institutions for creating meeting spaces where Native and non-Native people can gather. I asked gkisedtanamoogk, when he taught at the University of Maine, if he thought something like the Gatherings could be created within a university setting:

> They'd have to be open to having a fire in the classroom! Just kidding. I think universities are a natural venue. Keep in mind that a forum such as the Gatherings needs to have some consistency and the university, by its nature, has a constant turnover of students, but I still think it's possible. For example, if a campus organization were created that included Native American students along with whoever else wanted to be part of it, and membership were voluntary, then I believe it could work. One thing that made the Gatherings work was

that people wanted to be there, and so we made the time. The organization could be guided by the same sorts of principles that guided the Gatherings, with perhaps a Native and a non-Native advisor.

While it is not exactly an ongoing group with consistent members, an experiment has been started in a government department in Canada aimed at giving those who work in Native communities help and advice in understanding the cultures in which they work. Getting advice from the Elders themselves offers non-Native workers a window into Native culture they otherwise would not have, as Miigam'agan explains:

In a government building in Ottawa – Indian Affairs – they have a section called *Kumik*, or Grandmother Lodge. It's an Elders' center and there they have ongoing Talking Circles and discussions. If any of the workers there are dealing with a situation in a Native community, or a situation involving an individual Native person, they're invited to come to the Council of Elders and present their issue for guidance or to better understand what is going on. That kind of consultation is helpful both for non-Natives and Natives, because what holds us back is fear of making mistakes ... on both sides. We hold back and then we perpetuate our assumptions. We've lived side by side for so long but we don't know each other.

Working Together on a Cause

When Native and non-Native people do come together to work on a particular issue or cause, hopefully the intended outcome is to serve the best interests of all, with particular regard for Native concerns that are so often overlooked or disregarded. Regardless of the purpose or how the collaboration comes about, we share here a few insights into working together, based on our experiences with one another. There are also other helpful resources that have been published in recent years.*

Indigenous people are experts on the Western world in which they must live and work, but Western society knows very little about Indigenous culture, philosophy, or science. If the two are to work together as equals, a certain balance needs to be restored. We non-Natives must learn to listen more than we speak, observe more than we act – especially in the beginning – and ask questions instead of assume. Making the effort to travel to Native communities in order to work together can engender goodwill and contribute to our cultural education, but we need to be invited rather than rushing in. If the cause is Native initiated, non-Natives should look for those opportunities where we can be helpful *under the advice and direction of the Native people involved.* A Native-led pace and process may look different from the dominant culture's way of doing things, but is just as valid and may be more effective in the situation.

Betty shares what she learned from her many years spent in activism alongside the Lubicon Cree and the Innu:

> You know, like all good people everywhere, you come in with your head full of plans. I hope I was never too officious, but in the back of my mind I would think, "Well, if you're going to work on this, why don't you do that?" But I learned to keep my mouth shut, and gradually I fell under the spell of listening and learning, and began to live

---

* In "Suggested Resources" at the end of this book, see the section "How It Could Be Different: Reaching across the Cultural Divide, Examining Racism and White Privilege, Becoming Allies, a Future Decolonized," as well as the section "Posters, Etc." where you will find sources for the lists "How to Be an Ally to Indigenous Peoples" by the Two-Row Wampum Campaign, and the "Ally Bill of Responsibilities" by Dr. Lynn Gehl.

into their plan. And they did have a plan. Spend time together, and if they ask for help, ask what they would like you to do. Little by little, you know, we do give forth our ideas, if they want them. And sometimes they don't want what we suggest.

It's simply about listening and watching and learning. Gradually it comes over you, just as it did in our Gatherings, the whole spirituality of Native life. You don't necessarily believe everything they believe – their traditions and their culture and so on – but it affects you very much. It is rather close to Quakerism, I must say – the awareness of the Spirit within, and of course the Spirit without – the Great Spirit; and their reverence for life, which I feel I've had all my life.

Humility versus "White Guilt"

Non-Natives in alliance with Native people continually hear stories, and see the evidence, of the mistreatment and discrimination directed toward Indigenous people. At the same time, we become increasingly aware of the inherent privilege in our daily lives. As a result, we can be overtaken at times by what's known as "White guilt." Feelings of guilt and remorse for the tragedies inflicted by colonial society – in some cases by our own ancestors – and for current injustices are understandable and natural. When these feelings come, however, it is incumbent upon us not to burden Native allies and friends with them, in effect asking them to absolve us – they already have enough to deal with. Barb shares her perspective:

I want to have a genuine, respectful relationship working toward something, working toward an end goal. Working that way gives you a sense of humility, a sense of true humility, not the kind that comes from White guilt. White guilt is useless, and sometimes dangerous because some people will do anything to get out of that state of guilt. You get the feeling they are saying, "Please hit me. Please hit me so I don't have to feel that way anymore." That's an unhealthy relationship.

We non-Natives living today are not responsible for the past, although it is human to feel very sorry for it. And we cannot change current policies overnight. We *can*, however, do what we can do – our small part – that when carried out in relationship with others, both Native and non-Native, becomes a big part of the solution. Working through our White guilt enables us to be more fully present in our connections with Native people and to refocus on the work before us. When these feelings surface, it can be enormously helpful and healing to turn for support to other non-Natives engaged in similar alliance-building efforts, or to the wisdom in written and other resources. (Again, see "Suggested Resources" at the end of this book, particularly the section "How It Could Be Different: Reaching across the Cultural Divide, Examining Racism and White Privilege, Becoming Allies, a Future Decolonized.")

There also may be times in alliance work when we are experiencing a sense of camaraderie, even healing, that can feel so good it's easy to want more, to want to just keep "helping." That response may not be what is needed. Barb again offers a Native perspective on the issue:

There's another message that's important to say. It's important because once you get to that place in the relationship where you're working together and it feels so good … well, sometimes you have to be able to discern when you need to let us do our own thing. I saw the movie *Gandhi*, and that poor woman in the movie … I felt for her. This woman, who was the daughter of a nobleman, or someone equally important, came to Gandhi and she wanted to help. And she did help; she went through everything that the people went through. She was accepted and loved by Gandhi and his family, loved and trusted. But at a certain point, Gandhi said to her that it was time for her to go home. Gandhi said, "We have to do this ourselves. We have to be able to do this because otherwise it will be perceived as being done for us, and that we can't do it on our own."

So there might be points in the relationship – it won't be final – but there might be points in the relationship where we say, "We have to do this ourselves." We'll have to sort out the stuff that we can do, and know that we were the ones who did it. And when you can hear that, and not feel as if you've been rejected, that's respect … and humility. Because when you're in that place of starting to belong, and starting to feel that wonderful feeling, it's hard to give that up. But that's where wisdom comes. That's part of the evolution of our relationship – getting to the point where we can look at each other as human beings, but also as two distinct collectives.

Non-Natives Working with Our Own People

So sometimes we non-Natives may be asked to "back off" and leave our Native friends and colleagues to do work they must do. This is a time when non-Natives can continue to use our experiences and deeper understanding to inform and educate people in our own circles. Those of us simply born into the dominant culture and who have a reasonable number of connections within our communities have potentially far more influence than we might imagine. Possibilities for action include speaking up when we hear misperceptions, or misinformed or racist comments; writing a letter to the editor; calling or writing a local legislative representative, or otherwise working to change policies that discriminate against Native peoples or that dishonor existing treaty agreements (making sure that our facts, and our actions, have the sanction of those we're trying to support); attending public events that are organized by Indigenous people, or where Native speakers are featured, and then sharing what we learn (speaking from our own experience, not presuming to speak for Native people). All of these contributions add up and, in addition, provide our embattled Indigenous neighbors with a sense that they are not alone. Again, Barb shares a Native view:

> We can talk all we want to White people, but we may not have the words for them to understand what we're trying to say. That's when non-Natives who have taken this journey with us are really valuable in that they understand their people. They understand what words would work, to help them get an inkling of where we're coming from. If I try to say it, they'll think, oh, another guilt trip. They might listen to me, but truly they won't hear me.

As long as governmental structures remain intractable in terms of their dealings with Indigenous peoples, it is up to individuals and organizations that care about justice, healing, and reparation to take the lead in transforming the paradigm in which Native/non-Native relationships currently exist. Earlier, Miigam'agan spoke about deciding to be part of the Gatherings when she realized "maybe we should start talking to the grass-roots people because they are the voters in their system." She refers to a conversation she had with gkisedtanamoogk, who said to her, "You know, this relationship [that was forming in the Gatherings] is much different from our relationship to the federal government or to the state. These are community folks, and they can make change." Gwen echoes this point:

> We are not a people with power, and we often don't know how to work in those silos that the system has created. But there are people that have that knowledge, and we need their help. We ask for more than just support. We also want action if they can do it. They can work with the people of power, and help to set the record straight.

An example of what Gwen is talking about occurred in regard to the Penobscot Nation's lawsuit, mentioned earlier, against the State of Maine, in response to the state's claim that the Penobscot reservation does not include the river. Seventeen entities – municipalities and industries – had signed onto the lawsuit on the side of the state. These entities all had discharge permits into the river, and had been erroneously persuaded that the Penobscots, rather than the state, might gain authority over their discharges if they won the case. Penobscot leaders approached one of the towns involved in the lawsuit and asked to present the facts at a town council meeting. With the support of non-Native allies who lived in the town, they made their presentation and also held a larger informational meeting in the community. Town officials, upon learning the facts, and with pressure from town residents who attended the informational session, voted to withdraw their town from the lawsuit. This action was a tremendous morale boost, and subsequent actions were planned in towns up and down the river.

Grass-roots actions like this one capture the public imagination and help to educate non-Natives about Indigenous rights and concerns. This example also shows what can be accomplished when Native and non-Native people join together in service to a shared goal. Non-Native allies were motivated to assist their Penobscot neighbors out of a sense of justice, while both groups shared a deep concern for the environmental quality of the river. The Penobscot Nation, in order to protect the health of its community members who depend upon the river for sustenance fishing, monitors the water through its Department of Natural Resources. Allies living along the river felt that the Penobscot Nation's continued stewardship of the river helped to protect the quality of the river for all.[1]

There is much that we, Native and non-Native, can do together and yet, for most of us, being in relationship with one another is new territory. Opportunities are needed to gather, to get to know one another as individuals with common hopes and dreams. Existing Western institutions can be strengthened by incorporating Indigenous knowledge and wisdom. Alliances that exemplify and model nation-to-nation respect are needed in communities, governmental offices – local, state, provincial, and federal – and legislative chambers. Perhaps we need an image: a way to reimagine how we can begin again and go forward together on this continent.

Entering the Longhouse

Throughout the years of meeting in the Gatherings, and afterward, gkisedtanamoogk often spoke of the "longhouse." He talked about the longhouse as a structure indigenous to eastern and northern North

America, used both as a home for multiple families and as a communal meeting place for tribal council meetings. In the longhouse, families learned to be a tribe. They learned cooperation, sharing, conservation of resources, and consensual decision making. In Council Circles around the communal Fire, "No one is taller than anyone else."

gkisedtanamoogk also used the term "Longhouse" to refer to home in the largest sense of the word – our *Homeland*. This Longhouse encompasses "the life below our feet and the life above our heads – the union of Earth, Sky, and Cosmos." I began to understand that it is possible to think of all of North America as a longhouse as well. In this metaphorical Longhouse, the cultures of North America have an opportunity to relearn how to be, if not a tribe, perhaps a confederacy of tribes. We have an opportunity to share the knowledge that will allow us to better understand the needs and demands of the fragile ecosystem upon which we all depend. We have an opportunity to relearn the mutual regard, respect, and cooperation that is necessary for our survival into the next millennia.

I say "relearn" because the longhouse is also a structure that was indigenous to the peoples of modern-day England, Ireland, Scotland, Wales, Germany, France, Scandinavia – indeed all of central and eastern Europe. For those of us of European descent, the lessons learned in the longhouse are part of our heritage as well, a heritage that has been largely forgotten as we have succumbed to the hierarchical and individualistic paradigm that has dominated the Western world for the past five hundred years.

I have often imagined how life in North America would be different if, when my ancestors landed and were met by the Indigenous people of the area, they had accepted an invitation to enter the longhouse and sit in a Council Circle around the Fire. As was customary, they would have entered the longhouse by the eastern door. I imagine a Circle where the Indigenous residents and the new arrivals face one another, and my ancestor says, "Well, here we are. Can we stay?" Around that Council Fire, perhaps with a Talking Stick moving slowly around, and then around again, they would have worked out a way of coexisting that would be mutually beneficial, providing sustenance for all.

That is not how it happened. And the consequence has been unimaginable suffering and near annihilation for the Indigenous peoples of North America. There has been great loss for the rest of us as well. Certainly, we non-Natives have largely chosen to ignore, and even disparage, the invaluable knowledge and wisdom of the people native to this land. Perhaps another loss, less understood or acknowledged, has been to our souls, as we have inherited, and in various ways perpetuated, the unexamined and unreconciled violence wrought by many of our ancestors.[2]

There is still an opportunity to enter the Longhouse, to sit down together to revisit our history and to make history. Sitting together does not have to occur around a Sacred Fire, or in a traditional Council Circle. It can happen in schools, workplaces, churches, and communities; in environmental and other movements; and in the halls of government. It can happen anywhere that Native and non-Native people meet, if there is a desire and a willingness to work toward outcomes that promote justice and benefit us all.

The Gatherings of which we write occurred in the East, at the Eastern Door to this continent. Perhaps, by virtue of our mutual respect, concern, and commitment to one another, we walked through that Eastern Door and experienced, for a time, how to sit together, and how to live together, in the great Longhouse we now call North America. If that is so, may the prayers we offered to the Fire in those long-ago Circles be answered, and may our story, in sharing it with you, serve to light many Fires more.

The Seventh Generation is counting on us.

Being in the Relationship: An Afterword

Frances Hancock

I will always remember my first visit to Mi'kmaq country because I was convinced I would die before I got there. I was traveling in a car with Shirley H., who was driving, and persistent snow and black ice made the roads treacherous. Darkness fell with the snow and by mid-afternoon the daylight was gone. Shirley hugged the steering wheel and peered through a small opening in the otherwise ice-covered windshield. As the miles passed, cold penetrated my layers of clothing, making its way into my bones. We traveled at a snail's pace the length of Maine and into New Brunswick through terrain that was completely unknown to me. At every turn my South Pacific sensibilities were shocked by sensory experiences I never knew existed.

Every sensible person was off the roads, and I thought we should return to southern Maine where we both lived. But my calm companion was determined to complete the journey. She accepted the eleven-hour ride in these winter conditions and drove carefully. She pointed out cultural subtleties at work in local diners or truck stops, where we paused to rest, and told me riveting stories of other journeys she'd made to Mi'kmaq country. Shirley had made the arrangements to visit Miigam'agan and gkisedtanamoogk, and her determination told me that if we didn't push on we might have to wait some time before we could make the trek again.

I was a new Harvard graduate working for Tom's of Maine, an environmentally focused company co-founded by Tom and Kate Chappell. Tom and I had met and studied together at Harvard. On learning of his company's corporate ethic of social responsibility, I was persuaded to come to Maine to work for him. Among other tasks, I was to explore opportunities to extend their corporate donation program to include Indigenous initiatives. The first step, I advised them, was to make connections with Indigenous peoples across the bioregion and build relationships; hence the reason for the long car ride. Just when I thought we'd never arrive, Shirley cheerily announced: "Well, here we are, Burnt Church Reserve, or Esgenoôpetitj by its proper name." "Thank God we're still alive," I thought, before another idea rushed into my mind: "This woman is extraordinary."

If there was a monument to a burnt church, I had no hope of seeing it because it was pitch black outside. Soon after Shirley's announcement she carefully steered the car into a driveway lined on either side by a high wall of frozen snow. The car glided for the last few feet of its journey before coming to rest outside a two-story wooden house. Momentarily enveloped in silence, I became aware of a dull headache, vague nausea, and rock-hard shoulders. Before we could knock, the front door opened and, as we entered the quiet house, I realized I was just about as far from New Zealand as I could be. "How did I get here?" I thought, desperately wanting a bed.

Perhaps we looked the way we felt because gkisedtanamoogk grinned when he saw us. His Mohawk haircut and the etchings on his face immediately established his Indigenous identity. He wore a bear claw earring in one ear, studs in the other, and a string of beads made of bone around his neck. He was dressed much like us – in jeans and layers of upper-body garments – but wore moccasin slippers. As he embraced Shirley, his relaxed manner and smiling face suggested friendship. "Our ancestors would be impressed by your perseverance," he said, then added that Miigam'agan and the children were already asleep.

The temperature outside was well below zero but the house was warm and inviting. Since moving to Maine I had become obsessed with heating arrangements, as my life now seemed to depend on them. I scanned the open plan area and noticed a woodstove in the kitchen and another in the living room. Two woodstoves! "We also have electric heat," our host said, interpreting my startled look. Then, alluding to the purpose of my visit, gkisedtanamoogk looked at me intently and said, "The arrival of Christopher Columbus taught my ancestors to beware of strangers bearing gifts." Called to attention, I felt a stranger's discomfort. "Your ancestors were wise people," I said. He nodded. "Maybe tomorrow we could share stories of our ancestors as a way to get to know one another," I suggested. "Hmmm," he said, pausing to consider my suggestion. "That sounds good to me," he responded in that playful tone his friends enjoy, and then he led us upstairs, where freshly made beds were waiting.

That journey and late-night arrival was the beginning of a lifelong friendship, not only between two White women from opposite ends of the Earth but also between our Wabanaki hosts and me. Over the next four years I participated in the Gatherings and contributed to various collaborative projects, including a book with gkisedtanamoogk on Wabanaki spiritual traditions and justice concerns.[1] Those experiences created relationships that continue to this day and ground the hope I feel for Indigenous-settler relations and alliances for justice.

My White North American colleagues have spoken poignantly in
this book of their engagements in the Gatherings and related activities. So much of what they say resonates, especially the discomfort
and uncertainty of not knowing how to be or how to interpret relational encounters. I am also White like them. I therefore benefited
daily from that all-pervading White privilege, produced through
colonial structures and processes, that serves as a powerful shield
against the socio-economic inequalities experienced by Indigenous
peoples. Simultaneously, I was acutely aware of my distinct and different cultural location. As an Irish Pākehā (a New Zealander of
European descent),[2] I was from a distant land that was wrestling
with its own history of colonization.

Since the 1970s, Māori, the Indigenous people of New Zealand,
have been far more visible to mainstream New Zealand society
than Wabanaki are in Maine and the Maritimes. Various forces had
begun to galvanize the nation to reflect on its colonial history. In
1975 the Waitangi Tribunal, a permanent commission of inquiry,
was established to consider Māori claims of Crown breaches of the
Treaty of Waitangi, New Zealand's founding document.[3] Alongside
other efforts (such as public protests on the streets, law cases, and
treaty workshops), the tribunal's work began to raise public awareness of Māori experiences of New Zealand's colonial history, to
reinforce the status of Māori as *tangata whenua* (the people of the
land), and to challenge notions of cultural and national identity. In
the Gatherings, Wabanaki spoke of similar concerns, but Indigenous
interests were largely suppressed in White North American society.

When I was growing up, Māori were part of my everyday life. My
family moved a lot, and some of the time we lived in low-income
communities with a high proportion of Māori families. I was

exposed to Māori ways of thinking, seeing, doing, and being. My mother's closest friend was a Māori woman whose stories led me to question things I had taken for granted. As I got older I became increasingly aware of socio-economic inequalities and their impacts. My understanding of the colonial history of my country expanded during my undergraduate studies, when I began to encounter other critical Māori perspectives. I participated in treaty workshops facilitated by leading Māori activists. When South Africa's rugby team came to New Zealand in 1981, I joined thousands of New Zealanders in public demonstrations against South Africa's apartheid politics. These formative experiences challenged my thinking about the foundations of my country and exposed Pākehā myths about New Zealand having "the best race relations in the world."

Importantly, I was compelled to trace my own ancestral connections. My mother was a second-generation Pākehā but Irish to the core, so "always already" while growing up I knew who my people were and where I came from. My Irish ancestors fought for their land, their language, their culture, their faith, and their future generations. That ancestry and the journey of my great-grandmother to New Zealand in 1884 made me an Irish Pākehā. Inheriting this Irish legacy of struggle against colonial rule, encapsulated in the stories passed down to me, meant that by the time I reached my twenties I knew my life was dedicated to justice and inextricably linked to Indigenous peoples.

At Harvard I found myself in a privileged environment that largely excluded First Nations people. Also, Indigenous thought and concerns rarely registered in the classes I took on theology, ethics, and critical theory. The White North American imagination I encountered was grappling with a traumatic history of African slavery and seemed almost oblivious to or in denial of Indigenous histories, realities, and concerns. Finding my way to "Indian Country" after graduation led me home to myself. Participating in the Gatherings not only instilled a more global awareness of Indigenous-settler issues but also strengthened my cultural identity as well as my ethical and political commitments.

From time to time, between Gatherings, I visited Wabanaki communities (often with Shirley H. or JoAnn, or by myself). I recall one mid-winter's morning at Esgenoôpetitj when the temperature outside plummeted to minus thirty degrees. "Aren't your feet cold?" I exclaimed, when 'tjalenasi swept into Miigam'agan's home wearing thin cloth sneakers, known as sandshoes in the sunny South Pacific when I was growing up. "Yeah!" she said, her tone alerting me to my insensitivity; economic inequalities allowed me to have snow boots but prevented her from buying them.

How often did I say (or do) such stupid things – unaware, uninformed, unwise, ridiculous, ignorant, thoughtless, and tactless things – but still, 'tjalenasi and the Wabanaki contributors to this book welcomed, respected, and loved me. Generous and forgiving, their love only ever asked this of me: "Bestow [yourself] to silence, or a severer listening," adapting Adrienne Rich's words.[4] Sometime later Miigam'agan informed me of 'tjalenasi's passing; the Canadian health system had failed to diagnosis her life-threatening illness. "Oh my God," I said, confronted by an enormous loss. 'tjalenasi was not only a beautiful person and loving mother but also an adept Mi'kmaq language speaker and teacher. "That's how it is in Indian Country," Miigam'agan replied, matter-of-factly.

Eventually I returned to New Zealand, and nearly thirty years later I remain deeply engaged in those matters that called me to attention the first time I went to Esgenoôpetitj. In my fifties I completed a doctorate in relational ethics at Te Puna Wānanga, the School of Māori and Indigenous Education, at the University of Auckland.[5] Simultaneously I had been working alongside local Māori and their allies to advance the now nationally and internationally recognized SOUL (Save Our Unique Landscape) Campaign to #ProtectIhumātao.[6] This campaign seeks to protect a rare cultural heritage landscape a few miles from where I live and a stone's throw from Auckland International Airport.

Ihumātao is one of the places where Polynesians first settled in New Zealand more than seven hundred years ago and is a site of historical, cultural, archaeological, and geological significance. In 1863 the colonial government confiscated more than one thousand acres from the local iwi (Māori tribes) because they refused to swear allegiance to the British Crown. Local iwi were evicted from their lands and exiled. In 1867, the colonial government "granted" some of this land to a settler farming family whose descendants sold it in December 2016 for around twenty million dollars to a transnational corporation planning to build 480 high-cost houses, made possible through fast-tracked, developer-friendly legislation. The issue is complex,[7] but the implications are not. "If this development goes ahead, it will pour salt in the wound of the original confiscation," I said to the Social Services Select Committee at Parliament in April 2016.

Fast forward to July 23, 2019, when dozens of police arrived with corporate executives to evict a small group of "land protectors" they called "squatters." "Frances, come back in four years and see the community we build here," the chief executive of the company said to me. "A community already exists here," I replied, before being escorted off the *whenua* (land) by two policemen. Within days, thousands of campaign supporters had arrived, along with national and international media.[8] Since then, land protectors have refused to leave, and the struggle for justice continues, marked by their extraordinary witness.[9] In February 2020, the Campaign to #ProtectIhumātao entered its sixth year, but this shameful debacle has been going on for nearly 160 years. "Enough is enough," say local Māori and their allies, and many other New Zealanders agree.

Contributing to the campaign since its beginning, I have often reflected on the unrelenting struggle for justice of Wabanaki peoples over the past five hundred years. It matters hugely that on the other side of the world people I know through the Gatherings – Wabanaki and their allies – care about the injustice we are battling at Ihumātao and stand with us. Their prayerful support, moral courage, and long-standing witness of respectful engagement are a sustaining force for the SOUL Campaign. I received this e-mail from Miigam'agan while writing this afterword and helping to draft questions to Parliament concerning Ihumātao: "i can see more clearly how we become family ... being there for each other to the end. You are very much my family and i so love and respect you for your courage and honesty and in your whole being. And now you are standing for love (courage for justice) again in your area. I will continue to make prayer offerings to all of you in new zealand"[10] (lower case intentional). I believe that, like the relationships embodied in this book, the relationships forged through the SOUL Campaign will live forever. I also believe these relationships will become more deeply what they already are: a powerful source of hope for future generations, a hope that enacts a vision of relational justice. This book embodies and reassures that hope.

Over the past twelve years I have also walked alongside this evolving book project, noticing from afar that its contributors are still striving to enact the politics and ethics of relational justice that brought us all together decades ago. After a thirty-year gestation this book, by its very materialization, witnesses enduring, honest, and mutually beneficial relationships across a deeply conflicted and troubled hyphen: the Indigenous-settler divide.[11] How did the relationships in this book persist over so many years and, in my case, across a great ocean? "It comes down to love or something like that," suggests Professor Alison Jones, a Pākehā scholar working in the field of Indigenous-settler relations.[12] Recalling her words leads me now to reflect more particularly on the significance of the Gatherings for Indigenous-settler relations, drawing on scholarship in relational ethics. In discussing the following insights I am reminded, too, of something constantly reinforced around the Fire all those years ago – that my views are ever-particular as I look through a settler/Pākehā lens, and ever-expanding as I continue to embrace an "openness to exchange."[13]

The first insight is that this book enacts a politics of hope at a time in history when relational divides are proliferating, the survival and well-being of Indigenous peoples remain at stake, and the Earth's ecology is threatened by unethical or thoughtless human action. Here, Wabanaki Elders and leaders, alongside longstanding allies, tell stories that illuminate the absolute importance of productive cross-cultural engagement and relational integrity as a critical means to ensure human, cultural, and planetary survival. The stories contained here witness an exchange that made enduring relationships possible between particular individuals, whose peoples embody radically different ways of being, thinking, living, and doing.

Second, that "we are radically uncommon to each other, diverse in existence and therefore unique,"[14] calls for the kind of ongoing engagement discussed in this book, which Jones describes as "being in the relationship."[15] Sitting around the Fire, season after season, year after year, and visiting one another in between and since then, allowed for "learning through the skin."[16] Such learning can only arise *in relationship* – between persons/peoples, in situ/in specific contexts and, as it were, on the ground. Jones suggests that being in the relationship requires much more than a culturally sensitive approach; it demands a personal quality not directly teachable, but developed through an openness to being taught by experience, a tolerance for uncertainty, and an understanding of power.[17]

A third insight is that so often learning arises through "emotional collisions."[18] While emotional collisions were inevitable and at times disruptive (Shirley Bowen's story provides one example), they also marked the capacity of the Gatherings to foster learning across a troubled divide and become "productive sites of social justice dialogue."[19] This book reinforces that, for non-Natives, the Gatherings provided an opportunity to learn "from" rather than learn "about" Indigenous experiences and perspectives, a subtle but powerful distinction that disrupts a colonial legacy of objectifying Indigenous peoples.[20] Writing in an Australian context, McAllan reinforces this point, observing that when engaging with Aboriginal peoples, settlers confront and must negotiate their own "preconceptions regarding indigeneity" and "unrecognized privilege."[21]

Reading this book through the lens of relational ethics reinforces a fourth insight, noted by the Māori educational philosopher Te Kawehau Hoskins: that face-to-face embodied relations engender different ethical response-abilities.[22] Hoskins distinguishes these different response-abilities as settler responsiveness to Indigenous political interests (for example, Wesley's role as an ally during the stand-off in Miigam'agan's and Barb's community of Esgenoôpetitj over fishing rights) and Indigenous generosity toward settler learning (for example, Wayne's stories of continuing to engage with non-Natives seeking to learn, despite the discomfort he experienced when encountering their misguided assumptions). Looking back, the Gatherings were a genuine attempt to disrupt colonial relations of domination in favor of "relations of co-existence" that foster these particular response-abilities.[23]

A fifth critical insight is that "a complex reciprocity"[24] is needed for Indigenous-settler relationships to thrive. For a complex reciprocity to work, recognizing and valuing "otherness" and "difference" must become conditions for justice, suggests Canadian educational philosopher Sharon Todd, because these things inevitably give rise to the challenges, difficulties, and disagreements in relationships.[25] If we care about justice, she argues, then those things that create potential for disharmony, suffering, and violence in relationship warrant our full attention. She suggests that only by creating space for uncertainty and genuine engagement are new possibilities for justice likely to emerge. Here I am reminded of the work of Māori academic Hine Waitere, who adds that "the call to relationship" is also "a call to action."[26]

Perhaps a more obvious insight is that *how this book was made* is a case example of how settlers can work collaboratively with Indigenous colleagues. Because we settlers often struggle to engage productively with Indigenous colleagues and rarely, in my experience, go to the lengths that Shirley H. has in this book project, I want to reflect on her relational approach from a Pākehā perspective. For years now, I've witnessed Shirley H. striving to enact what the educational theorist Leigh Patel describes as a "decolonial praxis."[27] Put simply, she has exercised extraordinary care and diligence while co-researching and writing this book. She made herself answerable to contributors for the countless decisions required in creating a collaborative text, especially one tackling a hugely challenging subject – in this case, how do we (Indigenous peoples and settlers) live together?[28] Always, she put the interests of Indigenous contributors front and center. She sought to ensure that the book not only warranted their attention and contributions but also would help to advance their deeply held concerns. Māori academic Linda Tuhiwai Smith reinforces the importance of these and other ethical and political imperatives in her groundbreaking book on decolonizing methodologies.[29]

Another insight now occurs to me – the importance of humility. Māori and Pākehā scholars suggest that humility is a crucial quality for settlers seeking to engage productively with Indigenous peoples.[30] Notwithstanding Shirley's research and writerly talents, it is her humility, I believe, that has consistently defined her leadership in this relationship-building effort over so many years and been instrumental in this book project. She listens to understand, she acts on advice, and she keeps going until everyone agrees enough has been said. These qualities engender trust. When I sat at Wayne's kitchen table in November 2015 he summed up neatly what I am trying to say here in so many words. He said, "What I now care about the most is passing on the Passamaquoddy language and finishing this book ... Shirley can figure out the final changes; we trust her. She'll call when she needs to."

This book (the book itself, its deeply moving testimonies, and how it was made) symbolizes rich possibilities for Indigenous-settler relationships. It reinforces, as Hoskins argues, that "context and history, relationships and commitments *do matter* and can inform and shape the taking of political decisions."[31] Because these things *do matter*, Hoskins (a Māori scholar) asked Alison Jones to co-edit a journal on

Kaupapa Māori scholarship (Māori ideas, theories, and approaches) with her. Despite criticism, Hoskins argued that "*who* Alison is, exceeds *what* she is (i.e., a Pākehā middle-class professor)."[32] Years of working together had created an "intimacy of engagement"[33] – a friendship – that could only come about by relating respectfully to one another. Reflecting on Indigenous-settler relations, Jones further highlights what seems to matter most in the relationship: the "particular attitude," "orientation," "heart," "spirit," "mind" or, put simply, "the way a person *is*." My doctoral research reinforces that "who a person is" and "the way a person is"[34] can transform challenges in Indigenous-settler relations into meaningful engagements that are "at once always already political, profoundly ethical, deeply human, powerfully pedagogical, and that cultivate a way of life that, for some, is spiritual."[35]

As pedagogical (teaching and learning) engagements, the Gatherings encouraged Indigenous and settler participants to "work the hyphen"[36] in their relations with one another and in doing so made relational justice momentarily possible. In those moments – always substantive but inevitably fleeting – those of us around the Fire demonstrated what a bicultural reality could look like and perhaps collectively embodied a more just society as an example for others. Critically, the Gatherings cultivated in participants the political will to commit to an ongoing exchange. In Australia, the Mutitjulu Elder Bob Randall, when considering how to "open up relations" between settlers and Aboriginals, proposed that the two peoples "meet each other" and learn "oursness" in place of "mineness" as "we share this land together."[37]

Finally, looking back on my years in North America, I now see that I became immersed in two very different educational experiences: first at Harvard, in the lecture halls of one of the world's most prestigious universities; and later in gatherings of Wabanaki people and their White North American allies, which were held in various settings in Maine and the Maritimes. At Harvard I entered a realm of knowledge production that was deemed superior to others and defined by both age-old and newly created academic and professional disciplines. I encountered another realm of knowledge making in Wabanaki territories, however – a realm that was not only ancient and disciplined but also relational, holistic, embodied, co-produced and passed on within Wabanaki families, communities, and nations.

While both experiences were transformative, the relationships described in this book remain forever in my heart. Being with Wabanaki colleagues in a landscape and climate that were foreign to me but that they knew intimately and loved, I began to glimpse another way to see. I was reminded of my earlier engagements with Māori and became increasingly aware of the call to return home. After seven years in North America that call became an urgent longing. Sensing this longing, a Mi'kmaq man I knew, and whose kindness I appreciated, gently observed one day, "Frances, every day is a good day to go home." Ultimately that's where the Gatherings led me.

Thirty years later, I find myself at home in Aotearoa New Zealand, doing the work of justice at Ihumātao alongside another group of Indigenous people whom I have come to deeply respect and love. I think it is so important to somehow find the will, strength, and courage to persevere in enacting those ethical-political commitments that come to define your life. That can only happen because of relationships, and the relationships that seem to matter so much are the ones that endure over time and relish difference.

I owe each contributor to this book a debt of gratitude for all they taught me years ago when we sat around the Fire together and for the lessons I have learned over the past twelve years while contributing to this book project. "How have these particular relationships survived across time and a great ocean?" I asked earlier. Alison Jones's idea is worth repeating: "It comes down to love or something like that." Love, I learned at Harvard Divinity School and later experienced in the Gatherings, is another name for being in right relation, which is another name for justice.

 *Frances Hancock is based at the University of Auckland, where she is an honorary academic in Te Puna Wānanga, the School of Māori and Indigenous Education in the Faculty of Education and Social Work, as well as a research fellow for the Social Futures Research Hub in the Faculty of Arts. As an engagement specialist, writer, and researcher, Frances also undertakes commissioned assignments with diverse communities and organizations.*

Appendix: How This Book Came to Be

The Gatherings ended in 1993. Since that time paths have diverged, careers were launched, babies were born, perspectives shifted. Some of us lost touch, of course, but for many of us our friendships remained and deepened. In some cases, our values led us to support the same causes; in others, our work continued to bring us together.

The idea for this book originated in 2008 in conversations between Frances Hancock, the author of our afterword, and myself. Since returning to New Zealand in the 1990s, Frances has worked as a community developer, researcher, and writer. In numerous assignments with Māori, the Indigenous people of New Zealand, she has adopted a "co-research" approach that positions contributors as the authorities on their experiences; as such, their involvement in projects is more as co-authors.

As thoughts for the project began to take shape, Frances offered to return to Maine to co-research and write the book. We contacted gkisedtanamoogk, Miigam'agan, and Wayne to share the idea, which they enthusiastically supported, and the five of us became the planning group to guide the process. From the beginning, our intention was for all contributors to actively co-author their text and to have maximum involvement in the creation and development of the manuscript. Ultimately, we hoped to create an enduring document of our experience, one that would support positive change in Native/non-Native relations.

So began a three-year period during which we approached other Gathering participants and invited their participation, sought financial support for the project, discussed ethical responsibilities, and began organizing a reunion and planning meeting for contributors to be held at Wayne's home in 2011. Just as Frances was preparing to travel to Maine for this initial meeting, a medical procedure rendered her unable to travel for the foreseeable future.

The planning group agreed that the project must go on but, unavoidably, roles had to shift. Feeling daunted, but with everyone's encouragement and Frances's offer to act as a mentor, I became the co-researcher and writer. The group proceeded with our first meeting – a "reunion Gathering" held over a weekend just as our original Gatherings had been – and eight of us attended. Everyone agreed that the experience of the Gatherings had profoundly changed our lives, and that we wanted to share the lessons we had learned in our efforts to reach out to one another.

At that first meeting, we decided that all participants would have full authorial rights in relation to their contributions, and the planning group would take responsibility for the book as a whole. We identified several additional individuals whom we wanted to interview, bringing the total to fourteen in all. In the months to follow, I traveled over a thousand miles – several times in partnership with Miigam'agan, once with gkisedtanamoogk – from Halifax, Nova Scotia, to Cape Cod, Massachusetts, to record our conversations. Once home, I carefully transcribed each conversation and returned it to the contributor, making sure that their knowledge and insights were recorded as they wished, and making edits with their direction and approval.

Once all participants had reviewed their written transcripts, a second reunion/planning weekend was held in 2013 at Dana's home. There, we conceptualized the structure of the book, including the idea of presenting our stories as a Talking Circle. We also discussed emerging themes in our "lessons learned" and agreed on those offered as our Giveaway Blanket.

While writing the book, I gathered additional information in subsequent visits or in phone conversations with contributors, as well as doing other research. After eighteen months, the first draft of the manuscript was completed, drawing on the edited conversations and other sources while maintaining close contact with the planning group.

The manuscript was sent to all contributors for their review and, in the fall of 2015, Frances returned to Maine and together we visited each contributor except for Betty, who gave her response by phone. Our deep conversations with each individual reinforced the co-authorship of the book. We diligently recorded their feedback and recommendations in relation to their personal stories and to the book as a whole. During her extended visit, Frances generously edited the manuscript. I then spent the following five months reworking the first draft and including the feedback we received.

Another review by contributors followed in the summer of 2016. Each contributor, or their nearest relative in the case of our now-deceased members, had an opportunity to suggest any final edits. They subsequently approved the book's content and their representation in it. Eight years after we began this project together the possibility of publication was finally on the horizon, and the search was on to find a proper home.

We are deeply grateful to the University of Toronto Press for being that home, and for recognizing and believing in the contribution and implications of the experiences contained in this book.

Notes

Notes on Terminology

1 Elly Haney, *The Great Commandment: A Theology of Resistance and Transformation* (Cleveland: Pilgrim Press, 1998), 2.

Allies, Friends, Family

1 The concept of mutuality between groups of unequal power and privilege is thoroughly explored in relational-cultural theory, first expressed by Jean Baker Miller in her 1976 book *Toward a New Psychology of Women* and further developed by researchers at the Stone Center at Wellesley College. More information is available from the Jean Baker Miller Training Institute, accessed May 6, 2020, https://www .wcwonline.org/JBMTI-Site/the-development-of-relational-cultural-theory.

2 Centers for Disease Control and Prevention, *Fact Sheet – CDC Health Disparities and Inequalities Report – U.S., 2011*, accessed May 5, 2020, https://www.cdc.gov /minorityhealth/chdir/2011/factsheet.pdf; Saman Khan, "Aboriginal Mental Health: The Statistical Reality," *Heretohelp*, accessed May 5, 2020, http://www.heretohelp.bc .ca/visions/aboriginal-people-vol5/aboriginal-mental-health-the-statistical-reality.

How We Got Here

1 "*Dum diversas*," Doctrine of Discovery, accessed May 5, 2020, https:// doctrineofdiscovery.org/dum-diversas/.

2 "The Bull *Romanus pontifex*," Doctrine of Discovery, para. 4, accessed May 5, 2020, https://doctrineofdiscovery.org/the-bull-romanus-pontifex-nicholas-v/.

3 *Inter caetera*, Doctrine of Discovery, lines 3–7, accessed May 5, 2020, www.doctrineofdiscovery.org.

4 Elizabeth Prine Pauls, "Native American: Indigenous Peoples of Canada and the United States," section "North America and Europe circa 1492," *Encyclopaedia*

Britannica, accessed May 5, 2020, http://www.britannica.com/topic/Native
-American/Native-American-history#toc273135.

5   gkisedtanamoogk, "Native American Spirituality," lecture and public workshop
delivered at Chaplaincy Institute of Maine (ChIME), Portland, January 3, 2015.

6   Ker Than, "Massive Population Drop Found for Native Americans, DNA Shows,"
National Geographic News, December 5, 2011, http://news.nationalgeographic.com
/news/2011/12/111205-native-americans-europeans-population-dna-genetics-science/.

7   John Toland, *Adolf Hitler: The Definitive Biography*, vol. 2 (New York: Anchor
Books, 1976), 802.

8   Kevin Gover, "Nation to Nation: Treaties between the United States and American
Indian Nations," *American Indian* 15, no. 2 (Summer/Fall 2014), http://www
.americanindianmagazine.org/story/nation-nation?page=show.

9   U.S. Constitution, article VI, clause 2.

10   The Constitution Act, 1982, Schedule B to the Canada Act 1982, part 1, section 25.

11   Kevin Gover, "Nation to Nation."

12   "Study on Treaties, Agreements and Other Constructive Arrangements between
States and Indigenous Populations," July 1997, reported to the UN for the
"Working Group on Indigenous Peoples," https://www1.umn.edu/humanrts/demo
/TreatiesStatesIndigenousPopulations_Martinez.pdf.

13   Alex M. Cameron, *Power without Law: The Supreme Court of Canada, the
Marshall Decisions, and the Failure of Judicial Activism* (Montreal and Kingston:
McGill-Queen's University Press, 2009), 3.

14   Andrea May Simpson and Charlie Greg Sark, "Justice Recognized – Justice
Denied: The State of Aboriginal Treaty Rights in Canada," *Cultural Survival*,
June 2001, http://www.culturalsurvival.org/ourpublications/csq/article/justice
-recognized-justice-denied-the-state-aboriginal-treaty-rights-can.

15   Sand2300, "The Burnt Church Crisis," *Criminalizing Dissent* (blog), October 16,
2014, 2020, https://criminalizingdissent.wordpress.com/2014/10/16/the-burnt
-church-crisis/.

16   Letter from Hilary C. Tompkins, solicitor, US Department of the Interior, to Avi S.
Garbow, general counsel, US Environmental Protection Agency, January 30, 2015,
https://www.mitsc.org/federal-regulatory-decision, p. 3.

17   Judy Harrison, "Penobscots Lose Appeal over Policing River," *Bangor Daily News*,
June 30, 2017.

18   Colin Woodard, "Unsettled: The Passamaquoddy's Land Claims Case Takes
Shape," *Portland Press Herald*, July 5, 2014, http://www.pressherald.com/2014/07
/05/the-passamaquoddys-land-claim-case-takes-shape/.

19   Leadership Conference of Women Religious, "LCWR Assembly Resolution 2014
Doctrine of Discovery," accessed May 5, 2020, https://lcwr.org/sites/default/files
/resolutions/attachments/dod_resolution_2014.pdf.

20 Robert Coulter, "A Powerful Affirmation of Our Rights," in *United Nations Declaration on the Rights of Indigenous Peoples* (booklet) (Washington, DC: Indian Law Resource Center, 2012), 1.
21 Ibid.
22 Maria L. Girouard, "The Original Meaning and Intent of the Maine Indian Land Claims: Penobscot Perspectives" (master's thesis, University of Maine, 2012), 6.
23 Ibid.
24 Gale Courey Toensing, "Mixed Reviews on United Nations Declaration on the Rights of Indigenous Peoples' Progress," *Indian Country Today*, May 8, 2012, http://indiancountrytodaymedianetwork.com/2012/05/08/mixed-reviews-united -nations-declaration-rights-indigenous-peoples-progress-109471.
25 Christine Hauser, "Maine Just Banned Native American Mascots. It's a Movement That's Inching Forward," *New York Times*, May 22, 2019, https://www.nytimes.com /2019/05/22/us/native-american-sports-logos.html.
26 Jamie Ehrlich, "Maine Becomes the Latest State to Replace Columbus Day with Indigenous Peoples' Day," CNN, April 26, 2019, https://www.cnn.com/2019/04/26 /politics/maine-indigenous-peoples-day-columbus-day/index.html.
27 Donna Loring, "The Dark Ages of Education and a New Hope: Teaching Native American History in Maine Schools," *New England Journal of Higher Education* 26, no. 1 (Summer 2009), http://www.nebhe.org/info/journal/issues/NEJHE _Summer09.pdf.
28 Catherine Gewertz, "Maine Gov. Signs Order Proclaiming Local Control over Standards," *Education Week*, September 5, 2013, http://blogs.edweek.org/edweek /state_edwatch/2013/09/maine_gov_signs_order_proclaiming_local_control _over_standards.html.
29 Kristie Littlefield, social studies specialist, Maine Department of Education, interview by author, June 5, 2015. The statement's continued accuracy was confirmed in an interview with current social studies specialist Joe Schmidt on January 27, 2020.
30 Donna Loring, e-mail to Shirley Hager, July 6, 2017.
31 Maine-Wabanaki REACH (website), accessed May 5, 2020, http://www .mainewabanakireach.org/about. Current data are provided by REACH community organizer Barbara Kates in an e-mail to Shirley Hager, January 24, 2020.
32 Truth and Reconciliation Commission of Canada, *Canada's Residential Schools: Reconciliation*, Vol. 6 of *The Final Report of the Truth and Reconciliation Commission of Canada*, 2015, 128, http://nctr.ca/assets/reports/Final%20Reports /Volume_6_Reconciliation_English_Web.pdf.
33 "Truth and Reconciliation Centre in Winnipeg to Get $10M from Feds," CBC News, December 15, 2016, https://www.cbc.ca/news/canada/manitoba/trc -centre-winnipeg-1.3898651.

34   Kaila Johnston, acting manager for education, outreach and public programs, National Centre for Truth and Reconciliation, interview by author, January 31, 2020.

35   Truth and Reconciliation Commission of Canada, *Canada's Residential Schools: Reconciliation*, 223–41.

36   Insiya Mankani, "Canada Should Back Up Words with Action on Indigenous Rights," Human Rights Watch, June 21, 2019, https://www.hrw.org/news/2019/06/21/canada-should-back-words-action-indigenous-rights#.

37   Circles for Reconciliation (website), accessed May 5, 2020, https://circlesforreconciliation.ca/.

38   Maine Indian Claims Settlement Act of 1980, Public Law 96-420-Oct. 10, 1980, sec. 1735(b).

39   "Joint Resolution to Support the Development of Mutually Beneficial Solutions to the Conflicts Arising from the Interpretation of An Act to Implement the Maine Indian Claims Settlement and the Federal Maine Indian Claims Settlement Act of 1980," SP 0622, LR 2507, 129th Maine Legislature.

40   Mankani, "Canada Should Back Up Words."

41   Walter R. Echo-Hawk, *In the Light of Justice: The Rise of Human Rights in Native America* (Golden, CO: Fulcrum, 2013), 257.

How It Could Be Different

1   See the documentary *The Penobscot: Ancestral River, Contested Territory*, directed by Maria Girouard and Meredith DeFrancesco (2015; Indian Island, Penobscot Nation: Sunlight Media Collective), DVD and at http://www.sunlightmediacollective.org/.

2   See Walter R. Echo-Hawk, *In the Light of Justice: The Rise of Human Rights in Native America* (Golden, CO: Fulcrum, 2013), 249–79, for a comprehensive argument on the importance of apology, atonement, healing, and reconciliation for the perpetrators as well as the victims of violence.

Being in the Relationship: An Afterword

1   gkisedtanamoogk and Frances Hancosssck, *Anoqcou* (Bath, ME: Astarte Shell Press, 1993).

2   The English translation of Māori concepts provides, at best, simplified understandings. These Māori concepts are rich in meaning and express *something like* but much more than their English counterparts.

3   New Zealand Ministry of Justice, *The Waitangi Tribunal*, accessed May 5, 2020, https://waitangitribunal.govt.nz/.

4   Adrienne Rich, "Transcendental Etude," in *The Dream of a Common Language* (New York: W.W. Norton, 1978), 75.

5   Frances Hancock, "Becoming Just, Doing Justice: The Ethics and Politics of Māori-Pākehā Relations" (PhD diss., University of Auckland, 2018).

6   "SOUL/Save Our Unique Landscape: Ihumātao," accessed May 5, 2020, https://www.protectihumatao.com/.

7   T. McCreanor, F. Hancock, and N. Short, "The Mounting Crisis at Ihumātao: A High Cost Special Housing Area or a Cultural Heritage Landscape for Future Generations," *Counterfutures: Left Thought and Practice Aotearoa* no. 6 (2018): 139–48.

8   Q. Matata-Sipu and F. Hancock, "Rising Up in the Spirit of Justice," *Newsroom*, July 25, 2019, https://www.newsroom.co.nz/2019/07/25/699773/rising-up-in-the-spirit-of-justice.

9   F. Hancock, "Ihumātao: A Pākehā Ally's Perspective," *Newsroom*, January 21, 2020, https://www.newsroom.co.nz/@ideasroom/2020/01/21/995997/ihumatao-a-pakeha-allys-perspective.

10 Miigam'agan, e-mail message to Frances Hancock, August 31, 2016.

11 See, for example, Alison Jones, "Dangerous Liaisons: Pākehā, kaupapa Māori and Educational Research," *New Zealand Journal of Educational Studies* 47, no. 2 (2012): 100–12.

12 Professor Alison Jones, in discussion with Frances Hancock, March 2015.

13 Sharon Todd, *Towards an Imperfect Education: Facing Humanity, Rethinking Cosmopolitanism* (Boulder, CO: Paradigm, 2009), 155.

14 Ibid., 152.

15 Jones, "Dangerous Liaisons," 108.

16 Ibid., 108.

17 Ibid., 108–9.

18 Candace Kuby, "'Ok This Is Hard': Doing Emotions in Social Justice Dialogue," *Education, Citizenship and Social Justice* 8, no. 1 (2013): 29–42.

19 Ibid., 29–30.

20 Alison Jones with Kuni Jenkins, "Rethinking Collaboration: Working the Indigene-Colonizer Hyphen," in *Handbook of Critical and Indigenous Methodologies,* ed. Norman Denzin, Yvonna Lincoln, and Linda Tuhiwai Smith (Los Angeles: Sage, 2008), 471. See also Te Kawehau Hoskins, "Māori and Levinas: Kanohi Ki Te Kanohi for an Ethical Politics" (PhD diss., University of Auckland, 2010), 190–2.

21 Fiona McAllan, *Speaking-Writing With: Aboriginal and Settler Interrelations* (Newcastle upon Tyne, UK: Cambridge Scholars Publishing, 2013), 48.

22 Hoskins, "Māori and Levinas," 143–5.

23 Avril Bell, *Relating Indigenous and Settler Identities: Beyond Domination* (Basingstoke, UK: Palgrave Macmillian, 2014), 192.

24 Alison Jones and Kuni Jenkins, "Invitation and Refusal: A Reading of the Beginning of Schooling in Aotearoa New Zealand," *History of Education* 37, no. 2 (2008): 187.

25   Todd, *Towards an Imperfect Education*, 152.
26   Hine Waitere, "Cultural Leadership: Creating Futures Our Ancestors Can Walk In with Our Children," *Journal of Educational Leadership, Policy and Practice* 23, no. 2 (2008): 45.
27   Leigh Patel, *Decolonizing Educational Research* (New York: Routledge, 2016), 71.
28   Ibid., 73. Patel suggests "answerability" as a concept to think with and enact when seeking to practice decolonizing educational research.
29   Linda Tuhiwai Smith, *Decolonizing Methodologies: Research and Indigenous Peoples* (London: Zed Books/Dunedin, NZ: University of Otago Press, 1999).
30   Rose Yukich and Te Kawehau Hoskins, "Responsibility and the Other: Cross-Cultural Engagement in the Narratives of Three School Leaders," *Journal of Systemic Therapies* 30, no. 3 (2011): 65–7; see also Alison Jones, "Dangerous Liaisons," 107.
31   Te Kawehau Hoskins and Alison Jones, "Introduction," *New Zealand Journal of Educational Studies* 47, no. 2 (2012): 5, italics in the original.
32   Ibid.
33   Alison Jones and Kuni Jenkins, *Words between Us – He Kōrero: First Māori-Pākehā Conversations on Paper* (Wellington, NZ: Huia, 2011), 11.
34   Jones, "Dangerous Liaisons," 108.
35   Frances Hancock, "Becoming Just, Doing Justice," 260.
36   Jones with Jenkins, "Rethinking Collaboration," 471–86.
37   Bob Randall, quoted in McAllan, *Speaking-Writing With*, 48.

Suggested Resources

The following lists are not exhaustive. Rather, they are a compilation of materials suggested by contributors to this book and/or recommended by various ally organizations. Many thanks to Elizabeth Koopman, Diane Oltarzewski, and Arla Patch, all Quakers involved in ally education, for identifying and sharing a number of these resources.

BOOKS, ARTICLES, GOVERNMENTAL REPORTS

How We Got Here: Indigenous-Settler History and the Doctrine of Discovery

Awkwesasne Notes, Mohawk Nation (with Chief Oren Lyons, John Mohawk, and Jose Barreiro). *Basic Call to Consciousness.* Summertown, TN: Native Voices, 2005.

Berger, Thomas. *A Long and Terrible Shadow: White Values, Native Rights in the Americas 1492–1992.* Vancouver: Douglas and McIntyre, 1992.

Bigelow, Bill, and Rob Peterson, eds. *Rethinking Columbus: The Next 500 Years.* Milwaukee: Rethinking Schools, 2003.

Brown, Dee. *Bury My Heart at Wounded Knee.* 4th ed. New York: Owl Books, 2007.

Chandler, Sarah. "The Never Broken Treaty? Quaker Witness and Testimony on Aboriginal Title and Rights: What Cans't Thou Say?" Canadian Friends Service Committee, 2001. Accessed May 5, 2020. http://quakerservice.ca/wp-content/uploads/2011/10/The-Never-Broken-Treaty-copy.pdf.

Dunbar-Ortiz, Roxanne. *An Indigenous Peoples' History of the United States*. Boston: Beacon, 2014.

Harjo, Suzan S., ed. *Nation to Nation: Treaties between the US and American Indian Nations*. Washington, DC: Smithsonian Books, 2014.

Johansen, Bruce. *Enduring Legacies: Native American Treaties and Contemporary Controversies*. Westport, CT: Praeger, 2004.

Loring, Donna M. *In the Shadow of the Eagle: A Tribal Representative in Maine*. Gardiner, ME: Tilbury House, 2008.

Lyons, Oren, John Mohawk, Vine Deloria, Jr., et al. *Exiled in the Land of the Free: Democracy, Indian Nations and the U.S. Constitution*. Santa Fe: Clear Light Publications, 1992.

Miller, Robert J. *Native America, Discovered and Conquered: Thomas Jefferson, Lewis and Clark, and Manifest Destiny*. Westport, CT: Praeger, 2006.

Mohawk, John C. *Utopian Legacies: A History of Conquest and Oppression in the Western World*. Santa Fe: Clear Light Publications, 2000.

Newcomb, Steven T. *Pagans in the Promised Land: Decoding the Doctrine of Christian Discovery*. Golden, CO: Fulcrum, 2008.

Tinker, George E. *American Indian Liberation: A Theology of Sovereignty*. Maryknoll, NY: Orbis Books, 2008.

Treuer, David. *The Heartbeat of Wounded Knee: Native America from 1890 to the Present*. New York: Riverhead Books, 2019.

Weatherford, Jack M. *Indian Givers: How the Indians of the Americas Transformed the World*. New York: Fawcett Books, 1988.

An Indigenous Worldview

Dei, G.J. *Indigenous Philosophies and Critical Education: A Reader.* New York: Peter Lang, 2011.

Deloria, Vine, Jr. *God Is Red: A Native View of Religion.* Golden, CO: Fulcrum, 1973.

gkisedtanamoogk and Frances Hancock. *Anoqcou: Ceremony Is Life Itself.* Bath, ME: Astarte Shell Press, 1993.

Grande, S. "American Indian Geographies of Identity and Power: At the Crossroads of Indigena and Mestizaje." *Harvard Educational Review* 70, no. 4 (2000): 467–99.

Owings, Alison. *Indian Voices: Listening to Native Americans*. New Brunswick, NJ/London: Rutgers University Press, 2011.

Schaefer, Carol. *Grandmothers Counsel the World*. Boston: Trumpeter Books, 2006.

Senier, Siobhan. *Dawnland Voices: An Anthology of Indigenous Writing from New England*. Lincoln: University of Nebraska Press, 2014.

How It Could Be Different: Reaching across the Cultural Divide, Examining Racism and White Privilege, Becoming Allies, a Future Decolonized

Altvater, Denise, Maria Girouard, Arla Patch, and Elizabeth Koopman. "Peace Is Possible." *Friends Journal*, February 1, 2016. http://www.friendsjournal.org/peace-is-possible/.

Bell, Avril. *Relating Indigenous and Settler Identities: Beyond Domination*. Basingstoke, UK: Palgrave Macmillian, 2014.

Bloom, Liza M., and Berkley Carnine. "Towards Decolonization and Settler Responsibility: Reflections on a Decade of Indigenous Solidarity Organizing." *Counterpunch*, October 3, 2016. https:// · www.counterpunch.org/2016/10/03/towards-decolonization-and -settler-responsibility-reflections-on-a-decade-of-indigenous -solidarity-organizing/.

Davis, Lynne, ed. *Alliances: Re/Envisioning Indigenous-non-Indigenous Relationships*. Toronto: University of Toronto Press, 2010.

Deloria, Philip J. *Playing Indian*. New Haven, NJ: Yale University Press, 1998.

Echo-Hawk, Walter R. *In the Light of Justice: The Rise of Human Rights in Native America*. Golden, CO: Fulcrum, 2013.

Heinrichs, Steve, ed. *Buffalo Shout, Salmon Cry: Conversations on Creation, Land Justice and Life Together*. Waterloo, ON/ Harrisonburg, VA: Herald, 2013.

Heinrichs, Steve, ed. *Wrongs to Rights: How Churches Can Engage the United Nations Declaration on the Rights of Indigenous Peoples*. Winnipeg: Mennonite Church Canada, 2016.

Irving, Debby. *Waking Up White: And Finding Myself in the Story of Race*. Cambridge, MA: Elephant Room Press, 2014.

Jones, Alison, with Kuni Jenkins. "Rethinking Collaboration: Working the Indigene-Colonizer Hyphen." In *Handbook of Critical and Indigenous Methodologies*, edited by Norman Denzin, Yvonna Lincoln, and Linda Tuhiwai Smith, 471–86. Los Angeles: Sage, 2008.

Kimmerer, Robin Wall. *Braiding Sweetgrass: Indigenous Wisdom, Scientific Knowledge and the Teachings of Plants*. Minneapolis: Milkweed Editions, 2013.

Maine Wabanaki-State Child Welfare Truth and Reconciliation Commission. *Beyond the Mandate: Continuing the Conversation.* Report of the Maine Wabanaki-State Child Welfare Truth and Reconciliation Commission, Hermon, ME, 2015.

McFarlane, Peter, and Nicole Schabus, eds. *Whose Land Is It Anyway? A Manual for Decolonization.* E-book. Federation of Post-Secondary Educators of British Columbia, 2018. https://fpse.ca/decolonization_manual_whose_land_is_it_anyway.

McIntosh, Peggy. "White Privilege: Unpacking the Invisible Knapsack." *Peace and Freedom,* July/August, 1989, 10–12.

Mitchell, Sherri/Weh'na Ha'mu' Kwasset. *Sacred Instructions.* Berkeley: North Atlantic Books, 2018, pp. 93–105.

Moe, Kristin. "When Cowboys and Indians Unite: Inside the Unlikely Alliance That Is Remaking the Climate Movement." *Waging Nonviolence.* May 2, 2014. http://wagingnonviolence.org/feature/cowboys-indians-unite-inside-unlikely-alliance-foretells-victory-climate-movement/.

Pember, Mary Annette. "Intergenerational Trauma: Understanding Natives' Inherited Pain." *Indian Country Today Media Network.* 2016. Accessed May 5, 2020. https://amber-ic.org/wp-content/uploads/2017/01/ICMN-All-About-Generations-Trauma.pdf.

Sleeter, Christine. "Learning to Become a Racially and Culturally Competent Ally." In *Building Racial and Cultural Competence in the Classroom,* edited by K. Teel and J. Obidah, 82–96. New York: Teachers College Press, 2008.

Smith, Linda Tuhiwai. *Decolonizing Methodologies: Research and Indigenous Peoples.* London: Zed Books/Dunedin: University of Otago Press, 1999.

Sue, Derald Wing. *Racial Microaggressions in Everyday Life: Race, Gender and Sexual Orientation.* Hoboken, NJ: John Wiley and Sons, 2010.

Truth and Reconciliation Commission of Canada. *The Final Report of the Truth and Reconciliation Commission of Canada.* Vols. 1–6. Winnipeg: TRC, 2015.

Truth and Reconciliation Commission of Canada. *Honouring the Truth, Reconciling for the Future: Summary of the Final Report of the Truth and Reconciliation Commission of Canada.* Winnipeg: TRC, 2015.

United Nations. United Nations Declaration on the Rights of Indigenous Peoples. General Assembly Resolution 61/295. September 13, 2007. http://www.un.org/esa/socdev/unpfii /documents/DRIPS_en.pdf.

Wallace, Rick. *Merging Fires: Grassroots Peacebuilding between Indigenous and Non-Indigenous Peoples.* Halifax, NS: Fernwood, 2013.

Waziyatawin and Michael Yellow Bird. *For Indigenous Minds Only: A Decolonization Handbook.* Santa Fe: SAR, 2012.

Whaley, Rick, and Walt Bresette. *Walleye Warriors.* Philadelphia: New Society Publishers, 1994.

Whyte, Kyle P. "White Allies, Let's Be Honest about Decolonization." *Yes!* April 3, 2018. https://www.yesmagazine.org/issue/decolonize /2018/04/03/white-allies-lets-be-honest-about-decolonization/.

OTHER RESOURCES

Websites

Maine Wabanaki REACH (Restoration-Engagement-Advocacy-Change-Healing). http://mainewabanakireach.org/.

Oyate (Native-run website particularly for educators seeking to identify appropriate books and resources for young people about Native Americans). http://www.oyate.org/.

Truth and Reconciliation Commission of Canada. http://www.trc.ca/.
US Department of Arts and Culture. "Honor Native Land: A Guide
and Call to Acknowledgement." https://usdac.us/nativeland.

Films

The Canary Effect. Directed by Robin Davey and Yellow Thunder
Woman. 2006. DVD and online at https://www.youtube.com
/watch?v=lD7x6jryoSA.
Dawnland. Directed by Adam Mazo and Ben Pender-Cudlip.
Upstander Project, Boston, 2018. https://upstanderproject.org
/dawnland (features gkisedtanamoogk). See also the accompany-
ing teacher's guide at https://dawnland.org/teachers-guide/.
Invisible. Directed by Gunnar Hansen. Northeast Harbor, ME:
Acadia Film Video, 2005. DVD.
Is the Crown at War with Us? Directed by Alanis Obomsawin.
Ottawa: National Film Board of Canada, 2002. DVD and online at
https://www.nfb.ca/film/is_the_crown_at_war_with_us/ (a story
of the Esgenoôpetitj Mi'kmaq First Nation [Miigam'agan's and
Barb's community] fishing crisis during the summer of 2000).
N'tolonapemk: Our Relatives' Place. Directed by Gunnar Hansen.
Northeast Harbor, ME: Acadia Film Video, 2005. DVD (narrated
by Wayne Newell).
The Penobscot: Ancestral River, Contested Territory. Directed by Maria
Girouard and Meredith DeFrancesco. Indian Island, Penobscot
Nation: Sunlight Media Collective, 2015. DVD and online at
http://www.sunlightmediacollective.org/index.php/our-projects
/the-penobscot-ancestral-river-contested-territory.
Wabanaki: A New Dawn. Directed by Dennis Kostyk and David Westphal.
Mt. Desert, ME: Acadia Film Video, 1995. https://vimeo.com/6928369.

Audio

The Gathering: A Modern Thanksgiving Story. Produced by Barbara
   Simmons and Laura Jackson. 2002. Newtown, PA: Peace-Talks:
   Exploring the Alternatives to Violence, originally distributed by
   Public Radio International. https://beta.prx.org/stories/2251 (tells
   the story of our Gatherings described in this book).

Online Journals and Media

American Indian Quarterly. Edited by Lindsey Claire Smith. Lincoln:
   University of Nebraska Press. https://nebraskapressjournals.unl
   .edu/journal/american-indian-quarterly/.
Cultural Survival Quarterly. https://www.culturalsurvival.org/.
Indian Country Today. https://indiancountrytoday.com/.
Native News Online. http://nativenewsonline.net/.

Posters, Etc.

"Ally Bill of Responsibilities." Dr. Lynn Gehl, Algonquin Anishinaabekwe.   http://www.lynngehl.com/uploads/5/0/0/4/5004954/ally
   _bill_of_responsibilities_poster.pdf.
"How to Be an Ally to Indigenous Peoples." Josephine M. Cook,
   Onondaga, artist. 2013. Two-Row Wampum Campaign and
   Syracuse Cultural Workers. Poster, postcard, and bookmark.
   https://www.syracuseculturalworkers.com/products/poster-how
   -to-be-an-ally-to-indigenous-peoples.

Contributors

GWEN BEAR

Gwen Bear, a Wolastoqiyik/Maliseet woman, was born on the Tobique First Nation Reserve on the western border of New Brunswick. *Wolastoqiyik* means "people of the beautiful river," a reference to the St. John River that runs throughout Maliseet territory.

Gwen passed away on January 24, 2012, much too soon, but thankfully not before she could speak about her experiences in the Gatherings. She was an educator for twenty-five years, teaching Native Studies at the New Brunswick College of Craft and Design and Maliseet language classes at St. Thomas University in Fredericton. She also served as president of the New Brunswick Native Women's Council.

In her later years, Gwen was appointed Elder-in-Residence at the University of New Brunswick (UNB), the first person to hold such a position there. In her role, she supported Native students as well as the faculty who taught them, and helped Native students to connect, or reconnect, with their traditions. Since her passing, each year the Mi'kmaq Wolastoqey Centre at UNB hosts a memorial lecture in her honor.

As a Pipe Carrier, Gwen performed ceremonies, healings, and fasts for her people. She was a mother of three, a grandmother, and a great-grandmother.

SHIRLEY BOWEN

 *The Reverend Shirley Bowen is of Welsh and Irish descent. She grew up in the foothills of West Virginia, along the Ohio River in, as she describes it, "a typical blue-collar family" with a strong sense of place and history.*

Shirley's early career was in university Student Affairs where her experiences, over a span of twenty-four years, introduced her to diverse lifestyles and cultural experiences while teaching her compassion and a desire to educate others about the many forms of privilege and oppression.

During her last seven years at the university Shirley attended seminary part time, and in 2005 was ordained an Episcopal priest. She first served as a college chaplain, then as a parish priest, and now as executive director/chaplain at the Seeds of Hope Neighborhood Center in Biddeford, Maine. Seeds of Hope is a charitable non-profit that works with local communities to fight the causes of poverty, isolation, and despair. It also directly serves the poorest in those communities by providing for basic needs as well as offering education and training.

Shirley currently makes her home with her husband, Peter, on the southern coast of Maine where the Saco River joins the Atlantic Ocean.

ALMA H. BROOKS/ZAPAWEY-KWEY

*Alma H. Brooks/Zapawey-kwey is a
Wolastoqiyik/Maliseet woman from the
St. Mary's reserve situated in the center of
Fredericton, New Brunswick. As she says, "The
city of Fredericton grew up around us and so
that's where we are."*

*Alma is a Maliseet Clan Mother and member
of the Maliseet Grand Council. She is a widely
recognized environmental activist, particularly in the movement
against shale gas extraction ("fracking"), and has led numerous ral-
lies and marches in New Brunswick. In 2014, at the UN Permanent
Forum on Indigenous Issues, she represented Indigenous women in
the Western Hemisphere who are experiencing the results of resource
extraction. For her environmental work, Alma was given a lifetime
achievement award from the Conservation Council of New Brunswick.
She holds a Bachelor of Arts degree in liberal arts from St. Thomas
University in Fredericton.*

*In 2012 and 2013, Alma organized the annual Wabanaki
Confederacy Conference, and the Confederacy, with her guidance,
invited non-Native allies to attend – a first. There, Natives and non-
Natives together strategized responses to ongoing environmental
threats. Additionally, Alma has worked for years with ecumenical
groups throughout Atlantic Canada particularly in regard to prison
reform.*

*Alma is the mother of six, a grandmother of ten, and great-
grandmother of seven.*

GKISEDTANAMOOGK

gkisedtanamoogk is Wampanoag of the Otter and Turtle Clans. He is from the community of Mashpee, in what is now southeastern Massachusetts on the peninsula of Cape Cod. He would say these English place names reflect the "view from the boat" (e.g., the Mayflower) rather than the "view from the shore."

As a young man, gkisedtanamoogk attended Boston University thinking he would pursue a career in law. That plan changed with the American Indian Movement's occupation of Wounded Knee in 1973, which inspired him to put his studies on hold and return to his home community. There he immersed himself in understanding his people's history and in reclaiming his traditional culture.

gkisedtanamoogk has served as an adjunct faculty member in both the Native Studies and Peace Studies departments at the University of Maine. In 2013, he was seated on the Maine Wabanaki-State Child Welfare Truth and Reconciliation Commission as one of five commissioners mandated to gather testimonies, promote healing, and advocate for change in Maine's child welfare system as it impacts Wabanaki children and families. He is featured in the 2019 Emmy Award–winning documentary Dawnland, *which tells the story of the TRC process.*

gkisedtanamoogk is married to Miigam'agan, and they have three grown children and four grandchildren.

SHIRLEY N. HAGER

Shirley N. Hager is of English, Scottish, and German/Austrian descent, and grew up on a dairy farm in rural North Carolina. For the past thirty-eight years she has made her home in Maine where, with her husband Dave, she found her way "back to the country" in Maine's western foothills.

Shirley grew up in the 1950s and 1960s in the segregated South, an experience that left indelible impressions when, as a child, she witnessed inexplicable cruelty and injustice toward African-Americans in her community. In the mid-1980s, a lifelong interest in social justice as well as Indigenous cultures led her to the Center for Vision and Policy, and for two years she served as CVP's coordinator. Shirley organized the Gatherings under the auspices of CVP from 1987 to 1993.

For most of her career, Shirley has been an educator, retiring in 2007 as associate extension professor with the University of Maine. She is also a Circles of Trust© facilitator with the national Center for Courage & Renewal. Currently she serves with the Friends (Quaker) Committee on Maine Public Policy and chairs its Committee on Tribal-State Relations.

She is also a proud auntie to a number of nieces and nephews.

JOANN HUGHES

JoAnn Hughes was of Irish descent, born and raised in Quincy, Massachusetts, "the most Irish city in the US." For most of her adult life, she lived on Cape Cod, a place she loved and called her spiritual haven.

After raising her children, JoAnn trained and worked as a family therapist. During that time, she also studied at Weston School of Theology in Cambridge, MA, where she received her master's degree. Her growing understanding of feminist theology awakened her to the complexities of race, class, and gender in American society. Shortly after her time at Weston she became involved in the Gatherings, remaining a loyal participant and long-standing friend of many she met there.

In later years, with the support of her husband, Charles Weiner, JoAnn developed her natural talent as a painter, and her works have been exhibited throughout the northeast United States and elsewhere.

JoAnn passed away on November 1, 2015 surrounded by her family and community on Cape Cod. She was the mother of three and grandmother of six, with a great-grandchild recently born.

DEBBIE LEIGHTON

Debbie Leighton is of English descent. She was born and raised in New York City to parents who were social activists, working with immigrants and in the labor movement of the 1920s. In spite of her city upbringing, Debbie was drawn to the coast of Maine, where her family summered each year and where she has made her home for nearly forty years.

Debbie's social work career included the position of director of children and youth services for the State of Connecticut. As a lifelong peace and justice activist, she has been involved in movements for civil rights, women's rights, and gay and lesbian rights, including expansion of affirming and open policies in the United Church of Christ.

After moving to Maine, Debbie co-founded, with her partner, Elly Haney, the feminist Astarte Shell Press and was active in the Portland-based Feminist Spiritual Community. She was an integral part of the Center for Vision and Policy's development and all its activities until its dissolution. Her commitment to peace and justice has continued through participation in numerous organizations such as the Women's International League for Peace and Freedom and the administration of the Eleanor Humes Haney Fund.

Debbie is the mother of two social activists and a grandmother of three.

BARB MARTIN

Barb Martin is a Mi'kmaq woman from the community of Esgenoôpetitj/Burnt Church, New Brunswick. For the past thirty-five years, she has lived off-reserve in Wolastoqiyik/Maliseet territory, now in Upper Kingsclear. Since 1995, she and business partner Reni Han have co-owned Han Martin Associates, a consulting firm help-ing communities and organizations achieve their goals, particularly when these involve building relationships and working with diversity.

Between 2010 and 2013, Barb was project director for the Mawiw Council's Mi'kmaq and Maliseet Healing Networking Center. This innovative network provided healing services to residential school survivors and their families, using both traditional Aboriginal and Western healing practices. Barb is currently the program manager of Oeliangitsoltigo Mental Wellness Team (MWT), serving four Indigenous communities. She coordinates all aspects of the MWT, including outreach and service delivery, project oversight, reporting, communication, and governance.

Barb was the recipient of the 2011 Honouring Our Peoples Award from the Atlantic Policy Congress of First Nations Chiefs for her work with residential school survivors and in recognition of her contributions to improving the health of First Nations people in Atlantic Canada.

Barb has one son and takes seriously her role of auntie to her many nieces and nephews.

MIIGAM'AGAN

Miigam'agan is a Mi'kmaq woman of the Fish Clan from Esgenoôpetitj/Burnt Church Reserve on the northeast coast of New Brunswick, Canada. Her life has been devoted to Wabanaki cultural revival and to promoting an understanding of Indigenous matriarchal systems. She has extensive experience in behavioral and substance abuse counseling as well as community wellness planning.

Currently, Miigam'agan is Elder-in-Residence at St. Thomas University in Fredericton, New Brunswick. In this role, she provides support for First Nation students and offers opportunities for them to learn from Elders who are carriers of traditional knowledge. She is also an important link between the university and First Nations communities.

Miigam'agan sits on the executive committee of the Urban Aboriginal Knowledge Network at the University of New Brunswick, which sets research priorities and ensures that the research they support meets the needs of urban Aboriginal peoples. She is also a member of the steering committee on adult education initiatives for the Catherine Donnelly Foundation, and a member of the advisory board of the Association for the Study of Women and Mythology.

Miigam'agan is married to gkisedtanamoogk, and, as mentioned previously, together they have three grown children and four grandchildren.

T. DANA MITCHELL

T. Dana Mitchell is Panawahpskek/Penobscot from the Bear Clan. His people carry the name of the river they live on, the Penobscot, which runs through central and eastern Maine. Panawahpskek means "people of the river." As Dana describes it, the river is their highway, their lifeline, and their bloodline.

Dana grew up on Panawahpskek with thirteen siblings, descendants of a long line of tribal leaders. After graduating from the local public high school he joined the military, where he trained in electronics. This training led to a career with both NASA and the Atomic Energy Commission. Later returning to Maine and his home community, Dana went back to school in the building trades and made his living in construction.

Dana's return home in the 1970s ignited an interest in his culture's spiritual traditions. His commitment to the "Red Road" has taken him all over the world as part of two international Indigenous Elders networks, and he has spoken around the globe about his culture.

In addition to being part of original discussions about the creation of the Gatherings, Dana was an active participant in other CVP events in Maine.

Dana is the father of three children, a grandfather, and a great-grandfather.

WAYNE A. NEWELL

 *Wayne A. Newell is Peskotomuhkati/ Passamaquoddy, originally from the community of Sipayik/Pleasant Point on the easternmost edge of Maine.*

Wayne grew up speaking his native Passamaquoddy as well as English. He attended a Catholic church but also was steeped in his Native culture, primarily through his grand- mother. Legally blind from childhood, Wayne attended the reserva- tion school and the local public high school, and went on to complete a master's degree in education at Harvard University. He returned, in his twenties, to the neighboring Passamaquoddy community of Motahkomikuk/Indian Township, where he has lived for the last forty years with his wife, Sandy.

At Motahkomikuk, Wayne has made significant contributions to the local school, the health center, and tribal government while serving in the state legislature, on the University of Maine board of trustees, and on national education committees. He is a repository of Passamaquoddy songs and stories, which he has recorded and shared in numerous venues, including the Kennedy Center in Washington, DC. In recent years, he has helped to revive the Passamaquoddy lan- guage, and is currently editing a collection of Wabanaki stories passed down from generation to generation, unique in that each story will be presented in both English and in the particular Wabanaki language.

Wayne is the father of four, a grandfather, and a great-grandfather.

BETTY PETERSON

Betty Peterson was of English and German descent, born in Pennsylvania in 1917. In her early years, she studied, taught, and performed music in Syracuse, New York. In 1951, she and her husband, Gunnar, moved to the Chicago suburbs where she was active in civil rights and immigrant education.

In 1975, unhappy with US politics, they moved to Halifax, Nova Scotia, hoping to eventually retire on a small farm in Cape Breton. Tragically, within the first year Gunnar died of a heart attack, leaving Betty alone in their adopted land and wondering what to do with her life. A friend in Halifax said, "There's lots going on here ... stay and live with me." With the lure of companionship and meaningful activity, Betty accepted.

Experiences in Halifax led to her involvement, over the next thirty years, in peace, civil rights, environmental, and feminist movements throughout Canada. In 2000, Betty received an honorary degree of Doctor of Humane Letters from Mount St. Vincent University, Halifax, "for lifetime work to bring about a more humane and just society." In 2010, she was awarded the Peace Medallion by the YMCA of Greater Halifax/Dartmouth.

Betty passed away in February 2018 at age one hundred, leaving two children, two grandchildren, and two great-grandchildren.

MARILYN KEYES ROPER

Marilyn Keyes Roper is of Dutch, Scottish, and English descent, born in Oneonta, New York. She recalls two early experiences that significantly shaped her values: a high school boyfriend who was a conscientious objector and a month spent at a work camp on a Cherokee reservation.

Marilyn married Harrison Roper in 1955.

In 1962, the Cuban missile crisis and, with it, her fear for the future of her two boys compelled Marilyn to the study of archaeology and a master's degree from the University of Pennsylvania. Her research question: Are human beings innately warlike? Her first publication, which found no evidence for warfare among early humans, has been and continues to be widely cited.

Tired of "praying for peace and paying for war," Marilyn and Harry retired in 1982 to a small town in northern Maine close to the Canadian border, where they try to be good allies to their Wabanaki neighbors. They have contributed their skills to the local hospital and several day care centers and, in 1999, were named the "Adult Good Samaritans of Houlton." Marilyn currently serves as secretary of the Southern Aroostook Ministerial Association and volunteer administrative assistant of Aid for Kids.

They have two children, two grandchildren, and two great-grandchildren who, to their delight, live in Maine.

WESLEY ROTHERMEL

Wesley Rothermel was of German and English descent, growing up in Pennsylvania Dutch country. After years of living and working throughout the United States as a certified public accountant, he returned home to Pennsylvania to be closer to his family.

Wesley graduated from college amid the political and social turmoil that defined the 1960s. In the years following, while making his living in accounting, he was drawn into an awareness of the issues of the day, including a growing understanding and dismay concerning the realities faced by Indigenous peoples in the United States.

In the years since the Gatherings ended, Wesley used his accounting skills primarily in service to tribal governments, first in Montana, then on the Olympic Peninsula, and most recently in southern Arizona. As part of his job as chief financial officer for the Tohono O'odham tribe in Arizona, he also managed the tribally owned craft shop, drawing on his prior experience of owning a Native American arts and craft store in Camden, Maine. Additionally, he taught accounting classes at the community college located on the reservation, discovering a particular satisfaction in sharing his knowledge and experience with young people.

Wesley passed away on August 14, 2020, leaving two children and six grandchildren.

Map: Location of the Gatherings in the Gulf of Maine Bioregion / Traditional Wabanaki Territory

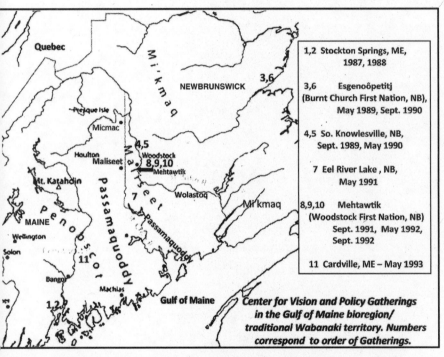

1,2 Stockton Springs, ME, 1987, 1988

3,6 Esgenoôpetitj (Burnt Church First Nation, NB), May 1989, Sept. 1990

4,5 So. Knowlesville, NB, Sept. 1989, May 1990

7 Eel River Lake , NB, May 1991

8,9,10 Mehtawtik (Woodstock First Nation, NB) Sept. 1991, May 1992, Sept. 1992

11 Cardville, ME – May 1993

Center for Vision and Policy Gatherings in the Gulf of Maine bioregion/ traditional Wabanaki territory. Numbers correspond to order of Gatherings.

Source: "Wabanaki Territory," *Headline News: Wabanaki Sovereignty in the 21st Century.* Based on map by Bill Nelson. Abbe Museum, 2011. http://archive.abbemuseum.org/headline-news /Wabanaki%20Territory/HeadlineNewsWabanakiTerritory.html. Map adapted by Marilyn Roper.

Reader's Guide

These questions were developed in conversations with several contributors to this book.

Introduction

- How did the author and other non-Natives in the Center for Vision and Policy begin to connect with Indigenous individuals? What did you notice about how the Gatherings were first formed? What decision enabled them to continue after the first two events?

- What do you think the author means when she says that the colonization of America is "a trespass and a violation that North America has never come to terms with, neither in relationship to the original inhabitants of this land nor within our own souls"?

- The author says, "in coming to know one another, we began to lay down the burden of our unresolved past, feeling the weight of that burden ease … just a bit." Have you ever been in a conflict, or had a misunderstanding, with someone and felt surprised at your relief when you found a way to talk through, or begin to address, the challenging issues you were encountering? Do you see any parallels with your experience and how the author describes the relationship between the Wabanaki and non-Indigenous people in the Gatherings?

GATHERING

Preparing

- How was organizing the Gatherings different from any experience you may have had organizing groups? What relational dynamics and practical concerns did Shirley H., as the coordinator, think about or struggle with? What was new or surprising to you in her description of the Gatherings?

- In general, how did the topics that the Indigenous and non-Indigenous participants raised in the Circles tend to differ? What are your thoughts about these differences?

The Talking Circle

- Why does Miigam'agan finally decide to join the Circle in the Gatherings? What caused the shift in thinking for her?

- Wayne talks about some of the elements of the Circles that served to make him comfortable being there. What were some of these elements? How could these elements apply to other circles you find yourself in, particularly those that consist of people from different cultures or socio-economic backgrounds?

- In his story, Dana suggests to a group of students that our world would be very different if, seven generations ago, we had been thinking about "the seventh generation," which would be those of us living now. What do you think the world would be like now, if seven generations ago everyone had been thinking that way? Why didn't we? Thinking about Dana's example of the bags of rocks (representing historical trauma) that are passed down and multiply through generations, how does this explanation of historical, or generational, trauma help you understand some of the challenges Indigenous peoples face today?

- Barb shared her observations of the White people in the Circles, and reflected on how she thought their experience in the Circle was different from the way Wabanaki people experience being together. Did any of her reflections resonate for you? How did she witness the non-Natives changing? How did her insights and feelings change over time?

- In her story, Debbie talks about how awkward she felt in the Gatherings, and how hard it was to make connections. What personal challenges did she encounter? Do you think it would have been similar or different for you in her situation? Why?

- Shirley B. talks about learning to hear and acknowledge the legitimacy of oppressed people's anger without taking it personally and without trying to "fix it" or diminish it. She says, "In that Circle there's nothing you can do but to be with the person speaking. It's later, in our own lives, that we can do something." After attending the Gatherings for a while, she says, "I started to look for ways to be an *active* ally …. to try to more actively make a difference in the world." What do you think it was about the Gatherings that inspired her intentions and motivations?

- Marilyn describes how her worldview has changed, especially about land and land ownership, based on her connections with Indigenous people. What are some of the differences she describes between Western and Indigenous perspectives concerning land?

- Wesley talks about how difficult it is for White people, especially White men, to give up some of their privilege. What were some of the privileges that the White people had who attended the Gatherings? In what ways did they try to "give up" some of their privilege or use their privilege on behalf of others as a result of their experiences in the Gatherings?

- Betty talks about meeting gkisedtanamoogk and Marilyn (and her husband Harry) Roper at the Gatherings and describes many activities they did together outside the Gatherings. What are some of the ripple effects over the years you noticed from connections made in the Gatherings by Betty and others?

- JoAnn had a deeply moving experience when she went to Ireland to connect with her ancestral roots and with the land there. She says, "Now, having had that experience in Ireland … even though I'm back on Cape Cod I feel that I'm grounded because I'm connected somewhere." She goes on to say "Once you have [that grounding somewhere], you want the environment to be healthy and you want to protect it wherever you are." What relevance might JoAnn's experience have for your life and your connection to the land and the environment?

- What do you think kept people, Native and non-Native, coming back to the Gatherings? And why?

The Last Gathering

- How do you understand the Gathering participants' decision to end the Gatherings?

THE GIVEAWAY BLANKET

The Circle and Ceremony

- Alma says, "You don't control a Circle. It will do its work. You just have to leave it alone and stop trying to manage it." What do you think of this idea, and how is it different from usual Western ways of meeting?

- What have you learned about the benefits of Talking Circles?

- Wayne and gkisedtanamoogk describe the elements of traditional Indigenous decision making in Council Circles. Reading their reflections, what benefits do you notice arising from this form of decision making? Drawbacks? Can you think of applications of these ways of decision making in your work, community, or family life that would be beneficial?

- Miigam'agan describes a shift over the years in her position on inviting non-Natives to participate in traditional Indigenous ceremonies, saying that she now feels it is important to share her culture with others. Yet when asked how she felt about non-Natives practicing Indigenous ceremony, she replied that there are responsibilities attached to that, which she describes. How do you understand the responsibilities she describes, and what would it mean in your own life to live up to them?

- Alma says that "when we invite someone to share in something of ours, like a ceremony, that doesn't mean that we're giving it to them, especially if it has to do with our culture or our identity." She's talking about cultural appropriation. What do you understand cultural appropriation to mean? What is the difference between appropriation and appreciation? What is the difference between participating in a ceremony (by invitation) and appropriating that ceremony? Have you seen instances of cultural appropriation around you, and how can you educate about, intervene, or interrupt appropriation effectively?

- How can non-Natives create and benefit from meeting in Talking Circles without appropriating cultural practices that are uniquely Indigenous?

Allies, Friends, Family

- What were some of the difficulties that non-Natives had in understanding what they were seeing and experiencing in the Gatherings? What were some of the difficulties that the Wabanaki people had? In either or both cases, what sorts of things helped them to overcome these difficulties?

- Wayne and Gwen talk about the issue of being "put on a pedestal" by non-Native people and how that made them feel. Wayne says those who put him on a pedestal in the Gatherings, and looked to him for answers, weren't the ones who stayed. How might putting someone on a pedestal get in the way of knowing them more authentically?

- Several women, both Wabanaki and non-Native, recall times of special bonding among the women. How do the Wabanaki women in the book (see Alma, Miigam'agan, Barb, and Gwen) talk about women's roles in traditional Wabanaki culture? Both Shirley B. and Shirley H. talk about being challenged by what they learned. Shirley H. says, "For me it was sometimes unsettling as well, calling into question beliefs and assumptions about being a woman that I had held my whole adult life." Did the Wabanaki women's descriptions challenge any of your beliefs and assumptions?

- In Shirley H.'s story, she says that "[t]he time spent together in our Circles seemed to enable us, slowly, to turn from looking at one another to facing outward together. I felt a subtle shift from seeing myself as primarily a listener and learner in relation to the Wabanaki participants, to feeling that we were partners in something larger than ourselves – our shared concern for the Earth and for one another's well-being." Others described a similar transition. What do you think caused this shift? Can you give specific examples of this transition in the participants?

- Studies show that, even when people of unequal societal privilege and position meet, if they are open to learning and being changed by the other, a sense of mutuality can still exist. The key is that what each has to offer is acknowledged and valued; in other words, there is an exchange. What helped a sense of mutuality and exchange to develop among participants in the Gatherings? What examples show that development? What was exchanged and how was it acknowledged and valued?

How We Got Here

- What does "colonization" mean and what were its origins in terms of the colonization of North America? What forms did colonization take when Europeans first came to this continent, and what forms does it take now?

- gkisedtanamoogk says that "[t]opography of the land was the determinant of cultural diversity – cultures differed because the land itself differed." Dana says his people carry the name of the river they live on. What does this tell you about the connection of Indigenous peoples to the land they have lived on for many thousands of years? Why do you think Indigenous peoples want to retain their identity and culture, as opposed to integrating into the Western culture?

- What did you learn that was new or surprising to you about US or Canadian history in terms of these countries' relationship to the Indigenous peoples of North America? What did you learn that was new about present-day realities for Native peoples?

- After reading about efforts in recent years to begin to make amends for past wrongs against Indigenous peoples in the United States and Canada, were you encouraged or discouraged about the future of these relationships? What action in particular encouraged you about the future, and why?

- John Mohawk, the Seneca scholar, said the real issue between Indian Country and North America is that, deep down, North Americans realize they aren't here legitimately and that's why they don't want to talk about Indigenous issues, or they want to pretend that these issues are in the past. He said North Americans suffer from not knowing that it's okay for them to be here. What do you think of his assessment? Can you think of evidence or examples that support his point of view?

How It Could Be Different

- Do you have a relationship to a particular plant, as the woman in this chapter did to sage, or to a particular animal or place on the Earth? Does this relationship strengthen your sense of belonging to the natural world, or to the Earth, in general? If so, how?

- How can non-Natives "belong" to the land they live on? Put another way, how can non-Natives be here in North America "legitimately"?

- Before reading this book, were you aware of the continued existence of treaties between the United States or Canada and Indigenous peoples, especially any treaties relevant to the territory where you live? How could you find out about them, and what would you do with this information as a resource for learning or other action?

- What is the language that is indigenous to where you live? What were the language(s) indigenous to where your ancestors originated?

- gkisedtanamoogk, Alma, and other Wabanaki contributors talk about an "Indigenous worldview." While understanding there are many differences among Indigenous peoples and their beliefs, can you draw some general distinctions between the "Indigenous worldview" as described and the "Western worldview"?

- The author writes, "Central concepts that have always been part of Indigenous cultures are now being understood and appreciated by environmentalists and scientists in the Western world as essential for our survival in an increasingly threatened ecosystem. Non-Natives have much to gain by understanding and incorporating Indigenous knowledge and perspectives as we seek to renew our relationship to the Earth." How is this idea different from cultural appropriation?

- Miigam'agan eloquently describes the need for opportunities, or forums, where Indigenous and non-Native people can meet and get to know one another. If you live in an area where Native and non-Native people are in reasonably close proximity, are there natural opportunities to get together? If not, what could you create in your own community, workplace, place of worship, and so on that might create such an opportunity? How could you "start small?"

- For non-Natives: What Indigenous groups, tribes, or nations lived on the land you currently live on? How could you find out? How could you acknowledge and honor their legacy of caring for the land that you now benefit from?

- What were some aspects within the section "Working Together on a Cause" that were new ideas for you in terms of working cross-culturally, or that seemed unique to Indigenous and non-Indigenous people working together? Why are these guidelines necessary?

- For White non-Natives: What is "White guilt"? If you think you've experienced this, what does it feel like? How might you deal with this feeling so it doesn't get in the way of your relationships with Indigenous people and other people of color?

- What did you learn from *The Gatherings* that was new or surprising about Indigenous peoples, about non-Native people, or about yourself? Did anything challenge or change an assumption that you had?

Afterword

- What are some of the important elements of creating and sustaining cross-cultural relationships described in the Afterword? What is one idea in particular you will seek to embrace, and why?

Index

Page numbers in italic represent photos/maps.

Tom's of Maine, 208
trauma, 39–40
treaties, 47, 162–8, 184–6
Truth and Reconciliation
Commission (TRC) (Canada), 44,
177–80
Truth and Reconciliation
Commission (TRC) (United
States), xxviii, 177–8

unci skat keq kisesinuhk, 23–4
United Nations, 33–4, 164
United Nations Declaration on the
Rights of Indigenous Peoples
(UNDRIP), 173–5, 180
University of Maine, 115
US Constitution, 163

Vienna Convention on the Law of
Treaties, 164
violence, 36, 37, 44, 55–6, 72
vulnerability, 26

Wabanaki Confederacy conference,
47, 121
Wabanaki peoples: community
life, 10, 14, 17, 40–2; curricula
in schools, 177; Gatherings
preparation, 3–6; map of territory,
255; and matriarchy, 151–2; and
MICSA, 179; migration of, 45;
and the present, 147; REACH, 178
Wabanaki Resource Center, 80–1

Waitangi Tribunal, 210–11
Waitere, Hine, 217
Wampanoag people, 61, 67–8, 75,
107. *See also specific people*
water, 188
Water Ceremony (Wolastoq), 47–8
Water Walk (Lake Superior), 94
Wayne, *125*, *251*; about, 251;
alliances, 193; Council Circles,
132–3; creating book, 218;
economic self-determination,
172; friendships, 153;
Gatherings experiences, 21–7;
LD 291 bill, 176–7; Native
peoples on pedestals, 148–9;
non-Native relations, 22–3,
169–70; sharing cultures, 138–9;
visibility of Native people;
vulnerability, 145
Wesley, 84–92, 119, *125*, *126*, 147,
254, *254*
White guilt, 198–9
Wolastoq River, 47–8
Woman Church, 111
women: authority of, 46; burdens
on, 14, 39–40; Clan Mothers,
134; comparing notes,
150–2; matriarchal societies,
150–1; meeting with White
organizations, 20; Moon Time,
4–5, 65–6, 79; and privilege, 16;
protesting Gatherings, 115–21;
violence against, 55–6